Commonwealth or Europe

The Commonwealth
Problems and Perspectives
General Editor: Gordon Greenwood

Commonwealth
or Europe

G. St.J. Barclay

University of Queensland Press

© University of Queensland Press, St. Lucia, Queensland, 1970
Text is set in Imprint 11/12
Printed and bound by Dai Nippon Printing Co. (International) Ltd.,
Hong Kong
Designed by Cyrelle
National Library of Australia registry number Aus 69-605
SBN 7022 0569 9

Distributed by International Scholarly Book Services, Inc. Great
Britain-Europe-North America.

*The Australian Institute of International Affairs as an organization does
not express opinions or advocate policies. The views expressed in this book
are therefore the author's own.*

Introduction to the Series

In introducing this series certain questions arise of which the most obvious is: why should it be thought that this is an appropriate point of time to produce a series centred about the Commonwealth? The Commonwealth, it would seem, is not in great favour among many of its constituent members, an attitude apparent enough in Britain itself. The high hopes, the optimism, of the late forties and fifties, when the Commonwealth was transformed into a multi-racial organization, have not been justified by events; they have been replaced by a much lower estimate of the political influence, the economic significance, and the advantage, nationally considered, of the association. This contemporary, perhaps more realistic, assessment of the Commonwealth should not be allowed to obscure either the extent of the influence which it has exercised historically or what is of continuing worth today.

There have been few defections, and with members in all quarters of the world the Commonwealth still facilitates meeting and provides sources of contact for member states. It provides also a network of organizational relationships, of an international character, which if they did not exist would in many cases need to be created. The economic links, though of diminishing importance, are by no means insignificant. For some members at least the cultural traditions of the United Kingdom have a continuing if subtly changed life in their own societies.

One legitimate way of approaching studies of the Commonwealth is to examine the contemporary consequences of earlier relationships. In almost all cases there are problems which are the legacy of British power, of imperial policy, or of Commonwealth linkage. There is too the historical contribution of the association in the various stages through which it has passed. To take but one example: it is, I think, clear that the very existence of the Commonwealth was of great assistance in the transition stages from colonial status to independence in Asia and, even more, in Africa. Whatever the merits or demerits of the Commonwealth, from a historical or a contemporary point of view, it is a phenomenon that cannot be ignored or lightly dismissed.

The approach adopted in this series is somewhat different from many traditionally employed. For clarity it may well be worth stating the things it is not. It is not a series dealing with the historical evolution of the association as such; it is not a collection of histories of member states, and certainly there is no intention of dealing with problems associated with every member state. Nor is it centrally concerned with studies of the functioning of the existing association, or of its machinery for consultation and co-operation.

This series is concerned rather with the recent and contemporary position in which member states find themselves, since all have problems peculiarly their own. For virtually all there are problems of adjustment to new circumstances, to new power balances, and to new associations. For many there are the difficulties and opportunities inseparable from recently acquired independence, together with the need of governments to satisfy the expectations of their peoples. In some countries examination may show that the Commonwealth connection is of continuing significance; in others it may prove to be of diminishing or even negligible importance. There are certainly major questions here, which are well worth probing.

The Australian Institute of International Affairs, with the backing of the Ford Foundation, thought it valuable to look at the situation of a number of member states, examining their recent history, the range of their relationships, and the character of their problems. Included in this approach is the assessment of certain specific issues, whether racial or religious, political or strategic, economic or organizational. Such a framework should be elastic enough to embrace from time to time the historical role of the association, or the contemporary directions in which it is moving. It will be my object as general editor to select issues for their intrinsic interest, or representative character, or crucial importance to an individual member state. The aim will be to provide a clear statement and analysis of the issues and an active and informed discussion of their ramifications.

The first of these volumes is concerned with a general question of undoubted import, a question which is crucial to the United Kingdom, of moment to the Commonwealth at large, and of special significance to some members — the process of European integration and its consequences for the United Kingdom and the Commonwealth. For this undertaking Dr. Barclay is well equipped, by training in history, politics, and related disciplines, by background experience in New Zealand and Europe of the issues associated with the possible entry of the United Kingdom into the Common Market, and through living with the problem with a scholarly absorption. A lively style is combined with an ability to focus the issues. Dr. Barclay has a definite point of view with which many will disagree. But those who do will need to marshal powerful evidence and argument to support their dissent. From his provocative analysis the central issues stand out boldly. It is a book which should stimulate discussion about a question of consequence.

I should like to thank the Ford Foundation and the Australian Institute of International Affairs for making the initiation of this series possible.

GORDON GREENWOOD
General Editor

Preface

There is no problem in outlining what this study attempts to do. It simply represents an endeavour to describe and interpret the changing attitudes adopted by British governments since the second world war to the phenomenon of Western European integration, and the reactions to these changes by the governments of other nations of the British Commonwealth. To say what it does not attempt to do is rather more difficult, though probably even more important. In brief, it does not purport to give an institutional analysis of European integration, nor to define how far progress towards integration has fulfilled or belied the hopes of its protagonists; it does not try to determine in any depth the economic significance of European integration for either those countries which are involved or those which are not; and it does not pretend to be a history of the Commonwealth in the past twenty-three years, except to the extent that Commonwealth interests were directly involved in the integration issue. Its concern is really only to answer the questions implied in the title, namely, to what extent postwar British governments have apparently tried to choose between the conflicting attractions of the Commonwealth and Continental Europe; whether such a choice was ever really necessary; and whether it did in fact exist.

Two points do perhaps call for some comment here. The first is that this study may well give a certain impression of inconsistency, in that British governments are portrayed in the opening chapters as having embarked upon a mistaken policy in choosing not to involve themselves in the Community Movement, and are then criticized in the later chapters for doing exactly the opposite. But the argument of the book is of course that the change in policy came at a time when changed circumstances in Continental Europe had rendered it inappropriate. A policy which on all the evidence would have been successful had it been tried in the 1950's proved in fact to be unsuccessful when tried in the quite different situation of the 1960's. This is merely restating the sad truth that there is such a thing as learning a lesson too late. It is possible to be wrong both ways. If this is indeed true of the British in this instance, one must remember that they are not the only people who have had such an experience.

The second point relates to the conclusion. There can of course be few final verdicts in history. One could hardly hope for finality in contemporary history, where one is dealing with a situation which is still actually evolving towards an outcome which is necessarily to some degree optional. At the same time, the historian can scarcely evade the responsibility of recording an interim judgment on the basis of the facts he has sought to interpret. And the conclusion which forced itself upon the author at the time of writing was that, far from there being no alternative to Europe, as British Ministers have recently been wont to argue, Europe is simply not available as an alternative in this particular sense in the foreseeable future. It thus seemed not so much appropriate as unavoidable to explore briefly what real alternatives might seem to exist.

I wish to record my great appreciation of the encouragement and assistance given me by Professor Gordon Greenwood, who first suggested that this book should actually be written, and who performed an editorial task on the original manuscript which was both invaluable and heroic. My thanks are also due to the Australian National University, which made it possible for me to carry out most of the initial research required for this study; to the University of Queensland, for their assistance with research grants in more recent years; and to the Australian Institute of International Affairs, under whose auspices this work has been prepared for publication.

Brisbane, 1968   G.B.

Contents

The British think of themselves as a separate continent, midway between Europe and North America.

Kaiser Wilhelm II

Maybe we can give you some advice . . .

Lester Bowles Pearson

1. Prelude to Integration

British policy towards European integration certainly came to be expressed in terms of a supposed conflict of interests between the Commonwealth and Europe. But the conflict that seemed most important at first was that between the Commonwealth and the United States. Any economic union between the United Kingdom and Continental Europe would necessarily involve some modification of the Preferential System formulated in the Ottawa Agreements of 1932, under which British manufactured exports enjoyed tariff preferences in Commonwealth markets in return for reciprocal advantages for Commonwealth primary products in the markets of the United Kingdom. The leaders of postwar Europe were concerned little with the Commonwealth and not at all with Commonwealth preferences. The Americans had long been concerned with and resentful of both.

This resentment had in fact shown itself in the aid agreements negotiated between the United Kingdom and the United States during World War II. Both countries had agreed under the terms of the Mutual Aid Agreement of 1942 to eliminate trade discrimination after victory, as a means of "promoting mutually advantageous economic relations". This had been clearly understood at the time, at least by the Americans, to forecast the abolition of Commonwealth preferences. Ideological and commercial interests reinforced each other, as usual. The Americans had obvious material reasons for disliking a system which they regarded as a discriminatory trading arrangement directed against themselves. But they could also disapprove of the preferential system as a technique for propping up an outmoded colonial system, incompatible with their own traditions. Moreover, the solidarity of the Commonwealth no longer appeared after 1945 to be important for the security of the United States. However, the Commonwealth had become more important to the United Kingdom at the very time that it became less so to the United States. And the preferential system itself acquired added significance in British eyes as a means of giving a tangible basis to the concept of Commonwealth unity, necessarily endangered by the erosion of imperial authority and the subsequent emergence of national governments in former colonial territories, possessed of traditions and aspirations often quite different from those of the United Kingdom and the Old Dominions. Reconciling these disparities in a multi-racial association of sovereign states would naturally appeal to the British as something good in itself. It was also something which would provide them with both a thoroughly benevolent form of national mission, and a means by which they might continue to exercise a significant influence in world affairs.

None of this would arouse sympathy from the Americans. They had virtually committed themselves during World War II to encouraging the dismantling of the remaining European empires; their own role as Superpower would only be complicated by the presence within the Atlantic system of another world power, claiming greater consideration than that accorded the views of the Continental Europeans; and their own material success naturally led them to dismiss anything that conflicted with the American concept of federalism as a substitute for all economic or political problems among states.[1] American spokesmen had no hesitation in recommending the British and Europeans to adopt the federal constitution of the United States, if they wished to attain to something like American prosperity and stability. If the British argued in reply that the Commonwealth connection made it out of the question for them to participate in any international federal union, that was merely another reason for objecting to the continued existence of the Commonwealth.

The American arguments were not easy to dismiss in the years immediately after World War II. It might have been a simple matter to show that the conditions in which the American Union was formed had literally nothing in common with those obtaining in Europe after the defeat of Germany. But it was equally obvious that the United States had achieved unparalleled material success, while the European states seemed to have accomplished their own ruin and impotence. It was difficult for Europeans to insist in the late 1940's that Americans were not entitled to tell them how to run their own affairs. What was still more compelling was the fact that the United States alone had the resources necessary to secure the strategic and ecnomico restoration of Western Europe. The primary task for British and Western Europeans alike was therefore to persuade the Americans to burden themselves with these tasks. Giving support to concepts of federal or customs union might seem a small price to pay, especially when there seemed little danger of having to translate these concepts directly into reality.

Hence on 23 November 1945 Ernest Bevin, the Foreign Secretary in the British Labour Government, and Anthony Eden, his opposite number in the Conservative Opposition, both gave tacit support to the federal ideal by agreeing in the House of Commons that modern developments had made traditional concepts of sovereignty obsolete.[2] The *New Statesman and Nation* commended Eden for expressing this view, and reminded him that Prime Minister Attlee's exhortation to Europe in 1939 to "federate or perish" had long been the slogan of progressive minds.[3] On 9 January 1946 R.A. Butler, another prominent conservative, went so far as to advocate the progressive and total integration of the United Kingdom with Continental Europe.[4] Philip Noel-Baker, Secretary of State for Commonwealth Relations in the Labour Government, agreed that what was needed in Europe was an international state with less sovereignty and more unity.[5] But the most eloquent and most misleading advocacy of federalism was that given by Winston Churchill in September 1946 in Zurich, where he claimed that the remedy that would make the "greater part of Europe as free and happy as Switzerland" would be to build "a kind of United States of Europe".[6] The only significant criticism of Churchill's speech was made by Morgan Phillips, the Secretary of the British Labour Party, who thought that international co-operation was likely to be stimulated by an organization sponsored by the Conservative leader. He accordingly urged that the Labour Government itself should take more positive steps to foster European union.[7]

European union could of course mean many different things. None of the party spokesmen quoted above had committed himself to any specific organization, except of course Butler. But the need to establish some form of international organization in Europe promptly was precipitated by the economic crisis of 1947. The British and French Governments had already taken a very innocuous first step by reaffirming their wartime alliance on 4 March, under the terms of the Treaty of Dunkirk, for mutual defence in the event of renewed German aggression. It had been intended by the British to extend the Treaty to include Belgium, Luxembourg and the Netherlands, united in the Benelux customs union on 18 April 1946. But economic considerations suddenly claimed prior attention throughout Western Europe. The United Kingdom and most other Western European states had already used up most of their reserves of foreign exhange in order to pay for imports of raw materials for their industries. Available supplies were then disrupted by an extraordinarily severe winter. Lack of coal brought industrial production to a standstill in both France and the United Kingdom in the second quarter of 1947. The American Secretary of State, George Marshall, then gave assurances that the policy of the United States was to help to revive an organic economy in Europe. However, he insisted that the first initiative would have to come from the Europeans themselves, who would have to prepare a joint programme of recovery, agreed to by the governments of separate states. Marshall's primary concern was to warn the Europeans that American aid would not be given unconditionally. This had indeed already been indicated by the decision by President Truman to close down UNRRA,[8] on the grounds that the United States paid over "seventy per cent of the bill, but had only one voice among nearly fifty in the determination of policy".⁹ But Bevin acted immediately so as to deny the Americans any excuse for not coming to the economic rescue. Within two days of Marshall's speech, he had begun discussions with the French Government. Within five weeks, sixteen European governments had met in Paris to draw up a joint programme of needs, resources and requirements.

The Commonwealth problem arose immediately. Almost the first act of the Paris conference was to appoint a study group to examine the prospects of forming a customs union among all or any of the European countries expecting to receive American aid. This was naturally welcomed by the protagonists of European union on the Continent and in the United States as being a logical step towards the fulfilment of their federal ideal. However, the leader of the British delegation, Sir Oliver Franks, objected that the Commonwealth connection would make it difficult for the United Kingdom to participate in any such union. The British Government nonetheless made a genuine and distinctly perilous attempt to meet American wishes. On 15 July it agreed to make sterling fully convertible, as a return for receiving American credits. An immediate flight from the pound took place. In two months the American credits had been overdrawn to the extent of $U.S.1,300 million. With only $U.S.400 million remaining, the British suspended convertibility in September. Bevin then suggested to a meeting of the Trades Union Congress in South-port that the Commonwealth Governments should consider forming a Commonwealth Customs Union.¹⁰ This obviously ill-considered remark was clearly only a symptom of the extent to which the idea of customs unions had been engaging people's attention since July. However, it provoked an extraordinary reproof from Robert Lovett, the American Under-Secretary of State charged with the administration of foreign aid. On the following day he warned the British that they could not have a Commonwealth Customs Union as well as a European Customs Union, and advised them to choose the latter.¹¹ The Europeans took the hint at once. France and Italy promptly set up a joint commission to study the possibility of forming a customs union of their own two countries. They transacted only 3 per cent of their total external trade at the time with each other, so the idea could be regarded as simply a bid for further American aid, as any other economic benefits could only be minimal.

Churchill replied directly to Lovett on 4 October, in a speech to the annual conference of the Conservative Party in Brighton. He insisted that the United Kingdom could continue to play an important part in the development of Western Europe only if it were not tied down to a choice between two rigid customs unions. The Conservative Party at least was not going to bargain away the Commonwealth preferential system, which had never prevented the growth of "an ever-warmer and more intimate friendship" between the United Kingdom and the United States. In conclusion, he developed the argument that the fundamental role of the United Kingdom in world affairs derived from its ability to act as the vital link connecting the "three systems" of the Commonwealth, European union and the "fraternal association" with the United States.

All this was in effect re-stating the basic claim that the position and potentiality of the United Kingdom in the world community was essentially different from that of the Continental European states. The United Kingdom had resources not available to the Europeans; it had in the multi-racial Commonwealth an ideal of international co-operation quite different from anything possessed by the French, Dutch or Belgians in their colonial empires; and it had developed during the wartime alliance a relationship with the United States which certainly no other peoples had had the opportunity to acquire. None of this was responded to in Washington. What came instead was an increasing insistence on the virtues of the federal solution as applied to European affairs. In his speech introducing the European Recovery Programme President Truman merely said that he considered the kind of mutual undertakings being entered into in Europe as essential "to give unity of purpose and effective coordination to the endeavours of the peoples of the sixteen nations".[12] However, at a hearing of the United States Senate Committee on Foreign Affairs on 20 January 1948, Senator Lodge suggested that progress towards the achievement of economic integration in Europe should be made a measure of the aid to be extended by the United States. Permanent presidential economic adviser Bernard Baruch supported the idea, if not the threat, which in any case could hardly be put into application, as the United States could not have afforded to let Western Europe collapse if it refused to become united. The Americans could scarcely do more than exhort, as John Foster Dulles, then Under-Secretary of State, did when he claimed that there was a vital need for a customs and monetary union in Europe.[13]

Vague exhortations could well call for vague reassurances. Bevin once again caught up the words of American spokesmen. Two days later, he told the House of Commons that the time was ripe for a consolidation of Western Europe. The British Government would seek to unite these countries by trade, social, cultural and all ties. The limits of Bevin's proposals were indicated by his comment that what he envisaged was essentially a spiritual union, such as existed among the members of the Commonwealth. This presumably need have meant nothing more than the fostering of a tradition of close consultations among the heads of independent governments. However, the Conservatives again seemed ready to contemplate more formal entanglements. On the Conservative side, Eden and Peter Thorneycroft both cited the Benelux Protocol as an example of the kind of relationship which the United Kingdom could enter into with Western Europe, without prejudicing its connection with the Commonwealth.[14] But Sir Oliver Franks had already argued just the opposite in Paris, and with far more obvious reason. In any case, it was Bevin's generalized idea of Western union and not Eden's specific idea of customs union, which was endorsed by Prime Ministers Fraser of New Zealand, Menzies of Australia and Malan of South Africa in the following weeks.[15]

Commonwealth relationships were affected in no way by the terms of the Treaty of Brussels, signed on 17 March 1948 as an extension of the Treaty of Dunkirk. The new treaty was described as being one of "economic, social and cultural collaboration and collective self-defence". Self-defence was provided for by an automatic commitment on all members to afford "all the military aid and assistance in their power" if one of their number should be the object of an armed attack in Europe.[16] In the economic sphere, the High Contracting Parties[17] undertook to "so organise and co-ordinate their economic activities as to produce the best possible results, by the elimination of conflict in their economic policies, the co-ordination of production and the development of commercial exchanges." However, this co-operation was not to "involve any duplication of, or prejudice to, the work of other economic organisations in which the High Contracting Parties are or may be represented ... "[18]

This clearly did no more than provide a formal basis on which

any one of the five nations involved could co-operate as closely
as it wished with any number of the others. It seems in any event
that the Brussels Treaty was never regarded by Bevin as more
than a demonstration of European solidarity, to induce the United
States to enter into a military commitment to Europe, as it had
already entered into an economic one. The actual form of this
American involvement seems to have been conceived first by
Lester Pearson, then Secretary of External Affairs in Ottawa.
It was alluded to by the Canadian Prime Minister Mackenzie
King in his description of the Brussels Treaty as "a partial reali-
sation of the idea of collective security ... which may well be
followed by other similar steps until there is built up an association
of free states which are willing to accept responsibilities of mutual
assistance".[19]

One further step which had great implications for the future
was the signing of the Convention for European Economic
Co-operation in Paris on 16 April 1948, by the countries receiving
aid under the European Recovery Programme. This specifically
pledged the signatories to "strengthen their economic links by all
methods which they may determine will further the objectives
of the present Convention. They will continue the study of
Customs Union or analogous arrangements such as free trade
areas, the formation of which might constitute one of the methods
of achieving these objectives."[20]

Prime Minister Attlee tried to allay any impression that
accepting the Convention had meant committing the United
Kingdom to early economic or federal union with the Europeans.
He admitted on 5 May that ultimately he believed that "we must
come to a federation of Europe", and that he had often spoken
against "the continuance of some absolute idea of sovereignty".
However, he insisted that: "after all, there is no exact definition
of what is sovereignty", and went on to say that he was disturbed
by the suggestion that "we might somehow get closer to Europe
than to our Commonwealth. The Commonwealth nations are
our closest friends. While I want to get as close as we can with
other nations, we have to bear in mind that we are not solely
a European power but a member of a great Commonwealth and
Empire."[21]

But it was becoming increasingly difficult to keep these
distinctions clear. On 7 May 1948 the Congress of European

Movements passed a resolution at The Hague calling for what amounted to complete political and economic integration in Western Europe. This resolution was officially supported by the French Government. On 11 June the United States took a further massive step into European affairs, under the terms of the Vandenberg Resolution, recommending that the United States participate in "such regional arrangements as are based on continuous and effective self-help and mutual aid . . ." Then the most venerated of Commonwealth elder statesmen, Field Marshal Smuts of South Africa, gave it as his opinion that the United Kingdom should directly participate in Western union, which could only mean that the United Kingdom should enter some association with Europe more binding than the Brussels Treaty or the Organization for European Economic Co-operation (OEEC):

> British participation is necessary and inevitable, both because European Union could not work without her, and also because Britain is part of Europe and no longer an island apart. . .
>
> Can she be a leading or important part of both Commonwealth and Western Union? Will the Commonwealth suffer from such a dual relationship of Britain? I have given the matter much consideration and see no insuperable difficulty.[22]

Western union might have meant many things in different circumstances, but there was no doubt now as to what it was being taken to mean by the Americans and Europeans. It was manifestly an issue of federal or economic union, or both. On 19 July French Foreign Minister Georges Bidault called on the signatories of the Brussels Treaty to formulate a political and economic union, first for themselves and later for any other European countries which chose to participate.[23] The American State Department gave assurance on 27 August that "this Government strongly favours the progressively closer integration of the free nations of Western Europe".[24] Bidault's successor, Robert Schuman, promptly submitted a project for a European Parliamentary Assembly to the Brussels Treaty Powers on 2 September. This proposal, if it could have been effected, would have meant the establishment of a genuine European federation, with a consequent loss of independence in foreign policy for the component states. The British suggested instead that a consultative Committee of European Ministers should be created, to meet at regular intervals over the next five years, to discuss matters of common interest. Federalist pressure was intensified in the United States. Both the Democrat and Republican parties endorsed Western union in their platforms for the 1948 presidential campaign. Governor Dewey of New York, the Republican candidate, indeed argued as Senator Lodge had that European aid should be used "as a means for pushing and ... prodding and encouraging the nations of Western Europe toward the goal of European union ... "[25]

There was no denying that on all the evidence it was only the British Government which seemed to require such persuasion. It was also true that it was only the British who had any reasonable expectations at the time of being able to maintain an important influence in the affairs of the world outside Europe. Certainly nothing they had done so far impaired their ability to play such a role. Reassurance on this score was sought in any case from the other Commonwealth Governments at the meeting of the Commonwealth Prime Ministers in London in October. The communique issued at the close of the Conference merely stated that there had been general agreement that "the association of the United Kingdom with her European neighbours (under the terms of the Brussels Treaty) was in accordance with the interests of other members of the Commonwealth, the United Nations and the promotion of world peace".[26] This has been interpreted as implying that Commonwealth support for the Brussels Treaty did not mean "a welcome for further steps towards a more far-reaching union".[27] It clearly did not. But the real point is that no such welcome was sought. All that was sought was the endorsement of policy decisions already taken.

And in the mind of one Commonwealth Government at least, other decisions would have to be taken. The Brussels Treaty may have been all that the Commonwealth Ministers said it was. But it could not guarantee the security of the West. On Armistice Day 1948 Premier St. Laurent of Canada reminded the governments of the Commonwealth and Europe of their vulnerability:

> ... the British Commonwealth of Nations does not constitute by itself a system of collective security. The same can be said of Western Union, left to itself ... Anything less than a North Atlantic Pact would leave us no real hope ...[28]

St. Laurent was talking only about defence. But other Canadians were ready to let their imaginations range almost without limit. Admittedly responding to a mood of national exhilaration, Lester B. Pearson celebrated the return of Newfoundland to the Canadian Confederation with the words:

> By union with Newfoundland we shall complete the work of federation begun long ago. By helping to create a North Atlantic Pact we shall have begun the work of uniting the North Atlantic Community.[29]

Pearson's words left a lot to the imagination. However, they could only serve to give further encouragement to the European as well as the American proponents of federalism. And both could draw even more concrete encouragement from the terms of the Treaty of the North Atlantic Organization, signed in Washington on 4 April 1949. NATO did not in fact provide for automatic armed support by the other signatories if one of their number were a victim of unprovoked aggression. It was merely agreed that in such circumstances the members should take such action as they individually deemed necessary, "including the use of armed force ..." The Americans declined to consider any more binding commitment as compatible with the constitutional authority of Congress. But the economic aspects of the treaty were spelt out in an obligatory if not particularly specific manner in Article II. Members were positively required to "seek to eliminate conflict in their economic policies and ... encourage economic collaboration between any or all of them".

This could easily be taken as a call to translate into action some of the closer forms of economic co-operation envisaged in the Convention of the OEEC. The British Government obviously did not feel required to regard it in that light. Scant attention was paid to NATO at the Commonwealth Prime Ministers' Conference held the following month. The Ministers had in any case sufficient problems of their own, resulting from the decisions of Eire to leave the Commonwealth and of India to become a republic. Prime Minister Nehru commented later that he had been informed about the Atlantic Pact, but that "there was no question of consultation, because we were not in it at all".
He also stressed that one essential difference between the Commonwealth and organizations like NATO was that "there was

no unwritten pact or convention according to which member states of the Commonwealth ... were bound by obligations of mutual defence in the event of war or external aggression".[30]

Nor did the Commonwealth leaders find it necessary to discuss the Council of Europe, created by a Statute signed in London on 5 May 1949. This organization gave formal effect to the proposal made by the British Government for a deliberative assembly of European governments, instead of the more ambitious legislative body sought by Robert Schuman. The aim of the new body was "to achieve a greater unity between its members ... by discussion of questions of common concern and by agreements and common action in economic, social, cultural, scientific, legal and administrative affairs ..." Defence matters were excluded from its competence, presumably because all of its members who had not opted for neutrality were already members of NATO. There was to be a Consultative Assembly, which would debate "matters within its competence", and a Council of Ministers, to which the Assembly would "present its conclusions, in the form of recommendations ..." The latter body reached its conclusions by majority vote, thus embodying the federal principle. However, it could present these conclusions to member governments only as recommendations, which the governments concerned were free to act upon or to disregard at discretion. It thus merely provided yet another debating institution, although admittedly one more comprehensive in membership than the Councils of Ministers of the OEEC or the Brussels Treaty Powers, since it did not confine representation solely to members of governments in office.

The fact is of course that the Council of Europe has proved an extraordinarily popular as well as unique forum for international debate, in which parliamentarians from member countries have been able to secure a wider audience for speeches which otherwise would have been heard, if at all, only within their own assemblies. It was, however, an institution incapable of satisfying the aspirations of the federalists, simply because it did not have legislative capacity. It was thus not in effect an alternative to Schuman's proposed European Parliament, whatever other uses it might have had in itself. Indeed, the point most obviously in its favour was exactly the one that made it most objectionable to the federalists. This was the fact that its membership was open to countries which would have refused to participate in a genuinely federal parliament. It thereby provided a forum for discussion and consultation among all the countries of the OEEC. But the claim of Western European federalists was precisely that countries prepared to contemplate federal or customs union were in a category essentially different from that of peoples like the Scandinavians, who had never endorsed the concept of Western union.

All this virtually guaranteed that the federalists would try again. But the economic circumstances of 1949 and 1950 seemed at first more likely to encourage the return of economic nationalism. Holdings of foreign exchange by the United Kingdom had fallen during the previous year by about 10 per cent, from U.S.$2,079 million to U.S.$1,856 million. They continued to fall at the same rate through 1949, to a level of $U.S.1,688 million. In the Council of the OEEC Sir Stafford Cripps, the British Chancellor of the Exchequer, rejected inconveniently timed American suggestions that sterling should be made convertible again. Then on 19 September the British acted decisively to restore their external financial position by devaluing sterling unilaterally. One can hardly in practice give much advance notice of one's intention to act in such a manner. It was nonetheless not easy to reconcile the British action with obligations accepted under the terms of Article V of the Convention of the OEEC, Article I of the Treaty of Brussels, or Article II of NATO. Cripps at least made the position of his Government clear when he told the Council of the OEEC that:

> We have made it clear from the beginning that our task is to try to combine our responsibilities as a leading member of the Commonwealth and of the Sterling Area with support for the development of Europe ... Our position is such that we could not integrate our economy into that of Europe in any manner that would prejudice the full discharge of these responsibilities.[31]

But the trouble was that it had not always been made clear to the Europeans that any such problem really existed. Sir Oliver Franks had certainly said that it did. But Eden and Thorneycroft had in effect denied this. So by implication at various times had Butler, Bevin and Attlee. And now Churchill once again confused the issue as he had previously done at Zurich in 1946, and as he was to do on almost every occasion on which he referred to the question of European union:

> I cannot think ... that the policy of United Europe as we

> Conservatives conceive it can be the slightest injury to our British Empire and Commonwealth or to the principle of Imperial Preference which I so carefully safeguarded in my discussions with President Roosevelt during the war ... there is absolutely no need to choose between a United Empire and a United Europe. Both are vitally and urgently necessary to our Commonwealth, to Europe and to the free world as a whole.[32]

Nobody of course ever knew exactly what Churchill meant by United Europe or by United Empire. But it was clear enough that he and Cripps agreed on the necessity to keep the preferential system intact. This would at least present difficulties if the question arose of the United Kingdom's joining a European customs union. What was not clear was how either the Government or the Opposition in the United Kingdom would now react to a proposal to join a form of European Integration which did not directly affect the Commonwealth connection in this way. The portents were hardly promising.

It would certainly not have been surprising if the British were indeed having second thoughts about the desirability of linking themselves too strictly with Europe. They had after all just emerged from the most damaging war in their history, fought against a Europe either subjugated by the enemy or actively co-operating with him. This experience had naturally encouraged them to turn more warmly towards their Commonwealth partners than perhaps had been the case between the wars. Moreover, the pattern of British trade had had to be substantially reorganized, due to the severance of European supplies. In 1938 trade with the Commonwealth had amounted to roughly 20 per cent of total British trade. In 1950 it amounted to nearer 40 per cent. Trade with Western Europe declined marginally from 12.4 to 12 per cent in the same period. This situation might be liable to change with European recovery. But European recovery itself was by no means certain even in 1950. And in any case, the Commonwealth had now acquired moral as well as material importance to the British. It provided perhaps the most convincing evidence that they were still a Great Power. British connections with the Empire and Commonwealth involved the United Kingdom in the affairs of every continent on earth. Also, as has been said, the multi-racial Commonwealth provided the British with a unique sense of mission, brilliantly compatible with the ideals of the United Nations.

No other European power could claim these distinctions. But in any case no other European power could pretend to anything like British material capacity. The United Kingdom had entered the war as the fourth economic power in the world. It emerged as the third. Moreover, British industrial production had suffered less and recovered more quickly than that of any other Western European belligerent except the Netherlands, as the table[33] below shows:

INDUSTRIAL PRODUCTION (% RATE OF INCREASE)

	1937	1946	1947	1948	1949	1950
United Kingdom	100	90	98	109	116	127
France	100	79	95	111	122	123
Belgium	100	80	95	102	104	109
Netherlands	100	95	95	—	—	140
Italy (1938)	100	85	95	99	105	119

The British success was partly due to the fact that they not only received a far greater amount of American aid than anybody else, but also devoted a far smaller proportion of it to overseas development than did other European colonial powers like France and Belgium.[34] The greater part went to reconstruct and redeploy British industry. By 1949 the United Kingdom was by far the largest and most efficient producer of steel in the OEEC. In that year it produced 33 per cent of the steel, 51 per cent of the coal and 56 per cent of the shipping in the whole Organization.[35] This great industrial development made possible an export drive spectacularly successful in compensating for the loss of invisible earnings from foreign investments capitalized during the war. In 1938 British exports paid for only 57.6 per cent of British imports. In 1950 they paid for 86.5 per cent. By comparison, export earnings as a proportion of import payments declined in the case of Belgium from 94.6 to 84.7 per cent, in that of Germany from 97.3 to 70 per cent, in that of Italy from 93.5 to 83.1 per cent, and in that of the Netherlands from 73.3 to 68.3 per cent. Only France matched the British achievement, with an increase of from 66.2 to 100 per cent. This success was reflected in a balance of payments position for the United Kingdom stronger, positively as well as relatively, than that of the five Western European countries and Luxembourg. In 1938 British reserves of gold and foreign exchange amounted to about $U.S.2,877 million. Those of the West European Six amounted to $U.S.4,855 million. In 1950 the relative figures were $3,300 and $3,195 million.[36]

The United Kingdom thus dominated the other Western Europeans materially after the second world war in a way which had not been possible since the German boom during the last quarter of the previous century. The British could thus well feel possessed of a capacity for a world power role simply not available to the Continentals. No other Western European state seemed to have such a destiny outside Europe, nor such resources with which to pursue it. But the very factors which encouraged the British to detach themselves from European entanglements made it inevitable that the Europeans would expect them to participate more actively. The Resistance had come to power throughout formerly occupied Western Europe, and the leaders of the Resistance had acquired through the years of Occupation the habit of looking to London for guidance and inspiration.

In doing so, they were of course showing themselves as indifferent to British preoccupations as the British were starting to seem to theirs. British conceptions of a world power role based on material strength and the Commonwealth were necessarily incompatible with any involvement in a European federalist organization. As Churchill explained in geometrical imagery:

> I feel the existence of three great circles among the free nations and democracies ... The first circle for us is naturally the British Commonwealth and Empire, with all that that comprises. Then there is also the English-speaking world in which we, Canada and the other British Dominions and the United States play so important a part. And finally there is United Europe. These three majestic circles are co-existent ... Now if you think of the three inter-linked circles you will see that we are the only country which has a great part in every one of them. We stand, in fact, at the very point of junction, and here in this Island ... we have the opportunity of joining them all together.[37]

The task of holding the circles together clearly involved to some degree that of holding them safely apart. It was this aspect of British policy which was not appreciated by either the Americans or the Western Europeans, all of whom had their various reasons for preferring to see the United Kingdom diminished to the part of a European rather than of a world power. In October 1949 Paul G. Hoffman, the new Administrator of the European Recovery Programme, told the Council of the OEEC that what the United States understood by European economic integration was nothing less than the creation of a single large market among the European states, similar to that existing in the United States. This meant simple customs union. Bevin replied flatly that the British Government was not prepared to yield any degree of economic sovereignty. "We are willing to consult, get advice, hear views and get opinions, but beyond that we cannot go."[38] Increased United States pressure in the OEEC for the British to free restraints upon European trade and payments merely evoked more determined opposition from British representatives. Again, the Americans could do little more than exhort. However, tempers in the OEEC were clearly becoming frayed. Hoffman now appealed to the OEEC governments to show some evidence of their will to unite, on the supposed basis of which the United States had been prepared to underwrite their recovery. On 2 November the OEEC Ministers agreed to eliminate quantitative restrictions on imports of at least 50 per cent of the goods exchanged in intra-OEEC trade. But British opposition to a further American proposal to create a European Payments Union for the multilateral settlement of accounts led to scenes of unprecedented ill-temper. Cripps insisted the new agency should have no power to intervene in the economic policies of governments; that existing bilateral arrangements should remain in force; and that the agency should have no decision-making powers beyond the day-to-day settlement of international payments. His further request that the United Kingdom should enjoy an associate membership affording privileged status as a persistent debtor drew threats of withdrawal from the Belgian representatives.[39]

It was not surprising that the leaders of the British Labour Government should have been reluctant to risk jeopardizing the social experiment they were engineering, by yielding any economic sovereignty to the Western Europeans. Nor was it surprising that they should feel a greater readiness to co-operate with the Scandinavians, whose financial situations and ideologies were alike less suspect than those obtaining in Western Europe. There were in any case good reasons of political expediency for approaching the Scandinavians. Norway, Denmark and Sweden had agreed in substance on 3 November 1949 to investigate the possibilities of forming a Nordic Customs Union.[40] The creation of such a bloc would have had the effect of leaving the United Kingdom confronted with a Europe divided into three separate customs unions, with ensuing complications for British trade. Accordingly, the British Government entered with the Nordic states into the Uniscan Agreement on 15 December, providing for closer but limited financial and economic co-operation.

Uniscan was not important at the time, although it acquired vital implications later. What was portentous, at least as far as the Western Europeans were concerned, was that the United Kingdom was prepared to enter into formal relations with countries outside the Brussels Treaty, closer than those which they would undertake with their treaty partners. This might well have seemed to answer for the time being the question of whether or not the British would themselves take any further steps towards joining in an effective Western union. The question still unanswered was how benevolently they would regard the formation of such a union without them. The element of doubt here derived mainly from the fact that such a union might well come to seem more important to the Americans than the United Kingdom itself, especially given the doctrinaire American preference for federalism over the Commonwealth Connection. There was only one way to find out.

NOTES

1. G. St. J. Barclay, "Background to EFTA", *Australian Journal of Politics and History*, XI, No. 2 (August 1965), 185-97.
2. U.K., House of Commons, *Debates*, Vol. CDXVI, col. 785.
3. *New Statesman and Nation*, 1 December 1945.
4. U.K., H. of C., *Debates*, Vol. CDXXVII, col. 1523.
5. U.K. Labour Party, *Report of the 45th Annual Conference*, p. 151.
6. C. Grove Haines (ed.), *European Integration* (New York: Johns Hopkins, 1957), pp. 53-54.
7. *Daily Herald* (London), 5 February 1947.
8. United Nations Relief and Rehabilitation Administration.
9. A.H. Robertson, *European Institutions* (London: Stevens, 1959), p. 6.
10. *Times* (London), 4 September 1947.
11. *New York Times*, 5 September 1947.
12. U.S. Congressional Record, *House*, XCIII, Part 9, 11749-51.
13. U.S. Senate, Foreign Affairs Committee, *Hearings*, 20 January 1948, p. 559.

14. U.K., H. of C., *Debates,* Vol. CDL, cols. 1316-19.
15. *Johannesburg Star,* 26 January 1948.
16. Preamble.
17. The United Kingdom, France, Belgium, the Netherlands and Luxembourg.
18. Art. 1.
19. Canada, House of Commons, *Debates,* 17 March 1948.
20. Art. 5.
21. U.K., H. of C., *Debates,* Vol. CDL, cols. 1316-19.
22. R.I.I.A., *Documents on International Affairs,* 1947-48, p. 241.
23. M. Bonnefous, *L'Idée Européenne et sa Réalisation* (Paris: Editions de Grand Siècle, 1950), p. 10.
24. U.S. State Department, *Bulletin,* 27 August 1948.
25. *New York Times,* 1 October 1948.
26. *Times,* 23 October 1948.
27. M. Mansergh, "Britain, the Commonwealth and Western Union", *International Affairs* (R.I.I.A.), XXIV, No. 4 (October, 1948), 498.
28. Canada, Department of External Affairs, *External Affairs,* 11 November 1948.
29. Canada, Department of External Affairs, *Statements and Speeches,* 10 February 1950.
30. This principle was affirmed thirteen years later by President Kwame Nkrumah of Ghana, when he protested against the decision of the British Government to send military assistance to India in its border war with China.
31. U.K., H. of C., *Debates,* Vol. CDLXIX, cols. 2214-15.
32. *Times,* 10 October 1949.
33. I.M.F., *International Financial Statistics,* 1951.
34. H.B. Price, *The Marshall Plan and Its Meaning* (New York: Cornell University Press, 1955), *passim.*
35. U.N., *Economic Developments in the OEEC,* 1951.
36. I.M.F., *op. cit.,* 1952.
37. Churchill, *op. cit.,* pp. 417-18.
38. U.K., H. of C., *Debates,* Vol. CDLXIX, col. 2210.
39. C. Zupnick, *Britain's Postwar Dollar Problem* (New York: Columbia University Press, 1957), p. 163.
40. Barclay, *op. cit.,* p. 190.

2. France Has Acted

International solutions certainly seemed to be called for to solve the international crises of 1950. The first involved the economic future of Western Europe. Three main elements were distinguishable, all deriving from the basic phenomenon of German industrial revival. The first and most obvious consequence of the German recovery was that it presented a challenge to French economic preponderance on the Continent. Between 1948 and and 1949 German industrial production had increased by 50 per cent, and French by only 9 per cent.[1] German steel production actually surpassed French in 1949, and German export prices were generally lower than French.[2] Meanwhile, low export prices were tending to make French coal production unprofitable. At the same time, the British and Americans had already decided to remove restraints on German production, by dismantling the International Authority of the Ruhr. They could indeed hardly have done otherwise. The experiences of the 1920's had made abundantly clear that the economy of Western Europe as a whole could not develop rationally unless its most naturally productive economic complex were allowed to grow unimpeded. Vital political factors were also demanding consideration. The Russians were beginning to offer West Germany greater access to the markets of Eastern Europe, in return for the neutralization of the whole country. Chancellor Adenauer could hardly hold out against this offer in face of mounting unemployment in the Ruhr and the Rhineland, unless he could be given greater opportunities to expand German trade with the West.

But this raised the second element in the crisis. German development had already helped to precipitate what appeared to be over-production in West European steel industries. A surplus of 8 million tons was anticipated by 1953. British, French and German steel owners had therefore begun secret talks in Zurich, with the intention of reviving the old International Steel Cartel. This in turn impelled Left-wing deputies in the Assemblée Nationale to demand action from the Government of M. Queuille, which depended upon their support to keep the Communists out of office.[3]

And lastly, progress towards further economic integration in Western Europe had broken down with the failure of the talks to unite the Benelux and Franco-Italian unions, and thereby give some validity to the latter. The reason for the collapse was the comprehensive one that the Beneluxers refused to enter any union which excluded Germany, at once their major market and chief supplier of imports; and the French and Italian industrialists refused to accept German competition on terms any freer than those applying already.

Adenauer himself tried to solve the triple problem by proposals increasingly more optimistic than practical. He first suggested on 19 January to John J. McCloy, the American High Commissioner in Germany, that the principle of international control should be extended to cover the Saar as well as the Ruhr. This drew an immediate response from Ottawa. Lester Pearson welcomed "the prospect of a closer economic cooperation among the countries of Western Europe", and argued that this might require some element of British participation, even at a certain cost to the Commonwealth.

> I would agree that any new economic bloc which might be set up in Europe should be so designed as to facilitate rather than retard progress towards this goal [of free trade]. It is often said in Canada that, in the short run at least, such a bloc might do some damage to Canadian trade. I would hope that it would not be serious. Nevertheless, it might be better for us in Canada to suffer some temporary disadvantages rather than to see the prospect of closer economic cooperation in Western Europe made impossible because the United Kingdom is unable to participate.[4]

Pearson's comment did not elicit a reply from the British or French, any more than Adenauer's original proposal had done. On 9 March 1950 the German leader tried again. He now told a representative of the American press that what he was really hoping for was the complete union of France and Germany. This time he indeed got an acknowledgment from Paris. The French Government said that it could not be expected to take seriously a proposal not conveyed to it through the proper channels. Adenauer then formally proposed that the economies of France and Germany should be unified as a preliminary to the complete fusion of the two countries. Schuman's reply to this was that meretricious suggestions of that kind should be treated with the contempt appropriate to jokes in bad taste.

Adenauer's proposals certainly seemed somewhat impracticable. But this was not the real reason for their unceremonious treatment in Paris. Schuman feared rather that they might jeopardize a plan of which he had himself become seized. This involved essentially placing the combined coal and steel industries of the participating countries under a common High Authority of international public servants, independent of the governments concerned. These officials would be charged primarily with ensuring that the liberalization of all restraints upon trade in these items did not lead to unemployment or the decline of living standards among the workers in the industries concerned. The plan was designed to cope with all three major problems at once. It would ameliorate the impact of German competition upon French industry by ensuring that this competition did not cause any fall in French living standards; it would make Germany inaccessible to Russian offers by involving German industry inextricably with that of other Western countries; and it would forestall the feared revival of the International Steel Cartel. The latter consideration would of course ensure its being opposed by French industrialists. Details of the Schuman Plan had therefore been kept as secret as might be, until it was considered opportune to release them. Probably only six people in the world had prior knowledge of the proposal Schuman presented to an astounded French cabinet on the morning of 9 May 1950. Eight hours later, the world was told. A press conference attended by 150 foreign journalists was called for six that afternoon, in the Salon de l'Horloge in the Quai d'Orsay. Schuman

> entered, his head bent forward, walking with catlike steps ... Having adjusted his glasses, he began to read in that harsh voice which, with him, compelled attention: "It is no longer a question of vain words, but of determined action, of constructive action. France has acted, and the consequences of its action could be immense. We hope that they will be."[5]

Schuman's proposal constituted quite literally a departure without precedent in the history of international organization. This was precisely what *Le Monde* called it ten years later, "a phenomenon very rare in history, a new conception of cooperation among people which will henceforth, whether one accepts it or not, leave its mark upon all the developments of international politics".[6] It was consequently hazardous as well as inspiring. Schuman accordingly acted to enlist the support of Britain, the nation whose participation would virtually guarantee the success of his initiative and whose opposition could make his task unimaginably difficult. Before the press conference, he had sent a note to the British Government, informing them that:

> In the conception of my Government this is a Plan of European scope. If in the presentation of it to the press particular stress is laid on the Franco-German aspect of the scheme, this is in order to give to the grand idea which is the inspiration of the scheme as striking a form as possible, particularly with regard to German opinion.[7]

Schuman could be reasonably sure of German support in any event, given Adenauer's obvious preoccupations. It was anyway to London and not to Bonn that he flew the following day. Schuman was well aware that a plan which proposed a solution for the most pressing problems of his own country might not seem to do as much for the United Kingdom. He warned newsmen at Orly "not to expect results too quickly. You know our British friends always give a lot of thought to what they will say."[8] Luck was certainly against him. Schuman's concern with the domestic French situation had led him to overlook the fact that the time that he had chosen as most felicitous for presenting the plan to his own Government was perhaps the worst imaginable for presenting it to the British. London was utterly unprepared to cope with the most adventurous diplomatic initiative in modern history. Attlee and Cripps were both on vacation; Bevin was preparing himself for major surgery against the disease from which he was shortly to die; and foreign policy was temporarily in the totally inexperienced hands of Herbert Morrison. Moreover, the last general election had left the Labour Government clinging to office with a bare majority of five seats in the House of Commons. British politicians could scarcely have been in a mood less receptive to the unprecedented and incalculable project from across the Channel.

It was not surprising that the British Ministers simply did not seem at first to have grasped the real gravamen of the Schuman Plan. Bevin expressed interest, but spoke of the problems of unemployment in Tyneside as an impediment to British participation, despite Schuman's explanations that the precise purpose of the plan was to ensure that rationalization of production did not involve putting people out of work. Similarly, Attlee told the House of Commons that the plan had far-reaching implications deserving very careful study, but welcomed it basically as a means of ending the Franco-German feud, despite Schuman's emphasis on the "European scope" of the plan, supported as this was by the fact of the presence of the French Minister in London.

Preliminary negotiations among British, French and American officials in the British capital failed to reach any definite conclusion. Meanwhile, British political opinion began to respond to the French initiative. The Liberals welcomed the plan warmly, urging British participation in the secure knowledge that they would never themselves be called upon either to reject or accept it. The *New Statesman and Nation* argued that British participation could well be necessary to safeguard the interests both of the United Kingdom and socialism in general:

> ... a Franco-German entente based on a revival of the old iron and steel cartel would lead straight to a German-dominated and reactionary Western Union. It would isolate Britain economically

and soon ruin our export market. On the other hand, a European administration of steel and coal, in which Britain participated, might become the nucleus of an independent Western Union — provided we were successful in obtaining the proper Socialist safeguards.[9]

On the other hand, *Reynolds' News,* representing the more conventional thinking of the Labour Party, dismissed the plan roundly as a capitalistic union of French and German steel makers, which was at least one thing it was not.[10]

The French officials associated with the plan had by now convinced themselves that its chances of success depended entirely upon rapid and decisive action being taken. Failure to elicit a direct answer from London accordingly began to arouse panic in Paris. Schuman's advisers warned him that the plan might now be doomed to failure unless British adhesion could be secured. Socialist deputies demanded that M. Queuille produce some evidence of British support. On 14 May, Jean Monnet, the chief of the French Central Planning Agency and Schuman's closest collaborator, himself flew to London. He and Schuman returned to Paris the following day, after having explained to Cripps and to Sir Edwin Plowman, the Chief Planning Officer at the Treasury, that the French Government believed that governments participating in the plan should accept at the outset the principle of pooling resources and establishing an independent High Authority, before considering how these procedures were to be applied in practice.

This was perhaps a very French way of doing things. It was not very English. Nonetheless, first impressions continued to suggest that British political opinion did in general welcome both the plan and the plea for British participation. On 16 May the British Labour Party Executive announced its intention of calling a conference of Western European socialist parties in London, to discuss socialist policy on the pooling of their coal and steel industries. On 17 May the Conservative David Eccles told the Eton College Political Society that the question was whether the United Kingdom should stay out of the coal-steel pool, or go in and direct it in the interests of the Commonwealth and the Atlantic Community.[11] On the same night, his fellow Conservative Harold Macmillan told the Essex and Middlesex Area Conservative Women's Advisory Committee that he hoped that the "rather tepid" reception given so far to Schuman's proposals did not mean that the British Government intended to stay out of the plan.[12] On 20 May the *Economist* and the *New Statesman and Nation* made history by agreeing in an attitude. The *Economist* argued that for "economic reasons as well as political Britain should participate in the scheme ... On this occasion, at least, no ground should be given for any accusation of 'dragging the feet'".[13] The *New Statesman and Nation* for its part published an article by Maurice Edelman favouring British participation in a coal-steel pool in which the international High Authority would be replaced by a European Coal and Steel Council, staffed by representatives of industry, trade unions, governments and consumers, and responsible to the Council of Europe.[14]

It was thus surprising to the French that the first formal reply to their approaches did not come from London until 25 May, and took the unexpected shape of a letter from Bevin to Schuman proposing that direct talks should be instituted between France and Germany. The British would wish to participate in these from the outset, with the hope of being able eventually to join in the scheme. It was no doubt unfortunate that the French Government did not simply accept Bevin's proposal and make the most of it. At the same time, it was manifestly not what they had been hoping for. Nor did it indicate any real appreciation of either the purpose of the plan or the difficulties the Government of M. Queuille was labouring under. Schuman and his advisers betrayed their exasperation in a peremptory reply despatched to London the same day:

> On 9th May the French Government sent to the British Government the text of a declaration which subsequently was published by the Ministry for Foreign Affairs ... The French document ... indicates the details on the basis of which the French Government are ready to open negotiations for a treaty to be signed by participating countries and submitted for the ratification of their Parliaments. From the outset the French Government have been anxious that the British Government should associate itself with the French initiative. To this end, in the course of conversations which took place in London on 11th May and on the following days, the Minister for Foreign Affairs and M. Jean Monnet sought to give additional explanations to certain members of the British Government and to certain high officials. They pointed out that if it were desired to reach concrete results it was necessary that the Governments should be in agreement from the beginning on the principles and the essential

undertakings defined in the French Government's document, but that the numerous problems which would arise from putting the project into effect would require discussions and studies which would have to be pursued in common with the object of achieving the signature of the proposed treaty.

Since then, the Chancellor of the German Federal Government has informed the French Government that he agrees to engage in negotiations on the basis indicated, and that in consequence he accepts the terms of the attached communiqué. The text has been transmitted to the Belgian, Netherlands, Luxembourg and Italian Governments ...

The French Government express the hope that the British Government will be able to participate on the same conditions in these negotiations from the outset.[15]

The draft communiqué read:

The Governments of ... are resolved to carry out a common action aiming for peace, European solidarity and economic and social progress by pooling their coal and steel production and by the institution of a new higher authority whose decisions will bind ... and the countries which may adhere to it in the future.

Negotiations on the basis of the principles and essential undertakings contained in the French proposals of 9 May will open on a date which will be proposed almost at once by the French Government with a view to working out the terms of a treaty which will be submitted for ratification to the respective Parliaments.[16]

The French note amounted to a request to sign on the dotted line and get down to business. Its tone was understandable enough from men preoccupied with the magnitude of the task they had set themselves and the importance of gaining prompt assurance of British participation if that task were to be fulfilled. However, they would have been justified in expecting a favourable reply only if they had reason to believe that the British Government did actually welcome the plan without important reservations. They could have had little more than hopes. These were soon disabused in any case. Schuman had asked for a direct reply. The one he received was as direct as might be. On the following day the British Government stated flatly:

The French Government ... will understand ... that it would not be possible for His Majesty's Government to subscribe to the communiqué, which it is intended to issue, or to accept in advance the essential principles and commitments contained in the French communiqué of 9 May.

But His Majesty's Government wish to reiterate their desire to participate in any discussions which may take place in the manner suggested in my message, and generally to adopt a positive attitude towards the French proposals. It should, however, be realized that if the French Government intended to insist upon a commitment to pool resources and set up an authority with certain sovereign powers as a prior condition to joining in the talks, His Majesty's Government would reluctantly be unable to accept such a condition. His Majesty's Government would greatly regret such an outcome.[17]

Just as it might have been more fruitful in the long run if the French had accepted Bevin's original proposition, so it might have saved embarrassment in the short run if they had taken the British reply as a simple refusal to participate in the plan, at least in its proposed form. The most convincing proof that the anxiety of the French to have the British endorse the plan had effectively blinded them to the possibility that the British might be unwilling to do so, is given by the reaction of the Quai d'Orsay to the British reply. Schuman and his aides seem literally not to have understood the British note. On 28 May the French Ambassador in London asked the British Minister of State if he were right in thinking that while the British were not prepared to commit themselves right away to the principle of pooling resources under a supranational authority, they were not adopting an attitude of hostility on principle, but were prepared to enter into discussions with the object of finding a practical method of applying the principle. The British Minister said that this roughly expressed the distinction. The Ambassador then said that he felt sure that this must be the case, and that he did not see how these reservations could in any way limit effective British participation in the negotiations.

Nor might they have, if the issue had simply been one of principles. But the attitudes of the two governments were materially irreconcilable. The French believed that they both required and deserved British support for an imaginative solution to the most pressing problems of Western Europe. The fact that the solution was expressly tailored to serve the interests of France did not alter the situation that a solution was needed, and that no one else seemed to have any practical alternative to propose. The British on the other hand were too engaged with the problems of their own economy and domestic politics to be receptive to an appeal from Paris which would complicate these and perhaps jeopardize Britain's independent role in world affairs, in the interests of an untried plan to solve the problem of people whose ideas the British distrusted, and whose industries competed with their own.

None of this seems to have occurred to the French. Otherwise they might have found it appropriate to bring to the notice of the British certain compelling practical reasons for responding to Schuman's pleas. These were: that the United Kingdom was in a sufficiently dominating position in Western Europe for it to be able to dictate to a great extent the future evolution of any organization it chose to associate itself with, so there could not be much risk involved; that it could not exercise such control unless it actually did participate; that British ideological interests would certainly seem to be served by a proposal aimed at forestalling both a Communist coup and a capitalist plot; and that the fate of Western Europe was really sufficiently important to the British for them to be obliged in reason to accept the Schuman Plan, if they could not produce a better one of their own.

But this was not done. The French persisted in believing that the difficulty in the way of securing British endorsement was purely semantic; that the British had merely failed to understand the real significance of the communiqué; and that all that was necessary was to explain it to them more clearly. This was duly done in a most painstakingly prepared note from Paris on 30 May, utterly different in tone and style from the curt summons of five days previously. It began by explaining that the French Government had "studied with the greatest care the British memorandum of 27 May". It was understood that the British justified their demand to preserve a special position in the negotiations on the grounds that the French intended to ask "as a prior condition, for full participation in the discussions, for an undertaking to pool coal and steel resources and to set up an authority with certain sovereign powers". However, the French said that they wished to confirm that this was particularly not their intention. As their communiqué had recognized, there could be no such commitment except by the actual signature of a treaty and its subsequent ratification by the Parliaments involved. What they had really wanted, they said, was to ensure that the preliminary negotiations should be "clearly directed by agreement between participating Governments on the fundamental objectives to be reached ..." Otherwise, "knowing the practical difficulties which the discussions will have to surmount", they did not believe that it would be possible to work out quickly enough the methods and supplementary arrangements necessary to give effect to the Schuman Plan. That was, they said, "the meaning which should be given to the French word *engagement* (undertaking) in the second paragraph of the draft communiqué". The note explained further that the French realized that the British were "of course legitimately preoccupied with following a policy of economic expansion, of full employment, and a rising standard of living for the workers". The Schuman Plan,

> far from obstructing such a policy, is calculated in the view of the French Government to avoid the dangers which may suddenly obstruct its course. For competition based on exploiting Labour will be substituted a concerted rise in workers' conditions; for the restrictive practices of cartels the development of outlets; for dumping and discrimination the rational distribution of products. The policy of full employment only reaches its true objectives if it provides labour with the most productive occupations — and it cannot finally be carried out under the pressure of unemployment in other countries.

The note concluded with the hope that:

> The French Government consider that the above explanations will clear up any misunderstandings about the scope of the proposed basis for negotiation. They do not think that there can be any difference of view between them and the British Government on the objectives put forward. They hope now that the British Government will consider it possible to take part in the projected negotiations on the same basis as the other Governments.[18]

This impresses as a thoroughly genuine attempt to present the plan to the British in a manner most appealing to Left-wing susceptibilities. However, it still contained the essential and basically objectionable feature that it would commit the British Goverment at the very least to attempting to pursue a course of action which was not obviously compatible with British domestic interests and external ambitions. The British Government repeated its argument that:

> it remained the view of His Majesty's Government that to subscribe to the terms of the draft communiqué...would involve entering into an advance commitment to pool coal and steel resources...before there had been full opportunity of considering

how these important and far-reaching proposals would work in practice...they feel unable to associate themselves with a communiqué which appears to take decisions prior to, rather than as a result of, intergovernmental discussions.

The British proposed instead an alternative draft paragraph stating that:

> The Government of the United Kingdom will participate in the proposed conversation in a constructive spirit and in the hope that as a result of the discussions, there will emerge a scheme which they will be able to join. But they cannot at this stage enter into any more precise commitment. They recognize the important and far-reaching character of the French proposals, and are in complete accord with the objective of pursuing a common policy aiming at peace, European solidarity and economic and social progress.[19]

This approach must have seemed reasonable and acceptable under most circumstances. However, two factors combined to make the existing circumstances abnormal. The first was that the four other Western European governments to which the French communiqué had been sent had already accepted it with greater or less enthusiasm. However, the British themselves produced as much coal and two-thirds as much steel as the six Western European states put together. There would thus be a practically equal balance of opposing interests in the proposed discussions. The past record of European organizations did not hold out much promise for the outcome of discussions in which the participants were not overwhelmingly agreed from the start on what they were trying to achieve. Of even more direct concern was the fact that the prestige of Schuman and his colleagues and through them of the Fourth Republic was by now dependent on the success of the spectacular initiative they had launched in the unfounded expectation of British support. Schuman had gambled his reputation and that of his country on a miscalculation. The British were certainly under no obligation to help him out. On the other hand, there were empirical grounds for asking if the inconveniences, to call them no more than that, of joining the Schuman Plan might not be outweighed by those resulting from the fall of the Fourth Republic and the economic collapse of the West if the plan failed through lack of British support, as was at least possible.

Schuman might as well have accepted defeat then, as he had to later in any event. However, face-saving considerations prompted a last bid. On 1 June the Quai d'Orsay replied again to London. It was noted that the text of the original communiqué, "which several Governments have already accepted, has through certain expressions used given rise to misunderstandings which have led to an exchange of Notes between the French and British Governments ..." A new text was accordingly proposed "to clear away this obstacle ..." The first paragraph of the new communiqué read:

> The Governments of ... in their determination to pursue a common action for peace, European solidarity and economic and social progress, have assigned to themselves as their immediate objective the pooling of coal and steel production and the institution of a new high authority ... [20]

The practical implications of the change in wording were not immediately obvious. The essential difference was that the first communiqué said that the participating governments were resolved to pool their coal and steel production and set up a high authority. The second said that they regarded this as their immediate objective. Presumably the implication was that the governments might find the objective unattainable or undesirable. They would then be free to try something else. If this indeed was the distinction, it might well have been conveyed more clearly. But semantics were really irrelevant. It was no longer credible that the British were still refusing to become involved with the plan because they had failed to grasp its purpose.

The British reply of 2 June substantially repeated earlier objections. They said that they would still feel committed, even under the terms of the new communiqué, "to the aim of preparing a treaty ... embodying the principles of the French proposal, without opportunity being given for their practical application to be worked out." They were nonetheless still anxious to do their best to see if a workable scheme could be produced that was "fair and just to all concerned", and would promote the agreed common policy. They proposed that this should be done by a "meeting of the Ministers of the countries interested at which the question of the most effective and expeditious method of discussing the problems at issue could be examined and settled".

This proposal might have been difficult to apply in the existing circumstances anyway, seeing that five other Western European governments concerned had already accepted the French proposal as a basis, not merely for discussing problems, but for positive action. It made evident in any case that the British could not be induced at that stage to give positive endorsement to the Schuman Plan. Schuman's strategy now was to terminate the exchange in a manner which would not give the impression of an Anglo-French breach, but would instead preserve the hope that British participation might only have been deferred. The note from the Quai d'Orsay on 2 June regretted that the attitude of the two governments had been defined without ambiguity in the course of the exchange, which was scarcely a wholly accurate commentary on the proceedings; and considered that a meeting of Ministers was not likely to clarify it further, which indeed might have been true. Meanwhile they would "lose no opportunity of engaging in exchanges of view with the British Government ... in order to enable the latter to participate in, or associate themselves with, the common task as soon as they feel able to do so". The British reply repeated the view that the French had taken the position that "the first step in the execution of their plan must be an international conference ... prepared to accept a commitment in principle to pool their coal and steel resources"; assured the French that the British Government "did not feel able to accept in advance, nor do they wish to reject in advance, the principles underlying the French proposal", which may have been a rational position, but was no help to Schuman; and explained that "an unhappy situation would arise if, having bound themselves to certain principles, without knowing how they would work out in practice, they were to find themselves, as a result of the discussion compelled to withdraw from their undertakings".[21] This was a risk which six other European governments had been prepared to take. It was of course true that the British were in a quite different situation, and that this accounted sufficiently for their different attitude. However, it would have been more immediately apparent to the Europeans if the British replies had concentrated on explaining the facts of the British situation, rather than on discussions of principle which could have given the impression that they had no substantial material objections to the plan.

It was clearly to the benefit of both governments to conduct themselves as if no serious clash of interests had taken place. The general tone of press comment on both sides of the Channel was one of puzzlement rather than recrimination. The *New Statesman and Nation,* which had been prompt to support British participation, with certain reservations, now asked if Prime Minister Attlee was "prepared to see the idea of European Union monopolized by an unholy alliance of the Vatican and the heavy industrialists of the Comité des Forges? ... These are questions which French and German Socialists can reasonably ask ..."[22]

They were scarcely questions that socialists anywhere could reasonably ask. However, the Continental Left soon did have occasion to question the position of the British Labour movement on this issue. At a press conference on 12 July, Hugh Dalton, the Chancellor of the Duchy of Lancaster, released to the public the Foreign Policy Statement of the National Executive of the British Labour Party. This document was challengingly entitled *European Unity.* Its main theme was the conditions under which the United Kingdom should participate in a closer association of European states. These were apparently extremely limited. It claimed that "no British government, whatever its political opinions, could save Britain from bankruptcy without retaining the general framework of control", so there could be no question of abandoning sovereignty in the economic sphere. Moreover, Britain was "not just a small crowded island off the western coast of Continental Europe. She is the nerve-centre of a world-wide Commonwealth which extends into every continent ..." Therefore the Labour Party could not regard European unity as an end in itself. But more serious still, in view of the timing of the publication, was a passage which appeared to be attacking the fundamental principle of the Schuman Plan, by rejecting the idea that it was either possible or desirable to form a complete union, political or economic, through imposing unity of action by a supranational body with sovereign powers. The manifesto considered that the European peoples did not need such a body anyway. What they needed was "an international machinery to carry out agreements which are reached without compulsion", such as the OEEC and the Council of Europe.

The basic objection to federal or customs union in Europe seemed to lie in the nature of the West European states themselves. The manifesto claimed that the Labour Party fundamentally rejected the theory that "the free play of economic forces within the Continental market ... would produce a better distribution of manpower and resources". Hence complete economic unity in Europe had to be excluded, since it would "demand an unattainable degree of uniformity in the internal policies of the member states ...(But) if a complete economic union is impossible, a complete political union is thereby also excluded." Moreover, as the manifesto pointed out, any representative body in Western Europe would necessarily be anti-socialist or non-socialist in character under existing circumstances. However,

> those European countries are most immune from Communist penetration which follow the policies of democratic Socialism. It would be criminal folly to wreck their achievements in the search for a unity whose main purpose was to restore Western Europe to economic and political health. No Socialist Government in Europe would submit to the authority of a body whose policies were decided by an anti-Socialist majority ... No Socialist Party with the prospect of forming a Government could accept a system by which important fields of national policy were surrendered to a supranational European representative authority.

There were many aspects of this argument open to criticism, even disregarding the circumstances of its appearance. The first was that it certainly seemed to treat the principles of parliamentary democracy rather lightly, if it were really being argued that the wishes of a majority should be regarded only if that majority were socialist. It was also not quite as certain as the writers assumed that the majority of a European parliamentary body would not in fact be made up of people who at least called themselves socialists of one kind or another. More seriously, it did appear to overlook the fact that the achievements of the Scandinavian socialists were very likely to be endangered unless something was done promptly to restore Western Europe to economic and political health.

But the most serious consequence of *European Unity* was certainly its effect upon Anglo-French relations at the time. This was admittedly not entirely Dalton's fault. He had certainly not conceived it as an attack on the Schuman Plan. Indeed, having become apprised of the nature of the Plan, he hastily appended a final paragraph referring to it in the most complimentary terms:

> The basic industries of iron and steel hold the key to full employment and stability in every country ... Until M. Schuman's historic proposal to pool the steel and coal industries of France,

Germany and the Saar under a single authority appointed by Governments, the unwillingness of many Governments to control their own basic industries obviously made European planning of coal and steel impossible. The opportunity now exists to fill the greatest gap in European co-operation.

This conclusion could only seem surprising after the severe comments on supranationalism in the rest of the manifesto, although the situation obviously was that Dalton had not envisaged the kind of supranationalism proposed by the Schuman Plan when he wrote the earlier part of the document, and that he did not have time to rewrite the earlier passages to make them more obviously consistent with his appreciation of the French initiative. From this point of view, the manifesto might have seemed positively encouraging to the French, since it implied that Labour Party publicists viewed the plan with far more sympathy than they had earlier proposals for Western union. However, the timing could only seem undiplomatic or at least inconsiderate. The French were unlikely to appreciate being told that the British Labour Party had always put a relatively low priority on Western union, and had in any event regarded their fate as less important than that of the Scandinavians. Inaccurate or exaggerated versions circulated in Paris, making the impact of the manifesto even more damaging to Franco-British relations than it would have been otherwise. Schuman hastened to assure French journalists that it could not have been accurately reported, as neither the Labour Government nor individual Labour members would take an attitude as intransigent as that now being attributed to them.[23] Other Frenchmen, their nerves strained by the length of the diplomatic exchange with London, and their tempers aroused by its failure, made no attempt to evaluate Dalton's views objectively. Guy Mollet, the President of the SFIO,[24] promptly declared his opposition to his fellow socialists in the United Kingdom, and expressed his determination to continue with what he called the building of Europe. On 14 June the SFIO officially deplored the fact that the manifesto denoted "profound modifications of attitude relating to the conception of Europe, modifications with which it could not associate itself".[25] On 15 June Léon Jouhaux, leader of the non-Communist French Trade Union Confederation Force Ouvrière, described the manifesto as the most unfortunate thing that could have happened at the time. Ironically, the manifesto was even less popular with the extreme Left. In England, the *Daily Worker* denounced it in improbable terms as a call to "workers, colonial slaves, capitalists, kings, presidents, maharajahs and sultans to unite — against Communism!"[26] Rather more analytically, *L'Humanité* commented:

> An American senator remarked ironically that Washington could "let English Socialism develop on its own — without dollars!" Let our senator be reassured! Our British Socialists are quite decided not to run that risk. The defence of "national socialism" is strictly limited to the defence of the position of Great Britain in Europe. In the set-up of the Atlantic coalition, they accept second place, but they want first place among the satellites.[27]

The most convincing display of Continental resentment, however, was provided by the members of socialist parties of all the six Western European countries, who confronted Dalton and Morgan Phillips in Transport House, the headquarters of the British Labour Party in London, on 18 June, demanding that they sign a document welcoming the Schuman Plan as "a bold example of European initiative", and declaring it to be, if properly developed, "a tremendous step towards European Unity, and thus worthy of the enthusiastic support of European Socialists".[28] This of course was little more than Dalton had said already in the last paragraph, which few except the Communists seemed to have read.

Once again, an overt breach between France and the United Kingdom seemed to have been avoided. Meanwhile, the Conservatives appeared to be mobilizing support for British participation. On 16 June Eden told a Young Conservative rally at Filey that the first task of British foreign policy was to promote peace and understanding throughout the world. To pursue that object the United Kingdom ought to be ready to work with any government, whatever its political complexion, which sought the same objective. He said that the Conservatives had always made it clear that the British Commonwealth and Empire would always come first in any clash of friendship. However, he considered that no such clash was involved in this case, as it was to the advantage of the nations of the Commonwealth that peace should grow in Europe, and to those of Europe that the Commonwealth and Empire should be united and strong.[29] This perhaps did not directly answer the question of whether in the existing circumstances the United Kingdom should join a Western European coal-steel pool. Such an answer was given the following day by fellow Conservative Harold Macmillan. He said in Bromley that the previous week had been a black one for Britain, for the Empire, for Europe and the peace of the world. The purpose of the Schuman Plan was to unite France and Germany. This would secure peace only if the United Kingdom participated. Without British participation, Franco-German unity would be a source of danger rather than of security. "In the not too distant future we may have to pay a terrible price for the isolationist policy which British Socialism has long practised, and now openly dares to preach in the Manifesto misnamed *European Unity*."[30]

Possibly heartened by these demonstrations of support from those who would presumably be among the leaders of the next British Government, Schuman told the leaders of Western European governments assembled in Paris to begin negotiations that:

> France has been blamed for its haste: there has been talk of rapid and brutal tactics; but experience has shown that the most hopeful initiatives die away when before seeing the light of day they linger too long amidst preliminary consultations ... We had earnestly hoped that England would be present at our delibera-tions. We cannot conceive of Europe without it. We know — and this reassures us — that the British Government desire the success of our work ... We continue to hope that the doubts and scruples which remained impervious to doctrinaire reasoning will finally give way before more concrete tests. The French Government will certainly be acting in conformity with the desires which animate all participating Governments in keeping the British Government informed of the progress of our discussions, and thereby affording them the possibility, if not of coming to join us, which remains our fervent wish, at least of communicating to us their observations, thus paving the way for future cooperation.[31]

It was obviously in Schuman's interest to pretend for as long as possible that the refusal of the British to participate had in fact been due only to "doubts and scruples", which were therefore liable to alteration. However, British statements soon began to indicate that the decision had in fact been made on the basis of the most solid material interests, which were not likely to be altered so readily. On 23 June the British Government performed what the *Daily Worker* called "an action of an abjectness unparal-leled in diplomatic history".[32] It was certainly an unusual position for a British government to find itself in. The British Ambassador in Washington presented Paul Hoffman with a letter to be read to the Foreign Affairs Committee of the United States Senate, explaining the attitude which the United Kingdom had adopted over the Schuman Plan. The letter enumerated the contributions made by the British to the cause of Western union in the past; claimed that they were at present working closely with other European governments to "develop and accomplish the common purposes which give increased strength and unity to all"; and asserted that it was the Commonwealth issue which had precluded British participation in the Schuman Plan, because "it is only as the focus of the Commonwealth that the strength of Britain can make its full contribution to European recovery and unity".[33]

This argument had a number of unusual and arresting features. The first was of course that neither the Commonwealth nor any other issue of material substance had been suggested by the British Government as an impediment during the exchange of notes with the French. The second was that the Commonwealth was in any event perhaps the argument least likely to be received sympathetically by the Americans, however relevant it may have been. The third was that it was genuinely difficult to see how the Schuman Plan itself could have materially affected the Commonwealth relationship in a seriously adverse manner. And the fourth and most singular aspect was that the only Commonwealth country which had yet conveyed an opinion to London, and the only one whose economic interests could possibly have been affected by British participation in the Schuman Plan, had already gone on record as favouring such participation. Pearson had publicly praised the Schuman Plan on 5 June as "a very important development ... the importance of which may well be as political as economic."[34] But more importantly, Prime Minister St. Laurent had written secretly to London, telling the British Government that the Canadians thought that "this was an important and far-reaching Plan ... and that ... it would be unwise for any Government not to fall in at once with the principles behind this Plan". Pearson revealed this démarche in September. He said at the time that they had not had any reply from London, and had possibly been interfering, but had merely been giving the British the benefit of their views.[35]

The motives behind the British refusal to participate were made possibly still more obscure in the full-scale debate on the issue which began in the House of Commons on 26 June. All that did seem obvious was that front-benchers in both major parties were not noticeably influenced in their choice of expressions by any concern for the feelings of Schuman and other European integrationists. Two hundred and fifty Conservatives packed the Opposition benches, while only 150 Labour members attended to give support to a policy already implemented. Anthony Eden opened the debate by moving a resolution that:

> This House requests His Majesty's Government, in the interests of peace and full employment, to accept the invitation to take part in the discussions on the Schuman Plan, subject to the same condition as that made by the Netherlands Government, namely, that if discussions show the Plan to be not practicable, freedom of action is reserved.

He went on to argue that the British had undertaken direct or implied commitments before without regarding them as incompatible with their position as the heart and centre of the Commonwealth and Empire. He referred to Prime Minister Menzies of Australia as one of the Commonwealth statesmen of every party who had supported the closer union of the United Kingdom with Europe and the United States. Eden then came to what might seem the heart of the matter, when he insisted that "the acceptance of European federation was no part of the political declaration signed by the Six Powers, and was at no time a condition of the negotiation". In saying this, Eden was presumably arguing that the Schuman Plan was a potentially valuable form of Western union, which the United Kingdom could commit itself to trying to implement, without at the same time committing itself to entering into a full federal union, which might have implications for the Commonwealth relationship. However, he then tended to confuse the issue by referring to Attlee on the subject of federating or perishing, and concluded:

> I do not personally take that view. I think that when these closer relations develop they are more likely to take the form of a confederation than a federation, and more likely to be Atlantic in area than European; but there was nothing in entry to these negotiations which compelled the Government to make up their minds on this issue.[36]

In that case, it might have been as well if Eden had not raised the issue at all, unless he were concerned to prove that while on past record he might favour the participation of the United Kingdom in a European customs union, he did not necessarily approve participation in a customs union as yet. This was something most speakers could agree upon, but which on Eden's own showing did not seem to have much bearing on the direct issue of participation in the Schuman Plan. Thus Cripps really left the debate where it was when he said that in the view of the British Government "participation in a political federation, limited to Western Europe, is not compatible either with our Commonwealth ties, our obligations as a member of the wider Atlantic Community, or as a world power", and argued that Eden's speech implied that the Opposition really agreed with this, as indeed they seemed to.

However, it was one thing to say that political federation was not acceptable or viable for the time being, and quite another to say that the Schuman Plan itself, which was not a federation, was also not viable. This was the point made by Arthur Greenwood, the Labour member for Wakefield, who made one of the less fortunate prophecies of the week by affirming that the "Schuman Plan as it stands holds out no hope for Europe, insofar as it is a European Plan only. Europe by itself can never save itself."[37] He might at least have mentioned that it was clearly not the fault of Schuman and the French Government if the plan were in fact confined to the Continent at the moment. David Eccles introduced a realistic if scarcely diplomatic argument in favour of British participation when asked if Cripps "would ... prefer such an authority, with all the dangers and things which he dislikes, to be set up in Europe without us, rather than that we should go in and try to make the power of the authority reasonable?"[38] Many Europeans would indeed have shared his sentiments, if not his words.

However, a considerably less respectful argument was then delivered by R.H.S. Crossman, the Labour member for Coventry East, from whom one would naturally have expected precision of language:

> The amount of enthusiasm for federal union in any country is a measure of its defeatism and of its feeling of inability to measure up to its own problems ... Look at the nations with self-confidence in Europe. They are not addicts of federal union ... We cannot be a member of a federation of Europe, even of a confederation — Switzerland is a confederation — and remain the motherland of a Commonwealth of independent nation-states.[39]

The most obvious comments on this analysis were that it had been generally agreed that federation was not at stake anyway; that the Swedes, Irish and Portuguese might indeed be more self-confident than the French, Dutch or Germans, but that this might be because they had altogether different problems to cope with; and that the only distinction that was worth making between a federation and a confederation was that legal independence was lost in the former and preserved in the latter, so that a nation could probably be a member of a confederation and retain almost any relationship it chose with other nations outside the confederation, especially if these were themselves fully independent. This again did not seem to advance the debate significantly.

Nor did even Churchill clarify matters as much as might have been expected. He began by asserting that the United Kingdom should help, sponsor and aid in every possible way the movements towards European unity.

> We should seek steadfastly for means to become intimately associated with it ... We are asked in a challenging way: "Are you prepared to part with any degree of national sovereignty in any circumstances for the sake of a larger synthesis?" The Conservative and Liberal Parties say, without hesitation, that we are prepared to consider, and if convinced to accept, the abrogation of national sovereignty, provided that we are satisfied with the conditions and the safeguards.

Then he too began to speak as if federalism were the immediate issue, claiming that "a hard-and-fast federal constitution for Europe is not within the scope of practical affairs", although he had certainly seemed to have been suggesting rather the contrary when he had advocated "a kind of United States of Europe" in 1946. He also warned that it would not be possible to accept the High Authority if that body had the power "to tell Great Britain not to cut any more coal or make any more steel, but to grow tomatoes instead", which was of course not its purpose and was unlikely to be its intention. In conclusion, he berated the French for making pedantic stipulations before sitting in council with their wartime comrades. Pedantry had certainly been one of the qualities most evident on both sides in the exchange of notes, but the overall tone of Churchill's address made it difficult to see whether or not he was actually supporting the resolution as it had been moved.

The debate naturally made the unhappiest impression possible on the Continent. Europeans who might have been encouraged by the wording of Eden's resolution found it difficult to comprehend the relevance of the arguments used on both sides in the debate; to see why it had been necessary to criticize the Schuman initiative and Western union in general in terms of quite such severity; or to equate some of the reservations now expressed with the enthusiastic support for even the most extreme forms of Western union made in earlier years, frequently by the same speakers. But the most shattering blow to what remained of Anglo-French good-feeling was yet to be delivered. On 1 July the British Secretary of State for War, John Strachey, referred to the Schuman Plan in a press conference at Colchester in the following terms:

> This is a plan to give the control of the coal and steel industries of Europe, including the British coal and steel industries, into the hands of a council of 8 or 9 men ... These dictators, responsible to no-one but themselves, were to have the power, for example, to close down half the coalmines of South Wales if they thought fit and if it would profit the shareholders of those industries to do so, and the British Government were not to have any say in the matter ... Now, what was the purpose of putting forward a plan like that? Is it not perfectly obvious that the real purpose was precisely to put up a barrier against the control of the basic industries of Europe by the European peoples...? Nationalisation ... is an alarm bell to the great capitalist interests of Europe, therefore they put up this sort of plan by which the real power in these industries is put in the hands of an irresponsible international body free from all democratic control ... The last time a plan of this sort was proposed was by the ex-Governor of the Bank of England, the late Montagu Norman ... Well, Labour had only, of course, to expose the plot in order to defeat it ... even some of the Tories could hardly stomach it.[40]

As has been seen, the Schuman Plan had had its point of origin in external as well as domestic political issues. That is to say, its essential purpose was to enable the economic development of Germany to take place in a manner consistent as far as possible with the interests of other Western countries. Nobody else had suggested any other practical technique by which this basic problem might be solved. The issue of the Schuman Plan was thus not primarily one between state or private control of industry. Even if it had been, all available evidence indicated that its intention was precisely the opposite of that attributed to it by Strachey. It was in the simplest terms an attempt to forestall a capitalist plot, initiated by governments many of which had already carried out more extensive schemes of nationalization and state intervention in industry than those essayed or projected by the British Labour Government. But the aspect of the Strachey analysis most disturbing to Europeans was not that the plan could still be presented in such a way by a British Minister. It was rather that a member of the British Government could be so unconcerned about the effect that his words would have on the Continent. *Le Figaro* described the incident as shocking.[41] The *Yorkshire Post* referred to it as a vicious attack on a measure put forward by a distinguished friendly statesman.[42] It was indeed hard to call it anything else. The *News Chronicle* perhaps made the most pertinent comment of all when it said that the Labour Government was certainly having no luck in its handling of the Schuman proposals.[43] Strachey was summoned to Downing Street to discuss with Prime Minister Attlee the new problems which he had created for the latter. On 11 July he made a formal retraction of his words in the House of Commons, which moved the *Manchester Guardian* to remark that it was difficult to recall any speech by a British Minister which had given the impression of a mind moving at quite so low a level.[44] Attlee said succinctly that Strachey had explained what he had said, and had said that "in certain respects what he said was unfortunate, and I agree". He then went on to affirm that the position of the British Government was "perfectly well understood by our friends in France ... we cannot accept in advance any supranational authority". The British Government had welcomed the French initiative clearly and explicitly, but had not been prepared to enter into discussions with a prior acceptance of the supranational principle.[45]

However, it was unfortunately obvious that the position of the British Government had indeed not been perfectly understood in France, and that there were people in the United Kingdom, in the British Government itself, and certainly in the Commonwealth who also seemed to be having difficulty. Dalton and Strachey, for example, as two socialists, seemed to have come to completely different opinions about the general desirability of the plan. The *New Statesman and Nation* also found it appropriate to change tack, commenting in stirringly patriotic terms, amended from Dalton's manifesto without apology to the author or regard for his later views, that:

> Great Britain is not just an island off the coast of Europe. It is the home of a people that mean to defend their right to live and of a great social experiment which the Government has no right to jeopardize in the interest of an unviable project of economic union in a tormented fraction of Europe.[46]

This was rather less than friendly. Meanwhile, the relevance of the Commonwealth issue still awaited definition. The Canadian Government had already chosen to regard it as insubstantial. The only Commonwealth Prime Minister actually to endorse the decision of the British Government was the Labour Prime Minister of New Zealand, Peter Fraser, who said in Wellington that the Schuman Plan would have placed the sovereignty of Britain under a body responsible to no one, and that the British Government had therefore done the right thing when it chose to stand by the Commonwealth of Nations.[47] But what still needed to be shown was that there was indeed some fundamental conflict between membership of the coal-steel pool and leadership of the Commonwealth. The nature of this conflict was not made any clearer by Patrick Gordon-Walker, the Under-Secretary of State for Commonwealth Relations in the British Labour Government, when he told the Canadian Club in Ottawa that the British Government welcomed the Schuman initiative, and wanted the maximum pooling of economic and military resources in Europe, but could not accept federation, because they would never accept any arrangement that would in effect take them out of the Commonwealth.[48] But the most obvious thing about the Schuman Plan was that it was a positive alternative to federalism. Even Anthony Eden had pointed this out. And in any case the Canadian Government did not seem to believe that entry into the Schuman Plan could significantly affect the Commonwealth relationship. Statements of this kind could only seem to be ill-chosen attempts to confuse the real issue of the independent world power role of the United Kingdom.

But what was most important in all this was the little real difference that had been made to European attitudes towards the United Kingdom itself. Western Europe still looked to London for leadership. It still waited for the British to become convinced of the rationality of the Community enterprise, and to nominate the terms on which they would consent to participate in it. The enormous moral authority of British power and prestige could

46

not be eroded entirely by the indiscretions and obfuscations of a few months. That unhappy task was to take years. It was to be substantially completed by a new confrontation, having its origin in events already in train even before the House of Commons began its first debate on the Schuman Plan, and destined to be enormously more protracted, more anguished and ultimately more injurious to British interests than the latter had been. The Schuman affair lost the British a unique opportunity to exercise their power to govern the destinies of Western Europe. The four-year crisis of the European army helped to ensure that that power would be safely transferred into the hands of General de Gaulle.

NOTES

1. U.N., *Economic Survey of Europe in 1950*.
2. Susan Strange, "The Schuman Plan", *Yearbook of World Affairs* (London: Stevens, 1951), p. 110.
3. France, Assemblée Nationale, *Débats,* 26 July 1950.
4. Canada, House of Commons, *Debates,* 22 February 1950.
5. *Le Figaro* (Paris), 9 May 1958.
6. *Le Monde* (Paris), 9 May 1960.
7. U.K., Cmnd. 7970, p. 3.
8. *Scotsman* (Edinburgh), 11 May 1950.
9. *New Statesman and Nation,* 13 May 1950.
10. *Reynolds' News,* 14 May 1950.
11. *Daily Telegraph* (London), 18 May 1950.
12. *Ibid.*
13. *Economist,* 20 May 1950.
14. *New Statesman and Nation,* 20 May 1950.
15. U.K., Cmnd. 7970, p.8.
16. *Ibid.*
17. *Ibid.,* p. 10.
18. *Ibid.*
19. *Ibid.,* p. 11.
20. *Ibid.,* p. 13.
21. *Ibid.,* pp. 14-15.
22. *New Statesman and Nation,* 10 June 1950, p. 645.
23. *Scotsman,* 13 June 1950.
24. Section Français de l'Internationale Ouvrière.
25. *Le Populaire,* 14 June 1950.
26. *Daily Worker* (London), 14 June 1950.
27. *L'Humanité,* 15 June 1950.
28. *Daily Telegraph,* 19 June 1950.
29. *Times* (London), 17 June 1950.
30. *Ibid.,* 18 June 1950.
31. *Ibid.,* 21 June 1950.
32. *Daily Worker,* 24 June 1950.
33. *New York Herald Tribune,* 24 June 1950.
34. Canada, H. of C., *Debates,* 5 June 1950.

35. Canada, Department of External Affairs, *Statements and Speeches*, 4 September 1950.
36. U.K., House of Commons, *Debates*, Vol. CDLXXVI, cols. 1907-18.
37. *Ibid.*, cols. 1958-59.
38. *Ibid.*
39. *Ibid.*, cols. 2039-41.
40. *Times*, 2 July 1950.
41. *Le Figaro*, 4 July 1950.
42. *Yorkshire Post*, 8 July 1950.
43. *News Chronicle* (London), 7 July 1950.
44. *Manchester Guardian*, 12 July 1950.
45. U.K., H. of C., *Debates*, Vol. CDLXXVII, col. 1159.
46. *New Statesman and Nation*, 8 July 1950.
47. N.Z., House of Representatives, *Debates*, 5 July 1950.
48. *Times*, 9 July 1950.

3. Gentlemen, Beware

If the handling of the Schuman Plan by the Labour Government left something to be desired, it was still considerably less unfortunate in its direct consequences than the attempts of the Conservative leaders to turn the situation to their own advantage. On 8 August 1950 Macmillan and Eccles proposed in the Council of Europe that certain modifications should be introduced into the Schuman Plan. These were an inter-governmental council of ministers to which member states could appeal against the decisions of the High Authority, the right of national veto, the right of unilateral withdrawal, and the liability to expulsion. The first of these was indeed provided for ultimately in the institutions of the coal-steel pool. However, the others would have necessarily destroyed the binding nature of the concept. As former French Premier Paul Reynaud explained to the Council of Europe:

> ... from the moment when you have set the Schuman Plan in

motion, when you have modified the economic situation in Western Europe, when you have closed down certain mines and certain factories, it will be impossible for one of the Members to be able to say to us: "I am going home, and now you will have to manage by yourselves!" Would you then be able to open your mines once more, to seek out those miners who have scattered in all directions ...[1]

All present had more serious things to think about, in any event.

The attack by North Korea against the regime of Syngman Rhee had given a new and practical urgency to the two greatest fears of the West. These were that the Cold War might escalate globally into a hot one, and that the Americans might be unwilling or unable to defend themselves and their scattered allies as well. On 10 August, as the first counter-attack of the United States Marines faltered before the Chinju Pass, François de Menthon, formerly Economics Minister under Bidault, chose to disregard the fact that the constitution of the Council of Europe denied that body competence to discuss military matters. He tabled a resolution in the Consultative Assembly, calling for the creation of a European High Commission of Defence, responsible to the Council of Europe and having responsibilities similar to those of national Ministers of Defence. Paul Reynaud intervened again to ask for "the immediate creation, among the free peoples of Europe, of an effective European Authority having at its disposal a single European Army subject to European control, cooperating with the United States and Canada". He turned while speaking to address the representatives of the British Conservative Party, who had earlier supported a resolution to take their country into the Schuman Plan, and who could therefore be expected to be responsive to this even more urgent call for common effort.[2] The challenge was apparently accepted by Churchill. He immediately matched Reynaud's proposal with one which seemed to make the supranational character of the proposed Army more precise. His amendments consisted in substituting "unified European Army" for "single European Army", "proper democratic control" for "European control", and inserting immediately afterwards the phrase "under the authority of a European Minister of Defence". These alterations could scarcely seem to have any purpose other than to stress the necessity for a federal political structure to administer the European army, since a minister naturally has to be a member of a government, and responsible to a parliament. What both resolutions also seemed to assume, though unfortunately without saying so, was that the United Kingdom would be participating, since there was no mention of the British army's being separate. In any case, the Conservatives had already given their support to British participation in the Schuman Plan, so it would not be surprising if they endorsed the European army as well.

It was also not surprising that the Labour Government should continue to endorse neither. The issue immediately at stake was of course that of utilizing German military capacity for the defence of Western Europe, just as the Schuman Plan had been intended to use their productive capacity for its economic revival. On 2 September Dean Acheson, the American Secretary of State, presented Bevin and Schuman directly with the problem in Washington. Bevin was able to obtain the consent of his Government to the proposition that German divisions should be enlisted to serve under the NATO Supreme Commander. Schuman for his part was unable to commit the French Government to accept German military resurgence except on the terms which they had already prescribed for German economic resurgence, namely, that it should take place in a manner which would preclude the possibility of its being used to the disadvantage of Germany's western neighbours. The new French Premier, René Pleven, accordingly brought forward Churchill's proposal for an integrated European army, indissolubly linked to a European Political Authority, and responsible to a European Minister of Defence. This was acceptable to the Americans. It was also acceptable to the Assemblée Nationale, which endorsed the Pleven Plan, as it was now called, on 25 October, rejecting the alternative of an autonomous German army. However, the Labour Government in its turn rejected the possibility of British participation on 13 November in a speech by Ernest Davies, the Under-Secretary of State for Foreign Affairs, who also rebuked the Council of Europe for discussing the matter in the first place. Indeed, the dying Ernest Bevin also argued that the French scheme, which had also been Churchill's, could only delay the building of Europe's defences. Security was to be found only in the Atlantic Community: "... in our view, Europe is not enough; it is not big enough, it is not strong enough, and it is not able to stand by itself."[3]

However, it was not the intention of the European army to make Europe stand by itself. It was rather to enable it to make a more useful contribution to Western defence, by utilizing German military potential in what seemed to be the only manner acceptable at all to the rest of Western Europe. Nor was it really logical to condemn the European army, any more than the Schuman Plan, as being limited to the Continent, when the most obvious desire of the Europeans was that the British should themselves participate. The British might have had sufficient reasons for refusing to do so, but it was hardly just to imply that they had not been invited.

In any event, the Americans persuaded the British Government to accept the European army as being worthwhile, at least for the Continent. On 14 September Acheson and Herbert Morrison made a Joint Declaration with Schuman in Washington, supporting the inclusion of a democratic Germany in a Continental European Community, on a basis of equality. But the crisis which had given impetus to the new project rapidly began to lose its urgency. The Van Fleet victories of June 1951 opened prospects of a negotiated peace by setting the Chinese armies up for destruction. They accordingly allayed the prime fears of the Europeans by proving that the Americans could indeed resist Communist aggression without sparking off a global war in the process.

Hopes for the European army project now seemed to rest entirely on the willingness of the new British Conservative Government to provide the necessary encouragement. This might very well entail actual British participation. Such would have been reasonably expected in any case from Churchill's sponsorship of the scheme, just as British participation in the Schuman Plan might have been expected from the attitude of the Conservatives in the debate of June 1950. However, no reference was made by the new Government to the possibility of British participation in the plan. Even before returning to office Eden had dismissed the possibility of their participation in the army. However, this could hardly be reconciled with the responsibilities which Churchill had taken upon himself in the Council of Europe.

Paul-Henri Teitgen, President of the integrationist Mouvement Républicain Populaire (MRP) and already six times a Minister of the Fourth Republic, accordingly put the issue directly to the new Government. He argued that British participation was necessary to the European army, not only for its own sake, but because "the day Continental States are called upon to establish this Confederation without Great Britain, they will gradually, one after the other, decline to establish it..."[4] However, Sir David Maxwell Fyffe, the new Conservative Home Secretary, replied by referring to Churchill's analysis of the three circles, which he said made it impossible for the United Kingdom to participate in any federal project. He did not consider that there was any widespread desire on the Continent for federation with the United Kingdom.

This again seemed a little misleading, although undoubtedly the European army scheme, as presented by Churchill, did have federal implications rather more evidently than had been the case with the Schuman Plan. But it was clear beyond question that there was a widespread desire and expectation in Europe for British participation in the European army, whether this scheme were intrinsically federal or not. And both the desire and the expectation were far more solidly founded than had been the case with the Schuman Plan. Paul Reynaud had obvious grounds for describing Maxwell Fyffe's speech as "a direct repudiation of the stirring motion as worded by the present leader of the British Government". He was also showing himself an accurate political forecaster when he continued:

> If the opponents of the European Army can say to our Assemblée Nationale: "Britain is inviting us to submerge the French Army in a vast European Army, but she is taking good care not to do the same herself; in this way she is retaining a military power which will give her the right to speak in international conferences whilst you will be left only with the right to keep silent" — if they can say that there will no longer be a French Army but there will still be a British Army, what will be the reaction of my colleagues? Here I wish to utter a solemn warning to our British friends. Britain's refusal to take part in the European Army would, I am very much afraid ... lead the Assemblée Nationale to reject the European Army, and I believe that no one here would in his heart of hearts dare to blame it.[5]

Further denunciations and warnings followed Churchill when he flew to Washington at the end of the year. Paul-Henri Spaak, the Belgian Foreign Minister, supported Reynaud's prophecies:

> We thought that the political change which had taken place

in Britain would provide us with a new opportunity of closer cooperation. We anxiously awaited what the Conservative Government representatives were going to tell us ... Gentlemen, beware! We Continental Europeans have said a number of times that we did not understand everything which the British told us about the Commonwealth and its difficulties, but sometimes — and here let me speak quite frankly — we had the feeling that these difficulties which you explained to us badly and invoked increasingly constituted some kind of pretext rather than any valid reason. But be very careful! Some time hence, public opinion will say that Continental Europeans are using the absence of Britain as an excuse not to create a United Europe.[6]

Certainly, a lucid and convincing statement on the relevance of the Commonwealth issue had not yet been made by any British leader. It was of course fully possible that the British might have thought that the projects currently in hand for uniting Europe were not desirable for the Europeans, or for themselves; but in any of these cases the Churchill resolution would have appeared to be a serious indiscretion, which demanded an explanation. And in any event the British were now faced with the situation, at least partly of their own making, that Europe might indeed be united without them, in a way which they had rejected, and that the leaders of this new Europe might well feel little gratitude or respect for British policies. And this development would certainly not be profitable to the Commonwealth or to anybody else.

France was obviously going to be crucial. The Netherlands socialist leader, Van der Goes van Naters, had said pertinently that Joan of Arc had had an easier job than the present generation of Europeans, since she had been able to do without the British while they could not: "Spirits have been conjured up without our having even the remedy of the stake. We have to convince both the French and the English; and this is not always possible."[7] President Eisenhower had a reputation as a reconciler of differences. The communiqué issued in Washington on 14 December indeed seemed to represent a working compromise among the parties concerned. Eisenhower, Churchill, Eden, and Pleven all joined in welcoming the decision by the Assemblée Nationale accepting the idea of the European army. It was also agreed that the British would enter into formal relations with the High Authority of the Schuman Plan, later to be known as the European Coal and Steel Community (ECSC), as soon as it was set up; that they would maintain armed forces on the Continent to fulfil their obligations in the common cause; that they would associate themselves with the new European Defence Community (EDC) as closely as possible in all stages of its political and military development; and that they would all stand together in true comradeship.[8]

This compromise did seem to accept that the United Kingdom would be remaining outside the scheme. The British would therefore be placing themselves in a category of power rather different from that of the Western European countries which joined the European army. There were convincing arguments in favour of the contention that the United Kingdom was in fact in a different category of power. Probably only one Continental country would have contested that view; and that one was the country whose acceptance of the scheme was indispensable to its success. The French could never have been pleased to accept the assumption that the United Kingdom had pretensions to consideration as a world power which were denied to themselves. It was more displeasing than ever to accept such a subordinate position as French economic and military power alike seemed to be collapsing under the strains of an ambitious external policy. The appearance of great power status became necessarily all the more important as its reality disappeared in the winter of 1951. Nothing could have been more bitter than the fact that the Van Fleet victories, which demonstrated the capacity of the Americans to contain and destroy an Asian challenge, should have been followed within a month by the Ho Chi Minh offensive in Indo-China, which demonstrated increasingly the inability of the French to do the same. Three years of frustrated counter-attack and humiliating withdrawal brought the French economy to the point of collapse, at the same time as they exposed the precariousness of French military and imperial pretensions. Mushrooming demands for munitions and supplies exacerbated inflationary pressures already latent in the French economic structure of full employment and high welfare costs. Spiralling prices and wages began to cause French industry to price itself out of world markets. French reserves of gold and foreign exchange consequently fell through 1951 from about $U.S.1,023 million to below $U.S.628 million, or barely enough for six weeks' imports.

Conditions of this kind naturally fostered the rise of aggressive nationalism in France. The most influential form was predictably that expressed by General de Gaulle. In a press conference on 21 December he stressed the need to base any new Europe upon a Franco-German entente, instead of trying to lose this basic problem in an overall European solution; opposed any abandonment by France of its national army, while insisting that precautions would have to be taken against the revival of a German hegemony in Europe; and argued that any consolidation of Europe would have to take the form of a Confederation of States, to which every state would delegate a part of its sovereignty. The Gaullists in the Assemblée promptly took up their leader's words. The Palewski-Triboulet Resolution, tabled a week later, called for a European referendum on the question of the establishment of a European Constituent Assembly with authority over defence, economic and cultural matters, and dismissed as valueless the Schuman concept of unifying Europe through the establishment of a series of functional communities.

It was always difficult to contain Gaullist demands within a mutually compatible framework, although the ultimate objectives were clear enough. It was for example difficult to argue simultaneously for a Confederation and for a Constitutent Assembly with real powers. But the important thing about the Gaullist proposals was that they struck simultaneously at both the idea of a federal solution for Europe, and the continuance of British predominance in European affairs. They would have retained national armies, which the federalists and integrationists were alike pledged to abolish; and they would have introduced a Constituent Assembly, which the British would apparently have been unable to join. The Gaullist ideal has always remained a Europe sufficiently united to exclude the United Kingdom, but not sufficiently so to prevent its being dominated by France.

All this was in the future. Meanwhile, plans continued for the development of further communities to be associated with the ones for Coal and Steel and Defence. In January the French Minister of Agriculture, M. Pflimlin, proposed in the Council of Europe that a single European market should be created for agricultural products along the lines of the coal-steel pool. The Assemblée Nationale also spelled out the form of the overriding European Political Community which was going to co-ordinate the activities of the functional communities. At the same time, it again rejected the alternative of an autonomous German army, and called for a European Defence Community, subordinate to "a supranational political body, with limited but real powers, responsible to the representatives of the Assemblies of the European peoples ..." Eden attempted to provide an institutional framework in which these Community projects could be associated with the other European states, by proposing the following month that the Committee of Ministers of the Council of Europe could function as the Highest Authority of the European Coal and Steel and Defence Communities. This could be done by appointing the Ministers of the six member countries of the Communities to act as a sub-committee of the Council controlling the management of the Communities. However, the Western Europeans were too actively engaged at the time to afford serious treatment to this bid for harmony. It was unfortunately not revived until circumstances had deteriorated so far as to deny it any chance of success.

At this stage, difficulties in the British position were considerably heightened by the decision of the Canadian Government to support the Defence Community, as they had previously supported the Coal and Steel Community. This decision is sufficiently explicable in terms of their own domestic preoccupations. The European army issue was clearly exacerbating relations between the Americans, the British, and the French; and the need to reconcile these three different approaches to reality had been the basic concern of Canadian politicians since before Confederation. One such reconciliation had been found in the NATO Alliance, which was of course the institution most likely to be damaged by the trans-Atlantic and cross-Channel tensions now developing. Pearson developed an oblique approach. On 26 January 1952 he began by hailing the European army as a move towards European unity, and noted that it had been alleged that the United Kingdom was delaying its development by its attitudes of aloofness. He did not comment on the accuracy of these allegations. However, he did affirm that Canadians had no right to quarrel with the decision of the United Kingdom not to join the EDC, "especially as she is making through NATO an important contribution to the defence of Europe". He then developed his own variation of the three circles theme, explaining that the three external points of reference of Canadian diplomacy were "North America, the British Isles and the Continental European group", forming the component parts of the Atlantic Community, which he described as "the grand design of the twentieth century".[9] This left the play much as it was, except to establish Canada's position as an interested party. Pearson sounded a more urgent note after his return from the meeting of the NATO Council in Lisbon in March. He told the House of Commons that he had originally feared that the EDC might develop a separate existence from NATO, and thereby damage the supremely important Atlantic concept. These fears had since been allayed by reciprocal guarantees between the two associations. These guarantees could nonetheless not come into force themselves until the EDC treaty had been ratified. Pearson accordingly warned Canadians to reserve their most enthusiastic plaudits against that day, because of the obvious difficulties in the way of legislative action in Bonn, Paris, "and possibly other capitals".[10] His next comment was similarly indirect, but certainly could be understood only as support for the idea of functional communities, and also as a deliberate rebuttal of Bevin's admittedly tragically inept criticism of the EDC:

> It is argued that European Unity is not only too late; it is also too little; that there must be Atlantic Federation or Union, if the Western World is to prosper or even to survive ... I think that normally it is better to proceed on a step-by-step and functional basis ... rather than to attempt to bring about, by one great leap, some grandiose plan for union now.[11]

Pearson's point may have been weakened by the fact that nobody was seriously advocating Atlantic union then. The "step-by-step" argument was also used by Anthony Nutting, the new British Under-Secretary of State for Foreign Affairs, for a rather different purpose. Nutting claimed that adherence to this principle in fact prohibited the British from participating in the proposed Agricultural Community. He also said that the United Kingdom could not merge its identity with any one of its three areas of interest without doing a disservice to them all. The British would therefore be unable to play a really effective part in European affairs if the development of a European Political Authority were to be entrusted to an Assembly outside the framework of the Council of Europe, and limited to the parliamentarians of the Six ECSC countries.[12] Paul Reynaud promptly accused the British of threatening to turn their backs on Europe, which seemed just about the opposite to what Nutting had been suggesting. Paul-

Henri Spaak repeated his anguished charge that "every time you could help us, every time you could cast a vote which might speed us and everyone else along the path to this restricted Community, either you vote against us or you abstain". And Guy Mollet commented: "It is impossible that, at the very moment when we are trying to meet you and have the feeling of having succeeded, with tireless persistence you should tell us: 'It is all right: you have amended your text, but it is no longer any concern of ours.' "[13]

Statements like this reflected the embarrassment of European politicians who had committed themselves to hazardous policies in the expectation of British support. The embarrassment was all the greater because no British Government had said or done anything since 1947 to justify these expectations, although undoubtedly members of the present Government had done so while in opposition. Again, feelings were not assuaged by the tendency of British spokesmen to justify the position of their Government by abstract arguments whose relevance was not immediately discernible. Thus Eden and Nutting replied simply that the House of Commons and the British people were not prepared to join in a political federation, and that both the Coal and Steel and the Defence Communities involved a commitment to federal union. But it was scarcely likely that any European national government would have been prepared at that stage to join a true federal union. The chief recommendation of the Communities seemed to be precisely that they offered an approach to more effective Western union with the minimum of federal implications. The British certainly seemed to carry this position to impressively doctrinaire lengths. Thus on 12 December 1952 Spaak proposed a European Health Community, to co-ordinate systems of sanitation and social hygiene in Western Europe under a supranational authority. This might have appeared both laudable in intention and innocuous in its implications. However, the British representative objected that the United Kingdom could not participate in any such organization of a supranational character.

These attitudes on the part of the British were of course tending to encourage French opposition to the EDC. The Canadians, in a characteristic display of bipartisanship, increased their vocal support for the EDC, and for any modifications of present British policy that might assist the creation of the European army. Pearson described the EDC as "the best and safest proposal yet made to bring Germany into the Western defence system". He hoped that the United Kingdom might find it possible to take even further steps than it had already in the way of closer association with the EDC, "steps which will not prejudice, of course, her Commonwealth and overseas interests and responsibilities". John G. Diefenbaker, the Leader of the Conservative Opposition, hailed the Schuman Plan as "an event of real symbolic and practical importance in the development of European integration", and went on to give support to the warning of John Foster Dulles that unless the Europeans moved towards unity they would risk peril from which it would be beyond American power to save them. He accordingly proposed that Canada and the United Kingdom should agree to extend the NATO Charter from a term of twenty to one of fifty years, to coincide with the duration of the EDC Treaty. "Building hope in Europe is a contribution all in America can make."[14]

It was fitting that in this combined North American attempt to influence British and European policies, the United States should have supplied the vinegar, and Canada the jam. But neither approach was likely to be effective now in restoring viability to the EDC. In the first place, there was no longer any possibility, if indeed there had ever been, of counting on British participation in the scheme. Indeed, the decision of the British Government to join with French industrial interests against the other members of the ECSC in squashing a proposal to rehabilitate dismantled German steel plants led Schuman to demand that the ECSC should be placed under a Political Authority limited to the Six, to get it away from British influence. The Beneluxers were already arguing that no effective progress in the Community approach could be made, unless the Six could first be united in a formal customs union. The proposed Constitution for the Political Community was not even considered by the Foreign Ministers of the Six when they met in Rome in March 1953.

In London, Churchill now asserted that the United Kingdom did not intend to merge itself in "the European Federation", by which he meant the EDC. The special position of the United Kingdom towards the latter was to be expressed "by the preposition 'with', but not 'of' — we are with them but not of them: we have our own Commonwealth and Empire". He then asserted that: "On the Continent we share their fate ... No nation has ever run such risks in times which I have read about or lived in and no nation has ever received such little recognition for it".[15] It was difficult to follow Churchill's reasoning here, as the British had indeed little choice but to commit their armed forces to the Continent to resist Communist aggression, since they could hardly hope any longer to be able to beat off an attack from within their own islands. However, the immediate effect of his speech was to accelerate the collapse of confidence in the EDC in Western Europe. In a meeting in Paris only two days later, Adenauer and Premier de Gasperi of Italy alone accepted the idea of a supranational authority for the Political Community. Even Bidault of France reserved his position. The Netherlands Foreign Minister, Dr. Beyen, affirmed that the only solution to the difficulties of the Six lay in the creation of a customs union in the manner of Benelux. On 16 May the Belgian Foreign Minister, Van Zeeland, said that he would unconditionally oppose the entry of his country into any continental federation which did not include the United Kingdom.

Dana Wilgress, the Canadian Under-Secretary of State for External Affairs, now intervened to avert European criticism of the British position. He said that it was not really correct to see the United Kingdom as having "its back to Europe, facing the Seven Seas", although it was inevitably true that "the people of Britain look out towards the Commonwealth and feel that, although they are in Europe, their history and their destiny are determined mainly by their interests overseas".[16]

This was surely true of the British. It had also become true in a rather different sense of the French. The British could still regard their overseas involvements as a fundamental aspect of their claim to be a world power. The French could regard theirs as liable to destroy any claim they had to be a power at all. Military and financial collapse loomed more menacingly than ever, after a delusive rally in the closing months of 1952. As the outfought French Expeditionary Force fell back through the Red River Basin in Indo-China, French holdings of gold and foreign exchange sank to below $U.S.600 millions, as far as could be gathered from the deliberately confusing figures released by the Bank of France. Defeatism, pessimism, and *je m'en fiche*-ism combined with the last shreds of a defiant nationalism to reject further foreign involvements and preserve at least the symbols of

French greatness and independence, even if the realities had to be abandoned.

These circumstances were distinctly appropriate for a new Gaullist intervention. It was lead by Michel Debré, the leader of Rassemblement du Peuple Français in the Conseil de la République. On 18 September 1953 Debré again ridiculed the idea of the functional Communities, on the grounds that they could have no real foreign policy, because they had no power to sign treaties of common defence. Debré argued that political authority in a United Europe could only consist in a system of Conferences of Heads of State, as de Gaulle had previously suggested:

> ... there at last is a democratic reality, there is democratic legiti-macy in Europe ... an elected Assembly could be set up ... which, without being a legislative body, would have financial powers, would be entrusted with supervising Europe's evolution ... Then there would be an administrative organization, working under the authority of the Conference of the Heads of Govern-ments ... It would, however, have to be a real administrative organization, governed as it should be by a democratic political power; it must not be an irresponsible administrative body as it is at present ... [17]

Debré's Confederal Conference sounded like the Council of Europe, attended by Heads of State instead of Foreign Ministers. More immediately relevant was his sudden claiming for France of external pre-occupations of a kind similar to those put forward by British spokesmen seeking to explain their country's inability to participate in supranational organizations:

> ... we consider that an associated Europe is the only system of political authority compatible with the maintenance of the French Union. If Europe is to include a United Germany — and that, surely, goes without saying — she must adopt a political form which will enable our primary demand to be satisfied, namely, the maintenance of French unity, the maintenance of the French Union. [18]

It was an extraordinary kind of argument that could identify the union of the two Germanies with that of France and its former colonies. But the most important implication was quite obvious. Spaak had been right. Continental Europeans were beginning to speak like Englishmen. Debré was simply stating the claim of France to be a world power of the same order as the United

Kingdom, and therefore to be justified as much as the British in endeavouring to retain full independence of action, instead of committing itself to an organization limited to Continental Europe.

The Gaullists altered the basis of their argument later on. At the time, their claims were rendered more credible by an upturn in the French economy even more rapid than its collapse over the previous two years had been. This recovery was itself of course primarily due to the very circumstances of external defeat which had inspired the Gaullist call to independence. The deterioration of the military situation in Indo-China had led to a repatriation of resources and investment capital, which helped to make an independent policy more credible, at the very time that the main objective of that policy was being lost in the Red River Basin. France could not afford to defeat its enemies in Asia, but it could afford to defy its allies in NATO.

The ally most inviting defiance was of course the United States, which had failed to provide the French with the kind of military intervention which they felt necessary in Indo-China, and was now putting intensifying pressure on the politicians in Paris to submit their country's army to the supranational control of the EDC. Dulles expressed American concern in a passage that was far more a warning against what the Europeans might do to one another, than a threat of what the United States might do to them:

> If ... the EDC should not become effective, if France and Germany remain apart, so that they would again be potential enemies, then indeed there could be grave doubt whether Continental Europe could be made a place of safety. That would compel an agonising re-appraisal of United States policy.[19]

The Assemblée Nationale responded to this reasoned appeal by resolving that it would continue to examine the EDC treaty "by the methods and at the speed which it had hitherto adopted". This gave no hope for the future of the treaty at all. Dulles thereupon adopted the self-defeating policy of forbidding American representatives in Europe even to discuss the possibility of any alternative to the EDC, thereby leaving himself unable to suggest what to do if the Europeans failed to be impressed. The Canadians characteristically moved with more finesse. St. Laurent again assured Canadian support for the EDC as the best and quickest means of associating Germany with the European system and the

Atlantic Community, and added that the proposal itself came originally, "we must not forget, from France . . ."[20] In Bonn, he suggested the possibility of some overall Atlantic solution, in the event of the EDC's not coming into existence. Pearson similarly praised the EDC as "a satisfactory arrangement and indeed the only one which has been put forward officially", while still leaving his Government room to manoeuvre by admitting that the EDC was not the only means to the ends of continental defence and co-operation.[21]

In any event, effective governmental action in France had been rendered impossible by mounting political crises. On 1 April Premier Lamiel removed Marshal Juin from his NATO posts for expressing hostility to the EDC. Two days later, René Pleven was assaulted by crowds demonstrating around the Arc de Triomphe in support of the Marshal. Rumours circulated in Paris that the British were considering not extending their commitment to keep troops on the Continent. On 12 April, as the Communist siege lines tightened around Dien Bien Phu, Lamiel resorted to coup techniques against his parliamentary opponents. A cabinet meeting was called at one hour's notice to authorize the signing of the Anglo-French Military Convention. When the Gaullist deputies, led by Michel Debré, protested at having been given so little time to study the documents, Paul-Henri Teitgen, the President of the dominant Mouvement Républicain Populaire, recommended that they follow the appropriate constitutional course and resign. Eden now tried to give support to the EDC by proposing on 14 April that the British armoured division on the Continent would in fact be placed under EDC command, and would operate within the framework of the EDC, but would not pass under its political control. He explained that the division "would not become part of what one might call the EDC amalgamation, but ... it is there available to them within one of their corps for as long as the Supreme Commander wants to keep it".[22] This would certainly have settled any European doubts about the determination of the British to commit their forces to the Continent, but this could scarcely have been doubted seriously, and was in any case not the main point at issue. The main point was that the British were not prepared to see their army merged into an integrated European military body. Debré again pointed this out to his colleagues:

What Great Britain does not want is the submission to a political authority ... at the moment when we sign an act of association saying to ourselves: "It is only the first step for Great Britain", you put in place the foundation-stone of a continental federation of which the British Foreign Secretary, supported unanimously on this point by the House of Commons, states: "It is exactly because they want us to go that way that we are not going any further."[23]

Meanwhile, French military defeat in Asia had been confirmed by the surrender of the recklessly exposed garrison at Dien Bien Phu, after the Americans had refused to provide assistance to the extent required, and the Canadians had refused to provide any assistance at all, in a conflict endorsed neither by the United Nations nor by NATO. At a time of the greatest French bitterness towards the Anglo-Americans, as the French Expeditionary Force fell back from Phuly to the ports of re-embarkation, Churchill criticized the EDC itself, in terms which no degree of linguistic analysis makes fully convincing. He now insisted that what he had originally proposed in the Council of Europe four years before was:

> ... a long-term grand alliance under which national armies would operate under a unified allied command ... My conception involved no supranational institutions, and I saw no difficulty in Britain playing her full part in a scheme of that kind. However, the French approached this question from a constitutional rather than a purely political point of view. The result was that when they and the other five Continental nations worked out a detailed scheme, it took the form of a complete merger of national forces under federal supranational control ...[24]

It is relevant to remember that Churchill had not called in 1950 for a long-term grand alliance of national armies, but for a unified European army; and that he had not then placed it under a unified allied command, but under a European Minister of Defence. One can only feel that it would have been helpful if he had asked at the time for what he had really wanted, or if, seeing that the Europeans had failed to grasp his actual intention, he had pointed out their mistake to them on some convenient occasion during the previous four years.

In any case, French opinion had been organized to reject a solution which could only seem to condemn them to an inferior status in Europe, simply because it was one which the British had refused to accept for themselves. Majority opinion in France preferred to risk the consequences of admitting Germany to the struggle for world power status, rather than to resign from the struggle themselves. The EDC had been judged to be worse than the *Wehrmacht*.[25] It was a judgment arrived at finally without even the trouble of a debate in the Assemblée Nationale. The EDC went down almost unnoticed, lost by a vote on the preliminary motion of General Aumeran. With it went the Political Community, the Health Community and the Agricultural Community. All that was left after five years of experiments with the Community technique was the original Coal and Steel Community.

The defeat of the EDC was the decisive step which ultimately left the main power of decision in Western Europe in the 1960's in the hands of France. At the moment, indeed, it appeared to return that power to the United Kingdom. Europeans in general assumed that the major lesson of the affair had been the danger of trying to unite Europe in a manner unacceptable to the United Kingdom. But in a wider sense the defeat of the EDC had simply left Western Europe open as an arena for conflicting aspirations to world power status. The British had allowed the EDC to fall in order to preserve their own capacity for independent action. In so doing they had also preserved that capacity for the France of General de Gaulle. Van der Goes van Naters had been more prophetic than he had imagined. Spirits had indeed been conjured up for which no remedy was to be found.

NOTES

1. Council of Europe, Consultative Assembly, *Reports,* 8 August 1950.
2. C.C. Walton, "Background for the European Defense Community", *Political Science Quarterly,* LXVIII, No. 1 (1953), p. 48.
3. U.K., House of Commons, *Debates,* Vol. CDLXXXI, cols. 1173-74.
4. C. of E., C.A., *Reports,* 27 November 1951.
5. *Ibid.,* 28 November 1951.
6. *Ibid.,* 11 December 1951.
7. *Ibid.*
8. *Times* (London), 19 December 1951.
9. Canada, Department of External Affairs, *Statements and Speeches,* 26 January 1952.
10. *Ibid.*
11. *Ibid.,* 5 April 1952.
12. C. of E., C.A., *Reports,* 28 May 1952.

13. *Ibid.*, 30 May 1952.
14. Canada, House of Commons, *Debates*, 12 February 1953.
15. U.K., H. of C., *Debates*, Vol. DXV, col. 891.
16. Canada, D. of E.A., *S. and S.*, 20 May 1953.
17. C. of E., C.A., *Reports*, 18 September 1953.
18. *Ibid.*
19. U.S., State Department, *Bulletin*, 15 December 1953.
20. Canada, H. of C., *Debates*, 29 January 1954.
21. Canada, D. of E.A., *S. and S.*, 25 March 1954.
22. U.K., H. of C., *Debates*, Vol. DXXVI, col. 1145.
23. France, Conseil de la République, *Débats*, 25 May 1954.
24. U.K., H. of C., *Debates*, Vol. DXXX, col. 498.
25. France, Assemblée Nationale, *Débats*, 29 August 1954.

4. Negotiation Under Threats

The British moved promptly to fill the vacuum left in Europe by the collapse of the EDC. They did so, however, not by introducing a new form of organization, but by a further modification of one already functioning. The Protocol of Western European Union signed on 23 October 1954 essentially extended the terms of the Treaty of Brussels to include Germany and Italy, just as the Treaty of Brussels had extended the terms of the Treaty of Dunkirk to include Benelux. There were other changes. Article 2 of the Protocol bound the Contracting Parties to "promote the unity and encourage the progressive unification of Europe". The British also accepted an undertaking not to withdraw their forces presently assigned to the Supreme Allied Commander, Europe (SACEUR) "against the wishes of the majority of the High Contracting Parties".[1] The radical French Premier, Pierre Mendès-France, claimed that this was evidence of a new departure in British foreign policy, representing "a veritable abdication of sovereignty". However, the British still reserved the right to withdraw their forces "in the event of an acute overseas emergency".

Commonwealth interest in the Western European Union (WEU) as in the EDC was manifested only by the one Commonwealth country outside the United Kingdom which was linked with Europe by NATO. Pearson's refusal to commit himself exclusively to the EDC now left him free to welcome the WEU without having to speak too severely of the governments responsible for letting the European army fail. He told the House of Commons that:

> I do not think that any Atlantic or European system of security really could be satisfactory or effective to which France did not willingly contribute ... Therefore a Western alliance which excluded France or which was forced on France against the wishes of the majority of the population is not, as I say, a prospect which would be faced with any satisfaction by the Canadian Government or people ... The initiative to restore the situation came from the United Kingdom, whose earlier refusal to join the European Defence Community had highlighted French distaste.[2]

Canada thus again attempted to heal any breach between London and Paris. This was being done anyway, as it happened, by the discovery of a common Anglo-French interest in developments in the Mediterranean. The British Government issued statements expressing at the same time their determination to retain control in Cyprus in the face of mounting civil disturbance there, and their support for similar actions by the French in North Africa. They indeed argued that it was absolutely necessary for the French to do this, if they were to continue to play an effective part in Western Europe and elsewhere.

But it would be difficult for France to sustain its role in North Africa if the economic consequences were going to be the same as those resulting from its Asian involvement. A massive diversion of French military resources from Asia to Africa was implemented by Jacques Soustelle, the most prominent Gaullist in the Assemblée Nationale, who had been appointed Governor-General of Algeria by Mendès-France, with instructions to apply a policy of "pitiless severity". Between May and December 1955 French forces in Algeria rose from 80,000 to 170,000 men, or virtually the same number as had been under arms in Indo-China, before the fall of Dien Bien Phu. Nonetheless, the resilience of the French economy enabled these renewed strains to be supported for the time being without untoward signs of inflation. Exchange reserves rose from $U.S.1,369 million at the beginning of 1955 to $U.S. 2,133 million at its close, an increase substantially greater than that recorded by any other major trading nation.

This buoyancy encouraged the integrationists to essay another attempt. Their new departure took place a bare eight months after the signing of the WEU Protocol. On 21 April 1955 the Dutch Foreign Minister, Beyen, reminded Spaak of his belief that the European states could be linked only by an effective customs union such as existed in Benelux. The European peoples would become genuinely committed to integration only when they believed it to be economically profitable to them. This may have been true, but the fact was that in any event the Benelux union itself seriously needed the stimulus of being associated with a wider trading area. On 23 April Beyen and Spaak invited Bech, the Foreign Minister of Luxembourg, to join them in calling a meeting of the Council of Ministers of the ECSC in the name of the Benelux Governments, to discuss a programme for the general economic integration of the Six states under a supranational authority.

The meeting opened on 9 May, a date made historic by the introduction of the Schuman Plan five years previously. On 18 May the Benelux Ministers formally presented their colleagues with a project for the integration of Europe by the creation of a common market and the harmonization of social policies. French support was enthusiastic, reflecting an anxiety to make amends for the defeat of the EDC, a desire to establish closer links with France's Continental neighbours in case international support was needed to deal with the African crisis, and understandable confidence in the brilliant performance of their country's economy. Maurice Faure, the first radical at the Quai d'Orsay after seven years of MRP control of foreign policy, was eager to continue the policy of his predecessors. On 26 May he told a press conference that a real European organization could not let itself degenerate into a mere club of ambassadors. "If the word 'supranationality' still scares people, let us admit that just the same it must be granted powers of decision."

On 1 June the Foreign Ministers of the Six met at Messina for the first time since August 1954, to begin work on a customs and economic union. Beyen himself had drafted the working paper for their discussions. The conspiratorial atmosphere of the Schuman Plan was re-created, in recognition of the fact that the Community Idea had now arrived at the moment of truth. The French Government refused to release anything more than cryptic and incoherent statements to the press. On 7 June Bech wrote to Macmillan, now Chancellor of the Exchequer in the Government of Anthony Eden, inviting him to take part in a Committee of Governmental Representatives, to deal with the formulation of treaties and other arrangements "concerning the questions raised by the Messina Resolution". He emphasized that he and his colleagues were unanimous in their hope that the British Government would participate in this work in the fullest possible manner. The resolution forwarded to Macmillan read:

> The Governments of the Federal German Republic, Belgium, France, Italy, Luxembourg and the Netherlands believe that the time has come to make a fresh advance towards the building of Europe. They are of the opinion that this must be achieved, first of all, in the economic field.
> They consider that it is necessary to work for the establishment of a united Europe by the development of common institutions, the progressive fusion of national economies, the creation of a common market, and the progressive harmonization of their social policies.
> Such a policy seems to them indispensable if Europe is to maintain her position in the world, regain her influence and prestige and achieve a continuing increase in the standard of living of her population.

The Ministers proposed to achieve these goals through "the creation of a common organization to be entrusted with the responsibility and the means for ensuring the peaceful development of atomic energy", and "the establishment of a European market, free from all customs duties and all quantitative restrictions".[3]

Bech can only have seemed somewhat optimistic in making such an approach to the British. Apart from anything else, the Common Market proposal at least would involve the Commonwealth relationship much more clearly than either the ECSC or the EDC. Whatever objections the British might have had to joining the less extensive Communities of the past would presumably be reinforced by new and even more compelling reservations. The only possible elements for hope lay in the facts that the British had accepted a further commitment to encourage increasing close European union under the terms of the Protocol of the WEU, and had not yet done anything about it; and that the material grounds for British independence were slightly less substantial in 1955 than they had been in 1950. The Gross National Product of the United Kingdom had for example declined from 48.3 per cent of the combined figure for the Western European Six in 1950, to 41.3 per cent in 1955; and the British share of total world trade had fallen in the same period from 11.7 per cent to 11.2 per cent, while that of the Six had risen from 17.6 per cent to 22 per cent. However, these figures did not yet indicate any significant change in the order of world economic power, and the importance in trade terms of the Six as against the Commonwealth had hardly altered during the five years under review. In both 1950 and 1955 the Six accounted for about 12 per cent of total British external trade, and the Commonwealth for about 42 per cent. British power was still unchallengeable in Western Europe, and British power was still supported by the Commonwealth far more than by the Continent.

Macmillan at first returned an evasive reply to Bech's invitation. The latter repeated his appeal on 30 June. Macmillan then replied, warning the Six that the British Government "were naturally anxious to ensure that due account should be taken of the function of existing organizations such as the OEEC, and that work should not be unnecessarily duplicated ... On this understanding, Her Majesty's Government will be glad to appoint a representative to take part in these studies". He added that: "There are, as you are no doubt aware, special difficulties for this country in any proposal for 'a European Common Market'."[4] This clearly referred to the Commonwealth connection.

Spaak persisted in anticipating from the British a will to closer union considerably stronger than either their words or actions had indicated for the past eight years. He welcomed the British representative at the first meeting of the Preparatory Committee of the Six at Brussels, expressing the hope that the word "representative" necessarily implied a relationship closer than that of "delegate" or "observer". This might have appeared excessively subtle. But in any case the appearance of the British representative in Brussels coincided with the adoption of attitudes by the British Government towards the only surviving European Community which certainly did not indicate any particular sympathy for that severely tried organization.

It began with a very minor affair. The British Foreign Office decided on 21 June to economize on extending diplomatic privileges to foreign representatives in the United Kingdom. They began with the ECSC. It was decided that the Chief Representative of the Community in the United Kingdom, René Mayer, should receive the same legal immunity as an envoy, but should have to pay the "non-beneficial" elements of the rates on his official residence. To that extent, he would then be financially worse off than an envoy. Other members of his delegation were to have no relief from taxes, and their privileges were to be made intermediate between those of foreign diplomats and the secretaries of international organizations. This was an appropriate classification, but one hardly calculated to enhance the prestige of the Community system at a critical moment of its existence. It was followed by a decision of the British Government which was both directly damaging to the Community, and also in some measure discriminatory against it. In July the British Government announced a complete ban on exports of coal to the ECSC, once existing contracts had been fulfilled. This put Mayer in a desperate situation. The Community was already short of coal. Loss of British supplies would mean that about 10 million tons would have to be found from other sources in 1956. The only alternatives were to import American coal, at twice the price of British; or to declare an emergency within the ECSC, which the member governments would be certain to oppose. The British Government claimed that their action had been necessary to save foreign exchange, as they would otherwise have had to import American coal themselves. However, it was pointed out that the saving actually achieved this way would be insignificant, and that in any event the ban was not being applied to the United Kingdom's non-Community trading partners in Uniscan.[5]

The Six nonetheless appeared to be seeking a genuine agreement with the United Kingdom in the preliminary negotiations. On 12 August they agreed to the request of the British representative that a representative of the OEEC should also sit on the Preparatory Committee, to meet Macmillan's requirement that the views of different countries affected should be heard. On 23 September a Treaty of Association was signed under somewhat unpropitious circumstances between the United Kingdom and the ECSC, despite the failure of a last-minute flight by Mayer to London, in search of a reprieve from the British ban on coal exports. In the Council of Europe Spaak insisted that there was nothing exclusive in the adventure of the Common Market, and hoped that all the states represented on the Council would join the Six in their enterprise. Thorneycroft referred in similar terms to the Treaty of Association with the ECSC, saying that: "The Association is not exclusive: the interests of other Western European countries must be considered, and Britain has its duty to the Commonwealth";[6] although it had still to be made fully clear how Commonwealth interests could be materially affected in an adverse way by the ECSC. In any case, the association between the United Kingdom and the Community did not appear to be particularly close. In short order, Thorneycroft refused to amend René Mayer's diplomatic status, to modify the ban on British coal exports, to agree to a common budget for the purchase of American coal by the Community, or even to discuss a proposal to revive the system of coal allocations used during the Korean War, to meet the present shortage. It might indeed have seemed excessive to expect the British to accept sacrifices in any form to assist the ECSC in its difficulties. On the other hand, their unwillingness to make some gesture in this direction was certain, humanly speaking, to generate resentment on the Continent which would have its own dangers.

This in fact happened. British and Community representatives clashed in recriminatory exchanges throughout the whole British-dominated framework of European Assemblies. On 6 December Sir Hugh Ellis-Rees, the British Chairman of the Council of Ministers of the OEEC, repeated Macmillan's warning that the work of the Spaak Committee was obviously going to duplicate that of the OEEC. He added the further considerations that the United Kingdom had particular difficulties with this kind of association because of the Commonwealth relationship, that the Six would probably not be able to achieve their aims any more quickly than by working through the OEEC, and that by going ahead on their own they were in any case in danger of creating a discriminatory bloc in Europe, which would certainly weaken the OEEC. In return, delegates of the Six in the Spaak Committee accused the British of having made up their minds in advance, thereby rendering discussion pointless; and demanded that the British state clearly what kinds of association they were prepared to support, and not merely what kinds they opposed.[7] Tempers deteriorated still further when Sir Hugh Ellis-Rees appointed Leandre Nicolaides of Greece as chairman of a committee to investigate the development of atomic energy in Europe, in disregard of the proposal for a European Atomic Community included in the Messina Resolution. In a closed session of the OEEC Spaak directly accused the British of working in the Organization to sabotage the projects of the Six.

Co-operation between the United Kingdom and the Six had thus become extraordinarily difficult, to say the least. It was not made easier by the fact that the Report of the Nicolaides Committee, in recommending that the Ministerial Council of the OEEC should itself appoint a steering committee to promote joint enterprises for the development of atomic energy, made no reference to the scheme for a European Atomic Community, or Euratom, tabled three weeks earlier. This appeared almost an invitation to the open rivalry that was declared when President Eisenhower offered 88,000 pounds of Uranium 235 to any agency that could develop atomic energy in Europe, making it clear at the time that he favoured Euratom rather than the OEEC for this purpose, if only because it seemed more promising to try to combine the efforts of six countries rather than seventeen. British representatives in the Preparatory Committee thereupon let it be known that their Government would consider association with Euratom once that agency was set up. On 28 February Macmillian told the OEEC Ministers that the development of atomic energy was "above all, an opportunity when Europe could act together". Similarly, Thorneycroft now said that he could see no reason why Euratom should not exist within the general European structure, though of course not on any discriminatory basis. On 29 February the OEEC Ministers passed a resolution affirming that there was no incompatibility between the forms of association pursued by the OEEC itself, and those pursued by certain member countries which were seeking to establish among themselves forms of co-operation closer than those envisaged in the OEEC.

This was certainly correct, as a matter of law, since one of the first tasks of the OEEC had been to study the possibility of forming among its members customs or other unions closer in nature than the union of the OEEC itself. However, it was also obvious that the OEEC had come to be regarded as an alternative rather than an encouragement to these closer unions. It was also literally unavoidable that the European Communities would have to discriminate to some degree against their OEEC partners, since the Communities could come into existence only if certain countries were prepared to treat one another differently from the way that they treated others. The real question was whether, questions of legality aside, the development of the Community system within that of the OEEC was going to result in a significant political split among the peoples of non-Communist Europe. It was genuinely difficult to envisage this really happening.

The resolution of 29 February did not in any event help Spaak's immediate problems. Euratom was being opposed by powerful interests in every country directly concerned with the venture. On the sixth anniversary of the Schuman Plan, of all days, the Belgian Federation of Industries expressed a preference for the looser form of association recommended by the Nicolaides Committee, on the simple grounds that they wanted to be able to continue to enjoy the advantages resulting from their monopolistic access to supplies of Uranium from the Congo.[8] At the same time, the French Government insisted on remaining free to make the atom bomb, and to keep it for themselves. Similarly, the Germans expressed fears that their own development of atomic energy might be retarded if they had to work with less industrially-advanced countries. In a wider area of dispute, French industrialists threatened to leave the ECSC unless the Germans gave them more concessions in the Saar; and German industrialists expressed a preference for the OEEC association, and rejected the whole Community system as an unwarranted interference by bureaucratic agencies in the working of the free market.

The Spaak Committee simply ignored these dissensions, being unable to do anything about them. During the weekend of 20-21 April it completed its report, recommending unanimously the gradual setting-up of a customs union, and the adoption of a common external tariff by its members, over a transitional period of ten to twelve years. Agreement had been possible only because the representatives of the United Kingdom and other OEEC countries had declined to associate themselves with the final stages of the Committee's work. The completion of the report was accompanied by a furious debate in the Conseil de la République, in which Michel Debré claimed that the ECSC had given rise only to deceptions, and insisted on the need to avoid a repetition of the EDC affair. In the end, it was unanimously agreed that the French Government should undertake no commitments in the field of atomic energy without first consulting Parliament.[9]

It had already been suggested that the British Government was counting on a repetition of the EDC affair, and had accordingly refrained from taking sides, in the expectation that the Euratom and the Common Market proposals would founder in the same way on the shoals of Continental parliamentary manoeuvring. This expectation might have seemed amply justified at the time. However, an approach of this kind carried its own dangers. There was no avoiding the fact that the British had repeatedly accepted commitments to help bring about a closer Western union of some form or another, and that their continued reluctance either to encourage movements in this direction by other governments, or to initiate alternative proposals themselves, was singularly likely to impel the Europeans to develop their own forms of union, without reference to British desires. The formation of a limited union of major Continental powers, animated by sentiments of resentment if not positive hostility towards the United Kingdom, was, as has been suggested, the least satisfactory outcome that could be envisaged. One alternative would be for the British simply to state a desire to join the Community system, counting on their tremendous material and moral predominance to be able to organize its development in a manner compatible with their Commonwealth interests. The other was to do as they were doing, and see if by chance the movement collapsed. There were few grounds on which to make a rational decision. The ECSC had succeeded, but to a far less degree than Schuman had hoped. The EDC and its associated Communities had failed. But a new factor had entered the scene. The United States was beginning to give specific backing to the new Community projects. And since one of the bases of British pretensions to world power was precisely their unique relationship with the United States, it would be difficult for the British advantageously to oppose

American wishes, however well or ill-founded they might be. There could be only one outcome worse from the British point of view than the emergence of a restricted European union, alienated from the United Kingdom: that would be the emergence of such a union, supported by the United States.

This was at least clear to the Canadians. And once again Canadian policy was to minimize the objections to British participation in the new European movement. There were many reasons for this. Ottawa would naturally adopt the approach most likely to establish closer relations between London, Paris, and Washington. But in any case the Canadians were uniquely placed to take the long view. With their external security guaranteed by the presence of the United States across their only land frontiers, and with the prosperity of their sixteen millions seemingly guaranteed by foreign trade and exchange reserves surpassed only by those of the United States, the United Kingdom, and Germany, the Canadians could afford to be objective. But for the first time even Lester Pearson indicated that his support for Western union did not necessarily take priority over commercial considerations. He warned the Six that the support of his Government for their enterprise was given on the assumption that the completed Common Market would not create restraints on world trade greater than those existing already. However, he commended the Common Market venture, and affirmed[10] that he could not

> see anything in this move towards European unity which should hinder in any way the growth and coming-together of the Atlantic Community ... [nor] anything necessarily inconsistent with the closest possible association of the United Kingdom with this European development, and the maintenance and even strengthening of its ties with the Commonwealth.

He added that he hoped that the British "would play an active and constructive part in the efforts now being made by European states to adapt themselves to new conditions which require their closer association". His inferences became more direct as the crisis of the Communities deepened. Repeating his earlier statements to the House of Commons, he said on 3 June that:

> While the other countries concerned have their part to play, it is, I think, true to say that European integration and the cohesion of the Atlantic Community — neither of which excludes the other — will proceed as far and as fast as the United States and the

United Kingdom make possible by recognizing the importance
of their own roles in bringing it about.[11]

The British Government was of course under no obligation
to accept Canadian advice or interpretations. On the other
hand, it was not easy for the British to sustain the argument that
membership of Community Europe was incompatible with the
Commonwealth relationship when the most powerful, resourceful,
and possibly most significant of their Commonwealth partners
persisted in implying just the opposite. But Canadian urgings
could still be safely ignored. It was less easy to ignore the
United States. And Washington now began to make its colossal
influence felt in a manner at once explicit and embarrassing.

On 5 June Monnet appealed directly to the British Government to help the Community movement out of its current
difficulties. He now claimed that Euratom at any rate could not be
created at all unless the British gave it their full support. Faure
flew to London on 15 June to try to secure a British commitment.
He was told that the British understood that association
with Euratom would involve common ownership of fissionable
materials. It would thus tend to disrupt existing military plans and
purchase agreements. The British had no intention of modifying
these. Further, they had just signed an agreement with the United
States to exchange confidential information on atomic matters.
The Americans would renounce this agreement if the information
exchanged had to be shared with the Six. However, President
Eisenhower immediately conveyed an assurance to the Six, through
his ambassador in Rome, that the United States would transfer
to Euratom any bilateral atomic agreements reached with other
countries, just as soon as the Community had been set up.

British relations with the United States as well as with Europe
were likely to suffer, if the Community movement were now going
to be carried on with American support in default of British. A
re-appraisal of policy was clearly indicated. Macmillan now said
that the Government was giving very careful consideration to
the implications of the Messina proposals, and suggested that the
matter could be discussed advantageously at the next Commonwealth Prime Ministers' Conference, "because we shall have
to consider its implications together with their views".[12] At the
meeting held in London 27 June–7 July 1956, the visiting
Prime Ministers were "informed of current proposals regarding

the political and economic activities of the North Atlantic Alliance, and the development of closer economic cooperation in Europe''. However, discussion was concentrated on the specific problems of the sterling area, the need for its members to restrict the value of their imports from North America, including Canada, and the continued demands of the under-developed Commonwealth countries for aid and capital investment from the United Kingdom. The last factor could easily be affected adversely by any move by the United Kingdom towards closer economic integration with Europe, since British capital would then presumably be needed at home to re-tool and readjust British industry to make it more competitive. On the other hand, this might be necessary anyway, if the United Kingdom were to sustain its exchange reserves at a level sufficiently high to permit a continued flow of capital investment to other Commonwealth countries. This situation could perhaps hardly be resolved at the time. The British Government said that it was determined to maintain and improve its capacity to serve as a source of capital for development in Commonwealth countries, without committing itself to a specific policy. The perplexing problem of how to deal with Community Europe was left in the air.

So was Euratom itself. Its fate, like that of the EDC, was now decided by a violent debate in France, between different but equally nationalistic interpretations of French national interests. Debré again attacked the Atomic Community as he had the EDC, by claiming that France should not accept restrictions of this kind if the British were not also prepared to accept them. He then reminded the Americans that France had watched over the cradle of American independence; asked if they proposed to repay the debt by presiding over the burial of French independence; and said that it might well be Spaak's vocation to help the Americans in this unworthy task, but that for Frenchmen to help him was "a scandal, a treason ... One nation does not have the right to manufacture atomic weapons, that is Germany. One nation has taken a step and even a lead in this field, that is the United Kingdom. One nation could have done as much but has not done it yet, that is France."[13] Warming to his theme, Debré then asserted that: "We must call things by their proper names: Euratom ... is a plot hatched and implemented by the foreigner against France."[14] Sir Robert Boothby, the Conservative member for

Aberdeenshire East, asked in the House of Commons if the British Government was prepared to stand aside as it had in 1954, and see Euratom go the same way as the EDC, and for the same reasons. Sir Edward Boyle, the Economic Secretary to the Treasury, repeated that the Commonwealth connection made close British association with the European Communities difficult but said that nothing would attract the attention of the Government in the months ahead more than the Common Market, whatever happened about Euratom. He pointed out that the Government realized completely the advantages which the countries inside the area should gain, "that is to say, a joint single market within which industry could be developed to its best economic use, possessed of great bargaining power in its negotiations against outside competition." He said that the Government was not ruling out any possibilities for the future, but in the meantime did not want to associate itself too closely at this stage "and then be open later to a charge of bad faith".[15]

It was certainly impossible to overlook the potential importance of the Common Market concept, if it ever were realized. Its chances of achieving fulfilment were enhanced by the final success of the Atomic Community, after French technicians had convinced the Assemblée Nationale that France's only hope of gaining nuclear independence lay in its collaborating as closely as possible with its neighbours. Foreign Minister Pineau was thus able to obtain an unexpectedly large majority of 342 votes against 183 in favour of a socialist measure authorizing the Government to continue with negotiations to conclude a treaty establishing Euratom. However, Faure served notice on France's Euratom partners that France would continue to manufacture its own atomic bombs, but would not explode any until four years after the signing of the Euratom Treaty. This was of course the earliest date by which the French expected to have any bombs to explode, so the concession was not remarkable.

Euratom was on the way. That left the Common Market. Negotiations on this most ambitious of the Communities were suddenly arrested by a completely new British initiative. A meeting of the Council of Ministers of the OEEC had been scheduled in Paris later in July. The Secretariat had proposed to place on the agenda the question of requiring members to reduce those areas of their trade still subject to quantitative restrictions on imports.

The Scandinavian representatives objected that their countries had already more than fulfilled their obligations to liberalize tariffs, and that it was not fair to insist on their reducing quota restrictions as well, without first dealing with the problem of those countries which had not met their original commitments on tariffs. They suggested instead a complex scheme for introducing tariff cuts on selected exports entering into intra-OEEC trade. The British representative criticized this as being impractical. René Sergeant, the French Secretary-General, then tentatively suggested that the Council might consider forming a Free Trade Area of the whole of the OEEC. The British representative supported this enthusiastically. Sergeant informed the Governments of the Six of his proposal on 16 July. On 19 July the OEEC Ministers resolved that a working party should be set up at once to:

> ... study the possible forms and methods of association, on a multilateral basis, between the proposed Customs Union [of the Six] and Member countries not taking part therein. As a possible method of association the Special Working Party shall take into account the creation of a Free Trade Area which would include the Customs Union and such Member countries.[16]

The Special Working Party began discussions on 21 July. Three days later, Macmillan explained the terms of the OEEC resolution to the House of Commons, assuring members that:

> ... no country is committed at this stage by the action which we have taken in this wide field of possible action ... The position of Her Majesty's Government is completely open. We welcome these studies because it is only in the light of them that we can see by what method — all methods being open in principle — we can most usefully cooperate.[17]

This was of course very much the kind of basis on which the British Government had wished to open discussion with the Western Europeans over the Schuman Plan. However, any fruitful discussions had to be deferred, pending the outcome of an external distraction which could hardly be overlooked. The Mediterranean crisis abruptly reached panic point. Two days after Macmillan's OEEC speech, President Nasser of Egypt nationalized the Suez Canal Company, in obvious retaliation for the decision of the United States and the United Kingdom to withdraw their offers of financial backing for the Aswan Dam project. Talks began immediately between the American, British, and

French Governments, and also between the last two Governments and their respective military advisers. Violence was fully implicit in the situation. Prime Minister Anthony Eden had decided that even if the British Government had to act alone, it "could not stop short of using force";[18] and the French Government was resolved, for its part, not to allow any victory of Arab nationalism at one end of the Mediterranean to encourage resistance to French colonial rule at the other.

Guy Mollet had accordingly decided upon an "energetic and severe reply" to Nasser's action. He suggested initially that the reply should take the form of "a joint action by the Western Allies". However, the Americans were reluctant to admit that vital Western interests were in fact endangered by Nasser's move, despite Eden's insistence to the contrary.[19] Nor indeed did any other Government except that of Israel appear to support the Anglo-French case at the time. The Scandinavians, Germany, Spain, India, and South Africa within the Commonwealth, as well as predictably the whole Arab world, urged moderation on the United Kingdom and France and down-graded the importance of the nationalization. The Americans, whose original refusal to finance the Aswan Dam had provoked the confrontation, now said that they were not prepared to support any action for which no clear justification could be found in international law. Indeed, on 5 August authority was given to American ships using the Canal to pay dues to the nationalized Egyptian authorities, albeit under protest and without prejudice. A Canal Users' Conference convened in London failed to agree on a proposition to be sent to the Egyptians. The Egyptians for their part rejected a proposal agreed to by the majority of the Users, and presented to them by Prime Minister Menzies of Australia, that the Canal should be managed by an international authority. It might of course have saved everybody a lot of trouble and themselves a lot of money if the Egyptians had accepted the proposal. The failure of the Menzies approach was charged to the United States by both Eden and Pineau. However, the British determined to refer the matter to the Security Council for further international consideration, despite a French objection that this would merely invite a rebuff which would strengthen Arab intransigence still further. The French themselves pressed on with plans for decisive action against Arab power. Military supplies greatly in excess of stated figures were rushed from France to Israel during August, while from the middle of the month Israeli commandoes launched attacks of mounting violence against their reluctant neighbours. The British finally had the matter of the nationalization brought before the Security Council on 12 September, but deferred to American wishes by not seeking any action from the Council. Three days later, British and French pilots were withdrawn from the Canal.

This was presumably an attempt to dislocate the operation of the Canal, and thus provide an occasion for international intervention. However, the United States again acted to frustrate the hopes of the interventionists by describing intervention under such circumstances as an act of aggression, to which the United States would not be a party. At the same time, the British still explored every possibility of securing American support for direct action against Nasser. A second Users' Conference was called in London on 19 September, this time limited to the eighteen powers which had supported the majority resolution unsuccessfully presented to the Egyptians by the Menzies Commission. The Americans did lend their support this time, at least to the extent that it was only through the diplomacy of Dulles himself that as many as fifteen of the eighteen governments represented agreed to form a new Users' Association. Dulles nonetheless still insisted that the Association had no intention of coercing Egypt. The British then persuaded the French to agree to approaching the Security Council again on 23 September. This renewed effort was opposed by both Dulles and the French themselves, who agreed to it only after the British had renewed their undertaking not to stand aside from the use of force, if the Security Council proved incapable of maintaining international agreements.

In this distinctly uneasy atmosphere, Macmillan sought the reactions of Commonwealth leaders to the Free Trade Area proposal. The matter was raised informally with Commonwealth Finance Ministers meeting in Washington 29–30 September, at a conference of the International Monetary Fund and the World Bank. Macmillan said later that he had told the Commonwealth Ministers that:

> Of course, the United Kingdom might stand outside the customs union [of the Six] altogether — but this would involve at the least a loss of advantage for our exports to European markets.

At the other extreme we might join the customs union — but this would involve the collapse of our system of Imperial Preference within the Commonwealth. Obviously, if such were the only choice, we could not hesitate. We must choose the Commonwealth. But is there a way out? Can we find a way of associating with this initiative in Europe in such a way as to benefit all? That is what we have to look for.

According to Macmillan, the answer was to be found in the creation of a Free Trade Area, which would preserve the United Kingdom from being made subject to the discriminatory common external tariff of the customs union, while enabling it to retain its own arrangements with other Commonwealth countries. At the same time, access of Commonwealth producers to the markets of the United Kingdom would be secured by limiting the scope of the Free Trade Area to industrial products only. The British Government "could not — and this is vital — include raw or manufactured foodstuffs, feedingstuffs, drink or tobacco in a free trade area of this kind".[20]

There was indeed little for most Commonwealth Governments to protest about here. As the Australian Minister for Trade commented the following day in a statement not remarkable for accurate drafting:

> The Messina Plan is open to acceptance by other European countries and the United Kingdom is considering whether to associate herself with the Plan in respect of commodities other than foodstuffs, drink and tobacco.
> The United Kingdom Government has asked Commonwealth countries for their reactions to the United Kingdom joining in the Messina Plan and the Australian Government has the question under consideration ...
> Moreover, the decision of the United Kingdom not to participate in the Plan in respect of foodstuffs means that our major trade with the United Kingdom will be protected.[21]

Rhodesia and New Zealand also gave reserved approval. The only Commonwealth country which appeared to have some misgivings was, ironically, Canada, part of whose trade with the United Kingdom was in fact likely to be affected. This was the more displeasing because the items affected would be precisely those for which the Canadians had been able to extract promises of assured access from the British in the previous December.

It was not the fault of Macmillan or of the Free Trade Area

proposal itself that the scheme was presumed in some quarters to be linked in some way with the developing Suez crisis. Italian politicians even described it as merely a bid by the British to secure allies on the Continent before moving against Egypt. Jean Fabiani of the now Gaullist *Combat* suggested darkly that it took some memory to recall when the European idea was put forward for the first time by an Englishman.[22] But the fact was that the Free Trade Area idea had in any case been put forward first by a Frenchman, as a response to circumstances which had developed quite independently of the Suez crisis. At the same time, the background of Mediterranean developments made an unfortunately ironic commentary on the terms being used by British representatives to present the Free Trade Area to the Europeans. Thus on 10 October the French and Israelis agreed secretly to co-ordinate military operations against Egypt, subject on the French side to the scheme's being approved by the British; on 16 October Eden and Mollet met in Paris, after which communication on the Suez issue was severed between London and Paris for a fortnight; and on 18 October Prime Minister Ben-Gurion of Israel designated the "Egyptian Fascist dictator" as the greatest danger facing his country. In these very uneasy circumstances Lord John Hope, Parliamentary Under-Secretary of Foreign Affairs in the Conservative Government, told the Europeans that the theme of the last ten years would tell not how Europe fell apart but how it came together, and that the part of the United Kingdom in this process would be included "in rather a special way". He admitted that a historian who was a devotee of form rather than content would criticize the United Kingdom for excessive caution. However:

> ... when it comes to concrete steps towards constructive membership of the European family, the historian will say, I believe that the United Kingdom did its duty ... There is no doubt that the enquiry in which Her Majesty's Government are now engaged opens up the possibility of unsurpassed importance in the whole of Great Britain's history. At the same time it is in direct line with the steps we have taken at each stage of our postwar journey ... The difficulty with which we have always had to contend is that some of our friends in Europe ... have never been able to feel that our actions lived up to our words.[23]

This was perhaps claiming a little too much. There was really no denying that at least six European countries had taken considerably more constructive steps than the United Kingdom had hitherto been prepared to take, although it was always open to question whether the formation of restrictive Communities was the ideal way in which to further the cause of Western union. Nor was there any doubt that the enquiries most engaging the attention of the British Government at the time were important enough. They were however scarcely conducive to helping Europe come together. Eden and his Cabinet allowed themselves to be convinced by Israeli arguments that the Russian military intervention in Hungary provided a convenient opportunity to carry out an attack on Egypt. The Israelis opened the attack. On 29 October the British and French Governments presented the two belligerents with an ultimatum requiring them to withdraw their forces from the Suez Canal region, and providing for the temporary occupation by Anglo-French forces of Port Said, Ismailia, and Suez. Air attacks on Egypt began on 31 October; paratroop landings followed on 5 November; and the seaborne invasion came the following day, only to be called off by the British Government the same afternoon, without prior consultation with the French, who could not bring themselves to halt the advance of their armoured columns for another twenty-four hours.

The most important lessons to be learnt from the Suez enterprise were not necessarily those that seemed most obvious at the time. Hugh Gaitskell described it as involving "not only the abandonment but a positive assault upon the three principles of British policy for, at any rate, the last ten years — solidarity with the Commonwealth, the Anglo-American alliance and adherence to the Charter of the United Nations".[24] But the fate of the venture served really most significantly to illustrate the enduring quality of all three bases of British policy. The three combinations of states regrouped, after a temporary disarray, in exactly the same pattern as they had presented formerly. Nobody left or was expelled from the Commonwealth, the Atlantic system or the United Nations because of what had happened at Suez. Nor did the venture necessarily indicate either the military or financial impotence of Britain or France. The military operations were finally successful, even though their planning and timing were organized with an almost total disregard for other than political considerations. And it is difficult to sustain the argument that the operations were halted for fear of the economic consequences. British reserves certainly fell from \$U.S.2,365 million in September 1956 to \$U.S.2,168 million in December, but this merely paralleled a similar decline the previous year; while the decline in French reserves during the crisis was actually at a lower rate than either before or after Suez.[25]

Suez certainly did have at least two measurable consequences. The first was to make it much more difficult for the British to sustain credibly certain positions they had held before. It was, for example, hard to argue the existence of a useful political cohesion within the Commonwealth, when Suez had demonstrated the existence of total differences of opinion on a specific issue; it was hard to estimate the importance of the "special relationship" between the United Kingdom and the United States, when the United States had apparently frustrated British attempts to solve a basically American-created situation, and the United Kingdom had acted in complete disregard of American warnings; and most important, it was hard to insist upon the superiority of British judgment in international affairs, when that judgment could be as unreliable as it appeared to have been over Suez. These considerations could not fail to cast some doubts upon British policy decisions both before and after. It was of course obviously unreasonable to suppose that because the British had blundered seriously once they were therefore prone to blunder all the time. It was very likely indeed that in fact the most dangerous blunders had been the American ones. But the real lesson was simply that the British, rightly or wrongly, did not carry the weight with the United States or with the Commonwealth that they had seemed to carry before. They were to this degree less important than had appeared to be the case. The impact on France was different. The French manifestly had compounded every sin which could be attributed to the British. They had been conspicuously more intransigent, more careless of world opinion, and more ruthless in conspiracy and action. The most they could claim was that they had not left an ally in the lurch, but this was only another way of saying that they were more reckless of consequences. But the French had a basis of strength in Europe which the British lacked, and which the circumstances of Suez made more important than ever. Community Europe obviously could be created without the United Kingdom. It could hardly conceivably be created without France. And France of November 1956, humiliated, embittered, defiantly bent on apparent self-destruction, was hardly to be placated by reasonable propositions reasonably negotiated. Its very weakness and intransigence would enable France to determine the course of the Free Trade Area negotiations.

First of all, the negotiations had to be set in train again. On 13 November Prime Minister St. Laurent of Canada produced the most elaborate analysis of the British proposals so far presented. In a statement remarkable for the scrupulous accuracy of the terms employed, he said:

> The Canadian Government has been informed ... of the proposals ... which would involve the United Kingdom entering a Free Trade Area in Western Europe along with France, Belgium, the Netherlands, Luxembourg, Germany and Italy (who are considering the establishment of a full Customs Union among the six of them) and other countries of Western Europe. The entry by the United Kingdom into such a free trade arrangement with European countries would entail the removal by defined stages of its customs duties on the products of such countries in return for reciprocal action on their part towards United Kingdom products. The United Kingdom proposes that this arrangement would not apply to foodstuffs, feeds, beverages or tobacco. In that event such advantages as are now accorded by the United Kingdom to imports of these types from other Commonwealth countries would not be affected.

> Even with the exclusion of such products, the changes in United Kingdom and European trading relations involved in the carrying out of these proposals would present a number of problems for Canadian trade with the countries concerned. The various possible effects upon Canada's trade and upon our existing trade arrangements will require detailed study by the Government and thorough discussions with the other Governments concerned.

> It will be important that the carrying out of these proposals proceed according to a definite programme and on a firm time-table and be accompanied by appropriate internal economic policies. The proposed new arrangement will have its most beneficial effects if it is brought into being with a minimum of discrimination against the trade of other countries and if the expansion of mutually advantageous trading relations with other countries is encouraged.

> If the proposals are carried through with determination, and at the same time the countries concerned proceed forthrightly with the removal of other trade barriers between themselves and also against other countries as they are pledged to do, it should be possible to surmount any difficulties which may be created and to increase the flow of trade, and maintain the ties, between this large European area and the rest of the world. On the other hand,

a partial development that resulted only in the creation of a new system of intra-European tariff preferences would interfere with trade between Europe and other countries, including Canada, without achieving the positive results which are expected from a full implementation of the plan. Similarly, it would be a matter of concern to us if the pursuit of this European objective, worthy as it is, were to result in an increase in tariffs against non-European countries or in less effort or willingness to reduce the other barriers to the development of competitive multilateral trade, which is the overriding objective of the Canadian Government and of the General Agreement on Tariffs and Trade.

Should the proposals be adopted and successfully carried through by Britain and the nations of Western Europe they should increase the economic strength and prosperity of the peoples of that whole great area and also their sense of solidarity and common purpose even beyond the economic field. Such a result could not fail to be welcomed by Canadians whose security, and cultural and political heritage, as well as economic welfare, have been, and are, so closely linked with that part of the world.[26]

Canadian commentators suggested that the measured arguments of the St. Laurent statement, and the long time taken to produce them, alike indicated something of an intensive and apparently agonising reappraisal of Canadian policy, rather than the quick and enthusiastic endorsement which past utterances might have been expected to produce. This might have been partially justified. On the other hand, the movements which the Canadian Government had supported previously had not been likely to affect significantly Commonwealth economic interests. There was nothing hostile in their reminding the Western Europeans that their experiments could have implications for the world outside which would not be met entirely by simply excluding agriculture from the Free Trade Area.

There was certainly no question that agriculture was to be excluded. This point was stressed by Harold Macmillan on 26 November. He insisted:

... the developing countries of the Commonwealth would not be prepared to remove their tariffs and quotas against European goods and ... the countries of Europe, not having our historical link with the Commonwealth, would be reluctant to grant entry to Commonwealth manufactures ... We must make it clear from the first that any projects we could envisage of a free trade area cannot be extended to foodstuffs ... We must remain free to continue to grant to this great volume of supplies the preferential arrangements we have built up ... It is absolutely essential that this exception should be made so that the preferential system can remain ... there is only one way out. It is simple but it is vital: it is to treat agriculture as an exception in the scheme.[27]

Macmillan tended to dismiss the 10 per cent of Canadian trade which would be affected, reminding the Canadians that they would still enjoy preference as against United States manufactures in the British market. It also could not be denied that the Canadians were better placed than most other peoples to accept a certain economic loss, especially if the Free Trade Area were developed so as to discriminate as little as possible against outsiders. There were in any case obvious limits to the number of reservations which could be introduced into the scheme. One could hardly have any kind of trading area if industrial and agricultural products were both to be left out.

But negotiations on the Free Trade Area had to be delayed in the meantime, while the Western Europeans tried to reach some agreement on their own Common Market. The kind of difficulty with which they were faced was shown on 20 November. In a démarche inspired by impending bankruptcy and the desire to extract the last possible sou from neighbours who had failed to support France over Suez, Faure demanded that the Common Market be extended to the overseas territories of the Six. In return, member countries would be allowed access to the dubiously valuable markets of the French Union. However, he also insisted that the Germans and Italians should give financial aid to France and Belgium to assist them to raise economic and social standards in their overseas territories. This amounted to asking the non-colonial countries of the Common Market to pay for the privilege of being labelled as colonialists, at the same time that they opened their domestic markets to the products of French and Belgian enterprises established in the overseas territories.

On 14 January 1957 Spaak flew to London to enlist the help of the British Government. He was told that he should try to get the Common Market treaty signed by the end of February, so that negotiations on the Free Trade Area could begin in March. As the new British Foreign Secretary, Selwyn Lloyd, told him: "There is one lesson from recent events that we have all taken, and it is that we must all be closer together." However, the very imminence of the Free Trade Area drew predictable demonstrations of panic and distrust from France. Socialists Gilles Gozard and Jean Le Bail warned about the basic isolationism and reservations of the United Kingdom;[28] Radicals Pleven and Mendès-France stressed the undeniable difficulty of trying to add to the Common Market, "with the same participants and with other countries, a complementary structure with different laws and rulings";[29] and Gaullist Michel Debré furiously denounced any concept of European solidarity on the part of countries which had not "desired to consider that the French action [at Suez] should be supported".[30]

British proposals for the Free Trade Area were fully spelt out in a White Paper presented by Thorneycroft and Eccles to the Council of Ministers of the OEEC on 13 February. The substantial paragraphs read:

> ... Her Majesty's Government are glad that the negotiations which were set in train in June 1955 for the establishment of a Customs and Economic Union ... are now approaching a successful conclusion. There are, however, substantial reasons why the United Kingdom could not become a member of such a Union ... Her Majesty's Government could not contemplate entering arrangements which would in principle make it impossible for the United Kingdom to treat imports from the Commonwealth at least as favourably as those from Europe ... Her Majesty's Government's concept of the Free Trade Area differs in some important respects from that of the ... Union now contemplated by the Messina Powers. The arrangements proposed for the ... Union include far-reaching provisions for economic integration and harmonization of financial and social policies and for mutual assistance in the financing of investment. These arrangements are to be effected within an appropriate institutional framework. Her Majesty's Government envisage the Free Trade Area, on the other hand, as a concept related primarily to the removal of restrictions on trade such as tariffs and quotas. Nevertheless Her Majesty's Government recognize that co-operation in the field of economic policy is of great and continuing importance ... There are special considerations which are of great concern to the United Kingdom in the matter of agriculture: the United Kingdom must be free to continue the preferential arrangements which apply to imports of foodstuffs from the Commonwealth ... The United Kingdom and most other European countries protect their home agriculture by one means or another for well-known reasons, and will wish to continue to do so ... Any special arrangements for agricultural produce, if restrictive in character, might clearly give rise to difficulty in securing international agreement. For these reasons Her Majesty's Government have throughout made clear

their view that the products in question ... must be excluded from the provisions of the Free Trade Area. Her Majesty's Government's proposal is accordingly for a European Free Trade Area defined in this sense.

The White Paper was particularly explicit on the subject of institutions:

> In the event of acute balance of payments difficulties it is clear that the imposition of quotas must be permitted and this without prior consultation, though it should be made subject to frequent and stringent examination. Apart from this, it seems unlikely that there will be circumstances in which unilateral action would be justified ... It had been suggested that there are certain disparities between the social regulations in different countries which are likely to distort the free play of competition, and that these disparities should be corrected by harmonizing these regulations at the beginning of the transitional period ... [However,] Her Majesty's Government do not consider it essential, as ... a necessary condition of the creation of such an Area ... Some departure from the unanimity rule will be necessary in certain carefully defined matters, for example, where a country seeks a release from one of the original obligations; or in procedure of a fact-finding or judicial nature concerned with verifying that a country is carrying out its obligations and with remedying any failure to do so.[31]

The *Economist* suggested that there were many places in the twenty-four paragraphs of the White Paper where the British Government could have struck a jarring note, and had in fact done so in very few of them. It was certainly clear that some arrangements would have to be devised to mitigate the impact of Common Market discrimination upon other OEEC countries. Nor was it a weakness of the White Paper that it should have stated the Commonwealth issue in direct and unambiguous terms. But it would also have seemed evident that negotiation on the basis of the White Paper itself was likely to be made difficult by its rejection of some of the basic principles of the Common Market. These of course were related to the questions of agriculture and the harmonization of social policies. The fact was that the French at least had been prepared to accept conditions of free trade with their Common Market partners only if it were agreed to harmonize wage levels and social costs. The British were now requiring them to compete with an economy more productive than that of any of the Common Market countries, without the same safeguards. The stringent requirements on quotas and other escape mechanisms also seemed directly aimed at the kind of action which the French Government was virtually certain to be planning to take. Negotiation was obviously going to require great tact, patience, and flexibility.

Just how much these qualities were going to be needed was illustrated by a severe setback administered to the Free Trade Area proposals on the occasion of their first being presented to the OEEC. In words no doubt intended to be reassuring, Eccles told the Europeans that the British, unlike the Six, were "not dreaming of a 'third force' or of a European bloc endowed with supranational institutions and anxious to rival Russia or the United States ... We are more prosaic and ... more practical."[32] But this more practical approach was scarcely welcomed by the other OEEC members. Only Sweden, Switzerland, and Germany actually accepted the British proposals as a reasonable basis for negotiations. Spaak demanded that the signing of the Common Market treaty should not be delayed for a single day to wait on the completion of the Free Trade Area. He also opposed the fundamental British plan to exclude agriculture. So did the representatives of Denmark, Greece, Turkey, Portugal, and the Irish Republic, the last four claiming in addition that the economies of their countries were insufficiently developed for them to be able to face competition from the industrial powers in a Free Trade Area. The Canadian and American repersentatives expressed concern that the interests of other countries outside the Free Trade Area should be considered. This was indeed the dominant note of the formal statement of American policy towards the new developments in Europe, issued on 15 January:

> The United States hopes that such free trade area arrangements as may be concluded ... would also encourage the expansion of international trade from which all of the free world countries and not only those participating in the common market and the free trade area would benefit.[33]

The Americans nonetheless welcomed both to the extent that they corresponded with "our consistent support of moves to further the political and economic strength and cohesion of Western Europe within an expanding Atlantic Community, and our long-standing devotion to progress towards freer non-discriminatory multilateral trade and convertibility of currencies".

Even a friend of the United States might have been pardoned for wishing that the Americans had shown similar devotion towards the removal of tariff barriers. However, what was mainly evident was that the Americans seemed to be expecting rather more from both the Common Market and the Free Trade Area than either could reasonably promise at the time. Moreover, signs of a genuine opposition between the two ideas were becoming evident. The Economic Secretary to the Treasury in the United Kingdom, Nigel Birch, hailed the news that the Six had composed their differences with the comment that it might be possible to pay too high a price for the Free Trade Area. Eccles repeated again on 12 March that no decisions of the Six affected the inflexible determination of the United Kingdom to exclude agriculture from the Free Trade Area. On the other side, the President of the Federal Association of German Industries said that the Six would welcome talks with the British Government at some future time, but were not prepared to delay the institution of the Common Market. Walter Hallstein, the German Foreign Secretary, similarly welcomed the idea of a larger Free Trade Area, but said that the Common Market was an essential pre-condition of its existence. Faure claimed that a Free Trade Area could be created only on the same conditions for all members of the European Club. Meanwhile the Common Market itself moved towards completion. On 25 March the treaties embodying the European Economic Community (EEC) and Euratom were signed by the Ministers of the Six Governments in Rome. Dr. Erhard flew to London immediately after the signing, to try to determine the attitude of the British Government, but returned to Bonn still undecided.

Other governments were also trying to determine the nature of British policy. In Australia, the Trade Minister John McEwen said that he could not give an unqualified assurance that Australian interests would not be impaired by the Common Market, but he did not think that anybody would wish to obstruct what was on the whole a beneficial arrangement because of some minute detail that might not be completely acceptable. The Australian Government assumed that the United Kingdom for its part was "not a completely free agent", but was bound by the General Agreement on Tariffs and Trade (GATT) and by its contractual obligations to Commonwealth countries to preserve existing preferential arrangements.[34]

But the United Kingdom was also clearly going to have to make certain concessions to the Europeans. And a singularly-timed programme of dumping subsidized British agricultural products in European markets did not tend to make the Europeans any more ready to meet the British position. On 30 April Hr. Lannung, the Danish Foreign Minister, protested against the invasion of Danish markets by huge quantities of eggs and cattle from the United Kingdom, dumped at prices little more than half the minimum guaranteed to British producers.[35] At the same time, the British concluded an agreement with New Zealand, under which they agreed to consider using quantitative restrictions against European meat exporters, if the New Zealanders felt that their interests in the British market were seriously threatened. The British Government refused to discuss the matter in the OEEC, and repeated that it could be asked to pay too high a price for the Free Trade Area, if it could be achieved only by sacrificing the interests of the Commonwealth.[36]

But this approach could be profitable only if the Europeans themselves were prepared to pay some kind of price for the Free Trade Area. And the ones most difficult to persuade would obviously be the Six. On 4 June the Conference of Socialist Parties of these countries unanimously recommended their governments to ratify the EEC and Euratom treaties, adding that other OEEC countries should either adhere to the Common Market or else conclude bilateral agreements with it. The British now tried another approach. Hitherto they had insisted on the uncomplicatedly economic nature of the Free Trade Area proposals. Now they began to attribute a high degree of political significance to them. Eccles visited the capitals of Western Europe, describing the Common Market as one of the masterpieces of history, but warning that Western Europe might fly apart if it were to come into existence without the Free Trade Area, and that some other powers might then look elsewhere for their trade and expansion. As he told the French:

> In the great questions of life, politics are more important than economics, and when we studied in England the text of the Treaty of Rome we did not let ourselves be deceived by the economic language. We see behind all the clauses dealing with tariffs, contingents, etc. that the Six States are seeking the path towards something very fundamental. Indeed, the political adhesion of Europe is essential.[37]

This was unlikely to be taken too seriously at the time, partly because it represented too sudden a change in British attitudes, particularly those of Eccles himself, to be immediately convincing; and also because it was once again genuinely difficult to imagine that Western Europe would be allowed to disintegrate under the impact of the EEC. However, Macmillan still insisted that Commonwealth governments had nothing to fear from European developments. He told the Commonwealth Prime Ministers' Conference in July that the Commonwealth would benefit if the United Kingdom were strengthened by arrangements that built up a stronger Europe, while if "there should at any time be a conflict between the calls upon us, there is no doubt where we stand: the Commonwealth comes first in our hearts and minds".[38] Nonetheless, negotiations on the Free Trade Area in the Interim Committee of the OEEC broke down on 13 September, with the Europeans complaining that the British refused to budge from their original unacceptable position on agriculture, despite warnings by the French and Dutch representatives that their governments would not accept a Free Trade Area that excluded agriculture. The Australian Government had already drawn the conclusion that some modification of the British position would be unavoidable. On 12 September McEwen told the House of Representatives that:

> ... it has become increasingly clear that the United Kingdom will be under pressure to be more prepared to examine the possibility of European agricultural products being included in a common market scheme embracing ... members of the OEEC than was thought by the United Kingdom to be the case in the first place. The Commonwealth Government is quite conscious of the implications for Australia of such a development.[39]

This would mean that the whole question of Commonwealth preferences would have to be discussed in an OEEC context. It also meant that something like eleven months of negotiations had been expended on principles that had seemed untenable from the outset. In the meantime, the Treaties of Rome had been signed; France still seemed to be pursuing a course towards economic and political disaster; and depression was beginning to radiate out from Detroit towards the world outside. The difficulty appeared to be to find some new impetus for the Free Trade Area. The British Paymaster-General, Reginald Maudling,

Eccles, and Thorneycroft all crossed the Atlantic to attend the Commonwealth Finance Ministers' Conference in Quebec from 28 September to 1 October, and to establish relations with the new Conservative Government of John G. Diefenbaker. During the talks, the British abruptly proposed a Free Trade Area between the United Kingdom and Canada, presumably with the idea of allaying Canadian anxieties about the impact on their overseas exports of the Free Trade Area of the OEEC. The Canadians agreed to send a trade mission to the United Kingdom in November. And in a speech at Vancouver later in the year Eccles emphasized the importance such a project might have in enhancing the unity of the Empire.

But first of all the Free Trade Area of the OEEC had to be achieved. The Federation of French Industries was now imploring its Government not to resume negotiations on the Free Trade Area, because of the alleged impossibility of linking the Common Market with any looser competitive structure. Nonetheless, the Council of the OEEC resolved unanimously on 17 October that it was determined to:

> ... secure the establishment of a European Free Trade Area which would comprise all member countries of the Organization; which would associate, on a multilateral basis, the European Economic Community with the other member countries; and which, taking fully into consideration the objectives of the European Economic Community, would in practice take effect parallel with the Treaty of Rome.[40]

Thorneycroft said that the question was simply whether they were going to have two Europes or one. They had decided to have one. He went on to assure the Europeans that the British would not now object to their concluding arrangements on free trade in agricultural products among themselves, on condition that the United Kingdom was authorized to make use of escape clauses to keep outside such arrangements. He also offered to make the British system of agricultural support prices subject to more searching review, but only on the understanding that decisions on its operation would have to be taken on a unanimity basis, so that the British Government would not be bound by the decisions of other governments. All this indeed involved some substantial modifications of the original British position. They had now admitted the introduction of agricultural arrangements, which they had originally insisted must be excluded altogether; they proposed the use of escape clauses as a means of preserving Commonwealth preferences, while these had been originally reserved for use in balance of payments crises; and they wanted the unanimity rule applied to safeguard their own agricultural policies, when the White Paper had specified that the majority rule should be applied wherever a country sought release from any of the original obligations of the Free Trade Area.

These modifications were certainly likely to be criticized on the grounds that the British were expecting the Europeans once again to submit to obligations which they were not prepared to accept themselves. However, the British representatives did not think it necessary to adopt a more conciliatory approach. Negotiations had now been entrusted to a ministerial committee, under the chairmanship of Reginald Maudling, whose political experience had been confined hitherto to Treasury matters and to trying to rationalize the British aircraft industry. He was assisted by officials of the Board of Trade, the Department of Sir David Eccles. The absence of any experienced diplomats from the British team helped to ensure that negotiations were conducted on a purely commercial basis, despite Eccles' conversion to a belief in the prior importance of politics. Maudling now told the Europeans that all that he had meant by saying that agricultural products should be excluded from the Free Trade Area was that they would have to be treated in it differently from industrial products, which was manifestly not the same thing. He said that the Europeans should therefore make their own arrangements to remove tariffs progressively on agricultural trade, but that the United Kingdom should be granted a waiver to maintain its own policies. He also warned that disunity in economic matters would be followed inevitably by disunity in political matters as well, and that this would be "tragic to contemplate".

But the fact that the British were obviously reluctant to admit was that the Europeans were simply seeking improved access to the British market for their agricultural products, in return for admitting the British freely to their industrial markets. And this affected the Commonwealth directly. Just how directly was illustrated by the collapse of the butter and cheese market in the United Kingdom, during the period from 1956 to 1958. In the five months from September 1956 to January 1957 the price of butter in London had fallen from 317s. to 254s. per hundredweight. It remained at about this level for the rest of 1957, then fell again in the New Year to 204s. per hundredweight until mid-1958. Cheese fell less sharply at first, from 293s. in September to 238s. in January 1957, but continued to fall during the rest of 1957 to a low point of 129s. per hundredweight. The situation was remedied by the warning of the British Government that anti-dumping measures would be applied against European countries which did not act to restrict their sales of subsidized agricultural products in the British market. This met the demands of the Australians and New Zealanders, whose vital economic interests were at stake. But it inevitably raised the question of whether Europeans would in their turn be prepared to accede to British demands without receiving some desired compensation in the form of increased access to the British market. And it was quite apparent that they were not in general consoled by the prospect of gaining free access to the British market for their industrial products, since only the Germans among the Six really believed in their ability to compete with the British on anything like equal terms.

The Canadians again tried to find a solution in the terms of their favourite treaty, NATO. Sidney E. Smith, Diefenbaker's first Minister for External Affairs, claimed, as Lester Pearson had done, and as his Liberal successor Paul Martin was to do, that Article II of the NATO Treaty could provide for the kind of review and consultation which would ensure that the Common Market and the Free Trade Area would strengthen all other countries of the free world, and not just the participants.[41] Nobody took him seriously. But neither had anybody been able to resolve the differences between the British and the rest of the OEEC over the problem of agriculture. By the beginning of 1958, all OEEC countries had combined to reject the new British position on agriculture as being just as unacceptable as the old one. Sir Hugh Ellis-Rees now said that there was no longer any question of either excluding agriculture or of including it, since everybody was more or less agreed that what would finally be signed was a Free Trade Area for industrial products, and a separate but parallel agreement for agricultural goods. This was at least something positive to work towards. But it had taken about eighteen months to get as far as that. It was becoming difficult to retain belief as well as optimism in the Free Trade Area.

This was largely because the deteriorating situation of France made a solution less likely with every passing week. The fault did not lie simply in a xenophobia which might or might not be more characteristic of the French than of most other peoples. It was simply that continuing experience seemed to prove the incapacity of the French economy to survive really free competition with any other major industrial power. The real seriousness of the situation was indicated by the decision of the Bank of France not to publish regular balance of payment statistics in the first half of 1958, after French reserves had fallen below the totally inadequate figure of $U.S.645 million. In a situation even more perilous and anguished than the crisis of the EDC, Maudling repeated the tactic of Dulles which had failed in 1954, of using exhortations and warnings to try to bring the French to modify their position. In February he said in Brussels that the whole strength of the OEEC and the European Payments Union would be threatened and undermined by the Common Market, if the Free Trade Area were not constituted at the same time. In March he warned the Western Europeans that it would be unfortunate for them as well as for the British if the United Kingdom were forced to choose between the Continent and the Commonwealth. Then, after warning the Danes and other OEEC countries of the danger of British retaliation if they joined the Common Market Six, he blamed France directly for the present impasse, and claimed that the controversy was not so much between Britain and France as between those who favoured freer trade and those who were protective by instinct. At the same time, inspired rumours were circulated around the Council of Europe, to the effect that the British might withdraw the Army of the Rhine from Europe if satisfactory free trade arrangements were not completed.

Once again, British arguments proved genuinely difficult to follow. It had been hard to imagine what adverse effects membership of the Coal and Steel Community could have had in reality upon the Commonwealth connection; it had been almost as hard to imagine how membership of the European army could have seriously altered the disposition of Britain's military forces in any circumstances in which they were likely to be deployed in war; and it was virtually impossible to imagine how the Atlantic Community was going to be disrupted because six of its most important members had grouped themselves into a regional trading organization, apparently approved of by the United States. But in any case there was no government in Paris after 21 April to consider Maudling's arguments. The Fourth Republic had yielded to the return of Gaullism. All that Maudling's injunctions had accomplished was to arouse a certain sympathy for the French among other European countries which agreed with the British in finding French economic attitudes intolerable, but were prepared to accept them as a price necessary to be paid for preserving Western unity.

Negotiations became formally possible again when the return of Charles de Gaulle to power brought a promise of political stability to France. His accession was greeted by John G. Diefenbaker, alert as his Liberal predecessors had been to the claims of Canada's other Motherland:

> In the complex and difficult world situation which confronts us all, I feel that the leadership of France can be of supreme importance in developing the basis for co-operation and concerted policy between Europe and North America, which I regard as fundamental to the solution of broader problems.[42]

Diefenbaker was certainly correct about the importance of French leadership. But de Gaulle was slow in showing his hand. He admittedly had prior claims on his attention. But in any case he was known to have no sympathy for either the Common Market or the Free Trade Area. The essential difference for de Gaulle lay in the fact that France was already committed to participate in the Common Market, and it was essential to French pretensions to be a great power that France should be able to fulfil its international obligations. There was no commitment yet to the Free Trade Area. And the Common Market had the further attraction that it represented a concept of Europe from which the British had chosen to exclude themselves. The role that de Gaulle had envisaged for France ever since the Liberation had of course required the exclusion of Anglo-American influence as a determining factor in European affairs. Moreover, the de Gaulle Government had a reason for confidence in the face of Common Market competition which the Fourth Republic had not been favoured with. The last legacy of the regime which had given a new dimension to international co-operation was a sudden recovery in France's external trading position which preceded de Gaulle's return to power by a matter of weeks. The Fifth Republic inherited from its predecessor both a policy and the means to pay for it.

The other OEEC countries had not failed to realize that the

Free Trade Area might well not survive the collapse of the Fourth Republic. On 19 April the Industrial Federations and Employers' Organizations of the United Kingdom, the Scandinavian countries, Austria, and Switzerland had agreed on the principle of a Free Trade Area which would exclude the Common Market Six. Consultations on this prospect were carried out secretly between the United Kingdom and Scandinavian Governments at a Uniscan meeting from 3 to 6 July. They were nonetheless not referred to during the Commonwealth Trade and Economic Conference held in Montreal 15 to 26 September. Neither was the earlier proposal that Canada should be linked with a Free Trade Area of the OEEC. The Conference merely reaffirmed Commonwealth support for outward-looking trade arrangements in Europe, approved the broad aims and objectives of the Six, and emphasized the importance of British guarantees to safeguard the agricultural interests of other Commonwealth countries in the United Kingdom market.

In October 1958 Maudling attempted to revive the Free Trade Area talks. He suggested that competition within the Area might be mitigated if countries were to adopt a voluntary code of good conduct. However, he refused to admit any restrictions on the freedom of members to alter their external tariffs unilaterally, or to allow members to evade obligations unilaterally by invoking escape clauses. French officials now suggested that the talks might at last be about to collapse. The Germans, who were at least not alarmed by the prospect of meeting the British in open competition, and therefore had a vested interest in salvaging the scheme, proposed a last-minute pre-negotiation conference between the French, the British, and themselves. The British Government ignored the first indirect German approaches, then rejected a formal German offer to mediate between London and Paris. Macmillan apparently still counted on the great power and authority of the United Kingdom, plus the basic economic good sense of the Free Trade Area idea, to induce the French to come to terms. He accordingly announced, as Dulles had done in similar circumstances in 1954, that he was not prepared to contemplate the failure of the Free Trade Area. Rumours were again circulated that the Army of the Rhine might be withdrawn from Europe if the United Kingdom were to suffer economically from Common Market discrimination.[43] But times had changed. Such methods would hardly have been necessary before 1956, and they could not have succeeded after 1957. France had always been essential to any construction of European union, and while the Fourth Republic would have paid almost any price to have the United Kingdom formally committed to European union, the Fifth Republic would have paid almost any price to have kept it out. On 14 November Jacques Soustelle, now de Gaulle's Minister of Information, told the OEEC Ministers that it was simply not possible to create the Free Trade Area as wished by the British, "that is, with free trade between the Common Market and the rest of the OEEC, but without a single external tariff barrier around the seventeen countries, and without harmonization in the economic and social spheres". He suggested that this did not mean that there could be no solution to problems of commercial relations between the Common Market and outsiders.[44]

Soustelle was perhaps merely stating the obvious. There was certainly no indication that any European country was really prepared, after over two years of considering the project, to accept the Free Trade Area on any conditions which the British had so far shown themselves willing to concede. It was thus reasonable for the French press to report his speech as if it had not signalled any change in the policy of their Government. It would nonetheless have been disingenuous to expect the British to regard it as anything less than a challenge. Maudling claimed that it had come as a complete surprise to him.[45] During the weekend, the British broke off the negotiations. The French press now suggested, possibly sincerely, that this might well prove constructive, since it showed that the British had at last realized that they could not get a Free Trade Area on their original terms. On the same day, the French Government announced that concessions on quotas to be applied on 1 January under the terms of the Treaty of Rome would be made available to other members of the OEEC as well, in order to minimize discrimination.

Negotiation had now turned into confrontation. On 15 November Maudling had warned that the Scandinavians, the Austrians, and the Swiss could no more adhere to the Treaty of Rome than the British could. The Swedish Government then presented formal notes to the Six, warning them that the tariff reductions contemplated under the terms of the Treaty of Rome would be incompatible with the maintenance of friendly relations with countries outside the Common Market, even if they were judged compatible with the GATT. The Swiss followed this up by threatening that they would consider withdrawing from the European Payments Union if discrimination against their exports occurred after the Common Market had begun operating on 1 January 1959. They also refused to consider any bilateral accommodations with the Six. On 1 December a meeting of British, Scandinavian, Austrian, and Swiss representatives was called at Geneva. The Portuguese were not called but arrived nevertheless. At the end of the meeting the seven governments affirmed their determination to pursue their efforts to find a satisfactory form of multilateral association between the Six and the eleven other OEEC countries, including themselves. They also formally rejected the principle of bilateral arrangements with the Six.

Dr. Erhard flew to London the following day, in an attempt to head off the impending collision between the two groups. Maudling invoked once more the danger of a breakdown in military co-operation if the present pattern of economic relations in the OEEC were impaired. However, he agreed with Erhard that the EEC proposals to mitigate discrimination should be discussed at a ministerial meeting of the OEEC. On 12 December the British Government decided not to put forward any new proposals themselves, and to reject the proposals already made by the Six. There thus seemed no basis for compromise, and no prospect of a solution either, unless one party or the other abandoned its stated position. The determination of the British at least to maintain their position seemed to be made manifest by the choice of Sir David Eccles to lead the British delegation. He opened his address on 15 December by claiming that the proposals of the Six amounted to discrimination, "whatever way you looked at them". However, he suddenly announced later in the evening that the British would be prepared to match the Six if they would extend their full quota liberalization to the rest of the OEEC. This offer, at once courageously generous and brilliantly statesmanlike, was clearly not expected by the representatives of the Six. Even the French could think of no satisfactory reason for dismissing it out of hand. They accordingly asked for time to consider the British proposal. Eccles demanded an immediate answer, presumably so as not to allow the French the opportunity to invent objections. The Ministers of the Six then left the conference room for a hurried consultation among themselves. On their return, they asked for the British proposals to be put in writing. Eccles thereupon asked the French representative, Couve de Murville, how his country could ease its trading policies towards its Common Market partners, while falling down on its obligations towards the other OEEC countries. He then warned angrily that the United Kingdom would reserve its right to take retaliatory measures against France to protect its trade. By this time, most of the Ministers were on their feet. In an extraordinary moment of historical irony, Germany, in the person of Dr. Erhard, sought to mediate between Britain and France. But no compromise was possible by this time. With the statement that France was not accustomed to negotiate under threats, Couve de Murville led his colleagues out of the conference room. It was the best answer he could have given at the time. But it was not his final reply to British attempts to exercise a controlling influence in Western European affairs. That was to come just four years later.

NOTES

1. Protocol of the Western European Union.
2. Canada, House of Commons, *Debates,* 20 January 1955.
3. *Times* (London), 8 June 1955.
4. U.K., Cmd. 9525, p. 10.
5. *Financial Times,* 11 November 1955.
6. *Manchester Guardian,* 18 November 1955.
7. H.J. Heiser, *British Policy with Regard to the Unification Efforts on the European Continent* (Leyden: Swythoff, 1959), pp. 98-99.
8. *Combat,* 21 March 1956.
9. *Le Monde* (Paris), 21 April 1956.
10. Canada, Department of External Affairs, *Statements and Speeches,* 30 April 1956.
11. *Ibid.,* 3 June 1956.
12. U.K., House of Commons, *Debates,* Vol. DLIV, col. 1207.
13. *Combat,* 26 June 1956.
14. *Ibid.,* 3 July 1956.
15. U.K., H. of C., *Debates,* Vol. DLV, cols. 1673-85.
16. Cmd. 641.
17. U.K., H. of C., *Debates,* Vol. DLVII, col. 210.
18. A. Eden, *Memoirs* (London: Cassell, 1960), pp. 426-27.
19. *Ibid.,* pp. 462, 475. .
20. *Times,* 4 October 1956.
21. Australia, Department of External Affairs, *Current Notes on Internationl Affairs,* 1956, p. 642.
22. *Combat,* 5 October 1956.

23. Council of Europe, Consultative Assembly, *Reports,* 22 October 1956.
24. U.K., H. of C., *Debates,* Vol. DLVIII, col. 1454.
25. I.M.F., *International Financial Statistics,* 1956 and 1957.
26. Canada, Department of External Affairs, *External Affairs,* 1957, pp. 38-39.
27. U.K., H. of C., *Debates,* Vol. DLXI, cols. 35-48.
28. France, Assemblée Nationale, *Débats,* 16 January 1957.
29. *Ibid.,* 17 January 1957.
30. France, Conseil de la République, *Débats,* 15 January 1957.
31. U.K., Cmd. 72.
32. *Times,* 14 February 1957.
33. U.S., State Department, *Bulletin,* 1957, p. 182.
34. Australia, House of Representatives, *Debates,* 1957, pp. 516-17.
35. C. of E., C.A., *Reports,* 30 April 1957.
36. N.Z., House of Representatives, *Debates,* 14 June 1957.
37. *Le Monde,* 18 June 1957.
38. N.Z., H. of R., *Debates,* 23 July 1957.
39. Australia, H. of R., *Debates,* 12 September 1957.
40. Cmnd. 648, p. 5.
41. Canada, D. of E.A., *External Affairs,* 1958, pp. 5-9.
42. *Ibid.,* p. 156.
43. *New York Times,* 12 November 1958.
44. *Financial Times,* 15 November 1958.
45. *Ibid.*

5. The World Awaits the Answer

For perhaps the first time since 1870, Paris had regained domination in Western European affairs. For certainly the first time since 1945, London had clearly lost it. The breakdown of the Free Trade Area talks nonetheless did not cause any real check to discussion between the Six and the rest of the OEEC. This was very evidently the case as regards the United Kingdom and France. There was no suggestion of any of the threatened collapse of military or financial co-operation. Instead, the British and French Governments actually combined on 27 December in seeking a replacement for the now outmoded European Payments Union, from which the Swiss had so vigorously threatened to resign. The French Government then proposed that a further ministerial meeting of the OEEC should be called as soon as the Common Market had become a reality. Talks with the United Kingdom on trade matters were set in train at once. On 28 January the

French also began discussing with the Germans ways of associating other OEEC countries with the Common Market. The two Governments instructed the EEC Commission to prepare a report on the subject. The British also acted swiftly to preserve their own markets in the EEC, despite their earlier condemnation of bilateral arrangements. On 5 February they signed a ten year agreement with Euratom for the supply of British fuel on commercial terms, and also began trade talks separately with the French. Negotiations were renewed with their Geneva partners[1] on 18 February, when a party of British Treasury officials left for a meeting of the Economic Committee of Uniscan in Stockholm. At the same time, Maudling explained to the House of Commons why the United Kingdom could not possibly adhere to the Treaty of Rome:

> We could not contemplate any system of working with Europe which was at the expense of our ties with the Commonwealth. It would be bad for us; it would be bad for the Commonwealth; and I think that it would be bad for the whole free world, if Britain were forced to choose between Europe and the Commonwealth ... to sign the Treaty of Rome would mean having common external tariffs, which, in turn, would mean the end of Commonwealth free entry, and I cannot conceive that any Government of this country would put forward a proposition which would involve the abandonment of Commonwealth free entry ... Finally, we must recognize that the aim of the main proponents of the Community is political integration ... The whole idea of the Six, the Coal and Steel Community and Euratom is a movement towards political integration. This is a fine aspiration, but we must recognize that to sign the Treaty of Rome would be to accept as the ultimate goal, political federation in Europe, including ourselves.[2]

Once again, the British had been prompt to discern political objectives which the Europeans themselves seemed less concerned about. The Treaty of Rome no more contained a commitment to ultimate federation than had the Treaties of the Coal and Steel Community and the European army.

It was quite certain that the goal of political federation had no more determined enemies in the world than President de Gaulle and Premier Debré of France. But that part of Maudling's speech which related to Commonwealth free entry did touch on an issue peculiarly difficult for the British Government at the time. Their immediate objective was to find some means of inducing the Six to resume negotiations on the Free Trade Area. They hoped to do this by confronting the Common Market with another trade bloc containing most if not all of the other OEEC countries. But to do this they would have first of all to discourage those countries from making their own accommodations with the Six. This was likely to entail offering them sufficient access to the market of the United Kingdom to compensate them for the loss of what they could otherwise have obtained in the markets of the Six. But the access which the Scandinavians at least were most concerned about was access for agricultural products, in which Denmark at least competed directly with Commonwealth suppliers. The Commonwealth Governments had obviously already agreed to accept some loss of preference in the United Kingdom market, or otherwise the British Government would never have been able to accept the principle of including arrangements on agriculture in the Free Trade Area. But the arguments in favour of Commonwealth Governments making these concessions had been very compelling in the case of the Free Trade Area. It had been a supremely sensible answer to European trade problems; it would have guaranteed continuing British access to European markets; and it was supposed to have been necessary to maintain the military and political cohesion of the Atlantic system. The last argument certainly seemed to have lost its relevance; it was by no means certain that Common Market discrimination was really going to injure the trade of other OEEC countries to any significant degree; and it seemed extremely probable that no pressure of any kind was going to induce the French at least to accept the Free Trade Area idea. The Commonwealth Governments would thus have to be persuaded to make certain sacrifices in the interests of a trading bloc whose activities were not likely to benefit themselves or the United Kingdom directly to any great extent, and whose chances of achieving its main objective were very far from certain.

The British Government was nonetheless committed to the attempt. Maudling flew to Stockholm on 1 March. He claimed to be going on a lecture tour. Meanwhile, Sir David Eccles visited Commonwealth countries, to discourage their governments from attempting to conclude the same kind of bilateral arrangements with members of the Six as the British Government was at that time concluding with the French. In Johannesburg he warned the South Africans that their country would certainly be injured by the Common Market, and told them:

> Commonwealth countries must stick together and not allow themselves to be picked off one by one by the Six ... You may get trade delegations from the Common Market countries saying: "Do a bilateral deal with us and we won't treat you too harshly".

He added that he had recently angered the British leather industry by rejecting a proposal that would have affected the importation of South African hides. "Unless you boys do the same for us, we won't be able to keep it up for long."[3]

Eccles had certainly developed a characteristic style in these matters. Meanwhile, the Anglo-French bilateral arrangements reached conclusion. The two Governments agreed to enlarge all their quotas on imports by 20 per cent for the coming year. In addition, the British undertook to import annually $U.S.3 million of French textiles, farm products and optical instruments, in return for French orders for an extra $U.S.10 million of cars and whisky.

This was undoubtedly sensible, but perhaps not an auspicious beginning to the opening of negotiations for a smaller Free Trade Association of the United Kingdom and other OEEC countries. The British tried first to exclude the Commonwealth issue by confining the proposed arrangements to trade in industrial goods only. This was no more possible now than it had been with the original Free Trade Area. The Norwegians flatly refused to consider any proposals unless they were allowed increased access to the British market, to offset the dangers they expected from allowing the more industrially developed Swedes and Danes freer entry to the domestic Norwegian market. The Danes also expected to be compensated in the British market for whatever they might have lost in Continental Europe through not joining the EEC. Hr. de Besch, the Secretary-General of the Swedish Foreign Ministry, managed with great difficulty to secure agreement among the Seven on a reduction of 20 per cent in tariffs on industrial products from 1 July 1960, to be followed by eight annual reductions of 10 per cent from 1 July 1962. These reductions were to be co-ordinated with cuts in the internal tariffs of the Six, and could be adjusted to meet any changes in the timetable of the EEC. The Danish Foreign Minister, Hr. Krag, immediately set off on visits to London, Brussels, and Bonn to learn what effects these arrangements were likely to have on his country's trade. The Germans assured him that Danish agricultural exports to the Common Market would not be endangered if Denmark entered another trade bloc. However, the Danish Agricultural Council violently demanded that Denmark should join the EEC, while the British Farmers' Union for its part objected to any concessions being offered to Denmark by the British Government.

On 6 July Krag announced unequivocally that Denmark would not join the new trade bloc of the Seven unless adequate tariff concessions were received from the United Kingdom. The British had little option but to meet the Danes at once. Commonwealth Governments were barely allowed twenty-four hours in which to endorse a British proposal that the 20 per cent duty on Danish canned pork, and the 10 per cent duties on Danish bacon and blue-veined cheese, should be halved on 1 July 1960, and abolished a year later. The Australian and New Zealand Governments were in a weak debating position, in any case. They had apparently already agreed to similar concessions in order to bring about the original Free Trade Area, and they had in any event little or no existing trade with the United Kingdom in these items. On the other hand, the original Free Trade Area had been far more obviously worth making concessions for, and New Zealand in particular had had hopes of developing an export trade in the items affected. They nonetheless conceded the point. This swift adjustment to a European demand indicated an approach on the part of the British strikingly different from that employed during the Free Trade Area negotiations. As Clifford Selby pointed out in the *Observer*:

> This smooth accommodation with the Danes is in marked contrast with all the doubletalk a year or two ago about the difficulty of reconciling industrial and agricultural economies when the European Free Trade Area was first projected. It was then said that in the interests of British and Commonwealth farmers agriculture must at all costs be excluded from the negotiations. It was only when the talks were breaking down that Britain conceded that there might be room for a reconciliation of agricultural policies ... It was not out of any tenderness for the British and Commonwealth farmers that the United Kingdom negotiators were reluctant to discuss agriculture. They were ... concerned ... to preserve the structure of Imperial Preference which brings the

twin advantages of cheap food for Britain's industrial workers
and safe markets for her industrial exports ...

This means however that the basic irreconcilability between
Britain's Commonwealth connection and the Common Market
still remains despite all the brave talk of bridge-building by the
Outer Seven. Many people in the Commonwealth have come to
realize this in recent months and to question whether their
interests in this issue are necessarily in line with Britain's. For the
Commonwealth farmer, for instance, the British market for his
produce is already pretty well saturated; would it not pay him to
develop a connection with the Common Market countries?
Similarly, the Commonwealth manufacturer is not always satisfied
that he is getting the best end of the Preferential deal.

It may well be that before long these Commonwealth voices
may be joined to those already to be heard here calling for a
joint re-thinking of Britain's approach to the Common Market.[4]

But they were not. And Selby's arguments did seem to
disregard a few fairly obvious considerations. The British had
indeed changed their approach, but they had done so simply
because the earlier approach was demonstrably inappropriate; the
British market might be nearing saturation, but the Commonwealth
producer was unlikely to be allowed any significant entry to the
markets of the EEC for as long as peasant votes were important to
European politicians; and the British Government had to be
tender to British farmers so long as it wanted to stay in office, and
to Commonwealth producers so long as it considered the preferential system important to the prosperity of the United Kingdom.
However, Selby was undoubtedly on safe ground in stressing the
extent to which the British had been compelled to modify their
bargaining position. On 14 July Krag, in an effort to conciliate
Danish farmers, revealed that the concessions just gained were
more extensive than those offered by the British to bring about
the original Free Trade Area. They at least achieved their aim.
On 21 July the Ministers of the Seven affirmed in Stockholm their
intention to establish a European Free Trade Association (EFTA),
the purpose of which would be:

> ... to facilitate early negotiations with the European Economic
> Community and also with the other members of the OEEC who
> have particular problems calling for special solutions. These
> negotiations would have as their object to remove trade barriers
> and establish a multilateral association embracing all members
> of the OEEC ...

The problem of course was simply that the Common Market countries might have solutions of their own to the problems of other OEEC members. The Seven would then serve no purpose other than the thoroughly useful one of enhancing and presumably rationalizing trade among its members. But this would not solve the particular British problem, namely, that the most important countries in Western Europe had formed a close union from which the United Kingdom was excluded. At the same time, the attractiveness of the EEC solution of bilateral deals was indicated by the fact that on 17 August the British and French agreed to raise their quotas on mutual trade in cars by 40 per cent. The British were meanwhile resisting a somewhat surprising Norwegian demand that processed fish products should be given full free trade treatment within the Seven as manufactured goods. The other EFTA countries had already agreed to this. However, the British Government was unwilling to risk offending its own fishing interests until after the general elections. This virtually halted all progress on the new bloc until after November. Similarly, the necessity for British parliamentarians to stay at home and campaign in their constituencies made the next meeting of the Council of Europe the most futile in its history. It was simply impossible for outsiders to form any idea of how the proposed EFTA was developing. John McEwen, questioned about the Seven in the Australian House of Representatives, could only say:

> The Australian Government has been concerning itself quite closely with this matter to see whether it can contribute towards its general policy of solidifying political cohesion in Europe without detriment to Australian trade opportunities. I had discussions only last week with the Minister of the United Kingdom Board of Trade ... and interested Australian industries. We are keeping in touch with this matter.

On the question of the Common Market, McEwen said:

> To the extent that the European Economic Community achieves its economic objectives Australia stands to benefit from any resultant rise in demand in the Community for food and raw materials. These benefits will be lessened, however, to the extent that the members of the Community adopt protectionist policies in favour of each other and at the expense of outside countries.[6]

This was indeed the danger, and the problem was how the world outside could expect to induce the Six to behave in any other way. The representatives of the world's fourth largest trading nation, a country more consistently helpful than any other in its attitudes towards all forms of Western union, now attempted to remind the Six of what might seem to be their responsibilities to their trading partners outside the Common Market. Canadian Finance Minister Churchill expressed in a meeting of the GATT his country's appreciation and sympathy for the "broad objectives" of the EEC initiative, and explained that Canada accepted the situation that "outside suppliers to the Six will face a tariff disadvantage vis-à-vis their competitors in the Community" because this was "the natural consequence ... of the formation of a Customs Union". However, he warned that Canada could nonetheless "not be expected to acquiesce to regional agricultural arrangements ... which intensify restrictions, increase tariffs or aggravate discrimination against our exports, and which might place outside countries in the position of marginal suppliers, to be permitted entry only after surpluses within the Community have been marketed..."[7] Nothing indeed seemed more likely. And the only hope marginal suppliers seemed to have was that demand within the Six might increase sufficiently for them to receive some increasing share, however slight, in the internal prosperity. Ten days later, Canadian Solicitor-General Leon Balçer expressed similar views in the same forum. He promised sympathy and understanding for the Six, and sympathy and judiciousness for the Seven when he had had a chance to find out what they were about. But he too demanded to know of the Six if they "as major manufacturers and exporters, wish to take advantage of world availability and world prices for necessary raw materials, or do they prefer to insulate themselves ... from the world markets and to protect limited local productions without adequate regard to the higher economic costs involved? The world awaits the answer."[8]

In Australia, the Federal Treasurer, Harold Holt, spoke in similar terms. He too emphasized the need to avoid political and economic division in Europe, and warned that "the degree of agricultural protectionism in Europe ... may be intensified as the European countries draw closer together". He added that he had sought and received assurances that the British Government would consult Australia fully at every stage of the developing situation in Europe.[9] The only wholly optimistic forecast was made by the Leader of the Labour Opposition in the Australian House of Representatives, Arthur Calwell:

> I see clearly the peculiar position of the United Kingdom in regard to this matter. Great Britain has to decide whether she will be just an island nation off the coast of Europe, or the centre of a very great Commonwealth ... Because these Six European nations will not concede her the right to exempt products should she participate in their scheme, naturally she wants to form some other body...Speaking only for myself, I would wish to encourage the formation of such communities. The European Economic Community will ease tensions, it will promote unity ... I do not share the fears of the Minister in regard to the European Economic Community ... I would not try to discourage ... the attempt of the Europeans to solve their problems. After all, the problems are their own and they have a right to settle them in their own way, even if at times it seems to our disadvantage.[10]

It was of course one thing to insist that the experiment of the Common Market should be conducted in a manner which would pay reasonable regard to the commercial interests of the trading partners of the Six outside the Market. It was something quite different to assert that the experiment of the Six was itself positively deleterious to the Atlantic system. This was in fact the argument which British Ministers continued to develop. In Birmingham Maudling warned again that the Six might become "inward-looking and restriction-minded".[11] A communiqué issued by the British Information Services in Bonn claimed that:

> The big question upon which depends the economic division or unification of Europe ... is whether the Six reciprocate the wish of the Seven for a European association or whether they do not wish to treat the Seven otherwise than as the rest of the outside world ... One cannot get over the fact that it will be a decision for the future of Europe, and for the creation of a counterpoise to the Soviet bloc with its rapid economic expansion ... a split within Europe, with the friction that would result, could mean that the entire Western world would have to compete in the race with the Soviet bloc under entirely new conditions.[12]

Similarly, John Profumo, then Minister of State for Foreign Affairs, told the United Kingdom's WEU partners that it was "hopeless to expect that the military and political cohesion of Western Europe could survive", if the development of the Communities of the Six were to result in a trade war in Europe. In an unfortunately memorable play upon words, Profumo invited the Six to come to terms with the Seven, denying that it "was part of our policy to set up a club of the Seven in opposition to the Six. No, indeed: we want the Seven to have Six appeal!"[13]

But facts to support this argument convincingly were not easy to find. The EEC had been in existence for nearly a year. No Western European institution had broken up. Nobody had left NATO. The British had not found it necessary to withdraw their troops from Germany. Cross-Channel trade consultations seemed to have been positively encouraged. Nor was it obvious that countries outside Europe were suffering from the effects of Common Market discrimination. This was evident least of all in the case of Commonwealth countries. Commonwealth trade with the EEC countries had certainly deteriorated during the recession year of 1958. However, it had recovered generally in 1959, the first year in which the discriminatory tariff cuts of the Treaty of Rome had actually been applied. Nor was there anything like a consistent pattern discernible. Australian exports to the EEC had fallen from £A232.5 million in 1957 to £A183 million in 1958 and again to £A139.8 million in 1959. New Zealand exports had fallen from £N.Z. 50.5 million in 1957 to £N.Z. 35.4 million in 1958, but had recovered to £N.Z.42.3 million in 1959. Canadian sales had similarly fallen from $Can.402.4. million in 1957 to $Can.239.7 million in 1958, and recovered to $Can.314.1 million in 1959. The United Kingdom had suffered least and recovered fastest. British exports had fallen from £stg.459.7 million in 1957 to £stg.419 million in 1958, and risen again to £stg.465.7 million in 1959.[14]

It would certainly have been difficult to plead present injury. Long-term trends might indeed present a different picture. And in any case the basic problem of the United Kingdom was not to be conveyed adequately in purely economic considerations. What was very clearly at stake were British claims to be regarded any longer as a world power. As Churchill had indicated, these claims to exceptional consideration were based on the three supports of Britain's predominant influence in Western Europe, its special relationship with the United States and its connection with the other countries of the Commonwealth. There could be no doubt that the first claim was severely called in question by the formation of a closed European union increasingly dominated by a country whose leader was at best unsympathetic to British interests, if not positively hostile to them. This was evidently a setback to British policy. What was even more serious was that any attempt to recover the situation was very likely to endanger one or the other of the remaining two supports. An attempt to restore British authority on the Continent by entering the Common Market was certain to endanger the Commonwealth connection. An attempt to impose such authority on the Common Market by pressure from the outside was likely to endanger the relationship with the Americans, whose preferred solution would clearly have been to see the United Kingdom safely installed in the EEC, having abandoned both the Commonwealth connection and any troublesome pretensions to influential status within the Atlantic system. EFTA undoubtedly appealed as a technique which, while being economically profitable in itself, might bring the EEC back within a British-dominated economic association, without testing the Commonwealth connection in any meaningful way. But it obviously could not place pressure on the Six sufficient for this purpose without the support of the United States. And this was being very clearly withheld.

Up to the end of 1959, American leaders simply refused to discuss the possibility of negotiations between the Six and the Seven. Their ultimate decision to intervene in the economic integration issue arose from pressing financial problems of their own. United States holdings of gold and foreign exchange had fallen from $U.S.24.5 billion in 1949 to $U.S.19.5 billion by the end of 1959. The combined reserves of the industrialized European countries had risen in the same period from $U.S.5.8 billion to $U.S.13.3 billion.[15] Washington had now become concerned that this adverse trend in the American balance of payments might be aggravated by economic regionalism in Europe. In December 1959 the United States Under-Secretary of State, Douglas Dillon, visited Europe for discussions on this issue. On the day that Dillon left the United States, the American Secretary of State, Christian Herter, refused to make a definite statement of American views towards the Seven. Asked if the United States would support the legality of the association of the Seven in the GATT, he replied:

> We, as you know, have been strongly in favour of the Six.
> We have certainly not done anything to discourage the Seven.

> We feel that if they should turn into rival organizations it might be a serious thing in Europe.[16]

In Brussels Dillon described the Common Market as "one of the most significant developments in the postwar era", but refused to say anything about the Seven.[17] He also refused to arbitrate between the Six and the Seven at a meeting of the OEEC. However, he did suggest that Austria should be permitted to come to a separate accommodation with the Six, with whom it transacted 60 per cent of its external trade. The British representative expressed astonishment at this proposal, although it would have seemed to have had little effect save to make Austria's external trade relations easier.[18] In a subsequent meeting Dillon managed to secure agreement to the proposal that reorganization of the OEEC should be considered. He suggested that the United States and Canada should be made full members of the successor organization, which would possess the dual functions of co-ordinating aid and improving the machinery of international co-operation. However, efforts to initiate useful consultations between the Six and the Seven failed. The United Kingdom and its associates insisted that the issue should be discussed in a purely European context. The United States and the Six preferred that the North Americans should be consulted as well. In Ottawa, Lester Pearson suggested that the four experts charged with preparing a report on the future of the OEEC should go beyond their terms of reference, and explore the possibility of a North Atlantic Free Trade Area. He claimed that nothing less would do, "knowing that a major Communist attack on the free world might soon develop on that front".[19] Finance Minister Fleming renewed the Canadian attack on European regional discrimination. He said that it was "understandable that the other European countries, which participated in the earlier postwar European initiatives, but which for political or economic reasons were unable to join with the Six, should regard the plans of the Six with mixed feelings..." However, he expressed fears concerning "some new form of discrimination against Canadian goods, some new European preferential system from which we were excluded..." In the sharpest comment yet made by the Canadian Government to its Atlantic allies he said:

> Any protectionist or discriminatory development in Europe against imports from Canada would in our view be particularly

indefensible in the light of the great increase in prosperity and economic strength in Europe during the past two or three years. Europe has built up its gold and dollar reserves to a substantial level, much of the inflow coming from the United States ... [20]

Fleming made it clear that he was speaking for other nations of the Commonwealth as well as Canada. Both Commonwealth and non-Commonwealth countries outside Europe had been in touch with Ottawa before the Dillon visit. But North American warnings against European discrimination were not in themselves generating support for the Seven. Both Canada and the United States indeed seemed to view the new association as a further complication to the European problem, rather than as a means to a solution. The British tried urgently to enlist positive American help. Selwyn Lloyd again prophesied that a trade war between the Six and the Seven might result in the breakdown of NATO. He was immediately challenged by Robert Abdessalem of the Republican Unity Group, who denied correctly enough that any trade war had yet developed. "The Community has harmed no one," he said. "The further it develops the more liberal become its policies."[21] Professor Walter Hallstein, President of the EEC Commission, said in London that he could see no reason why the Six and the Seven could not live peacefully side by side.[22] In New York Sir Harold Caccia, the British Ambassador to the United States, insisted that unless the Six and the Seven were united, Europe would never be able to play its full part in countering the Soviet economic threat, or in helping the under-developed countries to raise their standards of living.[23] The Americans did not respond. On 20 March 1960 President Eisenhower gave a "full-fledged endorsement" of the Hallstein Plan of bringing the date for the establishment of the common external tariff of the EEC closer by eighteen months. But at a meeting in Vienna the previous week the Ministers of the Seven had made it clear that they regarded the Hallstein Plan as a most unfriendly gesture by the Six.[24]

Macmillan made some kind of last appeal in Washington. His words were apparently made known to the *Washington Post* and subsequently reprinted in European papers. According to the *Corriere della Sera* he told Christian Herter that the United Kingdom was opposed for historical reasons to any attempt to unify Continental Europe, and was prepared to lead a new peripheral alliance against Germany and France as it had done in the days of Napoleon.[25] Herter himself refused to comment on the newspaper reports. Macmillan did not exactly confirm or deny what he was supposed to have said, and his own account to the House of Commons was described by the *Daily Telegraph,* normally sympathetic to the Government, as a display of "incoherent anguish".

> ... we should not allow an economic gap, a sort of division to grow up, which, gradually, I do not say in the short run, but in the long run, as all history has proved, will make another division in Europe ... It is not the particular groupings of Powers, but a division, and I have made the plea, again, that, somehow or other, we should, in the next period, try to make that gap so small that it is wearable and does not have these effects.[26]

The plea did not seem to have been sympathetically received in Washington. The Americans had in any case their own problems. It was in their interest that the EEC should settle their common external tariff as early as possible before tariff consultations began in the GATT in September 1960. The Americans would obviously be at an advantage if the Europeans had reduced their own tariffs substantially before global tariff-cutting negotiations actually started. This might well have seemed of more immediate importance to the Americans than the continued presence of two trade blocs in Europe, neither of which had yet proved to be of significant danger to countries outside Europe. But American support for the EEC meant the failure of British attempts to use the Seven as an instrument to re-open the Free Trade Area negotiations. The British were now at last in the clear position of having to make some manner of choice between Europe and the Commonweath, since their only means of at once retrieving their authority in Western Europe and re-establishing their relationship with the United States would be to achieve entry to the EEC.

Commonwealth Governments had already drawn this conclusion themselves. Panic signals began to fly. The Nigerian Government expressed alarm about the likely impact of Common Market arrangements on their external trade. In Canberra McEwen assured the House of Representatives that the British Government was keeping the Commonwealth informed on the progress of discussions with the Europeans. He referred to "quite frequent discussions in London at the official level and ad hoc discussions in Committees which exist for that purpose", and said that:

> The Australian Government has been careful from the outset to ensure that our interests, as embodied in the GATT arrangement, are not impaired by any arrangement such as the so-called Common Market or even the larger Free Trade Area ... we have not been reticent in making our views on this matter known to the United States of America and to Canada separately, as well as taking full advantage of the GATT.[27]

But the Europeans had now drawn the same conclusion. And events were moving too rapidly for existing methods of consultation to be adequate. On 9 May 1960 the Council of Ministers of the EEC over-ruled a proposal by Hallstein for recriprocal extension of tariff cuts between the Six and the Seven. They called instead for the immediate re-opening of trade negotiations with the United Kingdom. The British response could not have been quicker. On the following day, Maudling announced that the British Government would react positively to any initiative from the Six to break the deadlock between the two trading groups. He said that the attitude of the British Government could not be inflexible. Indeed, the British Government recognized that negotiation meant compromise and concessions on both sides, and "so great is the importance of maintaining European unity that all concerned should enter any negotiations in the spirit that such a prize is worth substantial sacrifice".[28]

This represented a considerable change in position from Maudling's own stance during the Free Trade Area talks, which could only rarely be described as flexible. His speech was followed coincidentally within twenty-four hours by the appointment of the first Australian ambassador to the EEC. The Minister for External Affairs, Sir Garfield Barwick, said that the appointment of Sir Edwin McCarthy was "prompted by the circumstances that this country has a very great interest in what happens in this organization in Europe".[29] Meanwhile the Australian Department of Trade began to study the possible effects of British entry into the Common Market, despite the protestations of Sir Harold Caccia in Washington that the United Kingdom could never do anything of the kind, because that would amount to a reversal of its vital economic, political, and military ties with the Commonwealth. Certainly, the meeting of Commonwealth Prime Ministers in London at this time was not forewarned of any impending change in British policy, although John G. Diefenbaker warned that the United Kingdom should "continue to maintain the closest possible cooperation with the rest of the Commonwealth in developing its own policies with regard to trade with Western Europe".[30]

The British indeed made one more attempt to recover the ground lost in Europe without involving the Commonwealth issue. John Profumo suggested in the Assembly of the WEU that the United Kingdom should contract into the membership of the ECSC and Euratom, but not the EEC. This would at least have established Britain within two of the European Communities. It did of course involve admitting that the federal implications which had been regarded as unalterable objections to British membership of these institutions in the past appeared in this light no longer. However, the objection actually urged by the Europeans was that they were about to amalgamate the three Communities at the time that the British were proposing to join two of them. This was said to involve impossible administrative difficulties. Even the friends of the United Kingdom among the Six professed to find the British initiative incomprehensible as well as illogical. They could well afford to take this position. They were not really rejecting British membership of two of their Communities. They were trying to make it impossible for the British to avoid becoming members of all three.

Maudling now told a joint meeting of the Trade and Industry, Foreign Affairs and Agriculture Committees of Conservative back-benchers on 4 July that the difficulties in the way of British adherence to the Common Market were as great as ever.[31] However, this attitude was challenged thirteen days later by Erhard, who appealed directly to the British Government to take the step towards Europe, assuring them that they would not be turned down if they took the plunge wholeheartedly. This call from Europe was attended to at last. Between 18 and 25 July 1960 the Conservatives began marshalling for a change of front. Selwyn Lloyd, now Chancellor of the Exchequer, told the House of Commons that:

> We in Britain regard ourselves as a part of Europe ... although we have welcomed the Six from the beginning, we have always been conscious of the danger that it might lead to a division between us ... In seeking to avert this division we do not wish

> to affect the cohesion between the Six as an independent entity, nor to prejudice the achievement by the Six of their political goal ... I think that we have to realize that another set of proposals of the same nature [as the Free Trade Area] would have no chance of acceptance ... Our purpose is a United Europe, and we accept the need for some political organization as a factor in that unity.[32]

Maudling was at once more precise and more ambiguous. He claimed that nobody would suffer if the United Kingdom were to be a member of both the Commonwealth and Western Europe, since it was ready to pay in full the membership fees of both associations. However, it was scarcely probable that the United Kingdom could be a member of both the Commonwealth and the Common Market without some measure of injury to somebody. He also said that while the United Kingdom could certainly join a common market within the meaning of the GATT, it objected to the particular form of Common Market created by the Treaty of Rome. But any kind of common market defined in the GATT would create substantially the same problem for the United Kingdom, namely, that it would have to agree to an external tariff against imports from outside the market, including those from the Commonwealth, while accepting imports without restriction from its partners in the market. If Maudling had really not appreciated this factor, then the unsatisfactory nature of much of the Free Trade Area negotiations would be easy to understand. In any case, the House supported with only four dissenting votes Selwyn Lloyd's resolution that:

> This House recognizes the need for political and economic unity in Europe, and would welcome the conclusion of suitable arrangements to that end, satisfactory to all the Governments concerned.[33]

The only dissidents were the Liberals, who argued that the Government should simply have made an immediate application to join the Common Market. Certainly, there seemed little way by which the stated goals of the British Government could otherwise be achieved. This was certainly true of its unstated goal. It was perhaps difficult to see that achieving the political and economic unity of Europe was really urgent at the time. Political unity could hardly be achieved at any time unless the neutrals were to join NATO, and, as has been stated, the degree of economic disunity existing had still produced no apparent adverse effects. But what was becoming urgent was the need of the

British Government to regain British capacity significantly to influence world events. This was the issue at stake. It was simply true that the United Kingdom could hardly be significantly influential in Europe so long as Gaullist France determined the destinies of the Common Market. And it was not clear that the United Kingdom could be significantly influential in the Atlantic system or even the Commonwealth unless it could again achieve predominance in Western Europe. But what was not clear either was whether this could be done even by joining the Common Market. Then de Gaulle of all people seemed to indicate a way in which the Common Market itself could become an instrument for national ambitions. In a press conference on 5 September he ridiculed both the prospects of ultimate federal union in Europe, and the means of approaching it through functional Communities. He admitted that it was necessary to unite Europe. "Il est banal de le dire."[34] But unity had to be built on realities, not on dreams. The true realities in Europe were the independent sovereign states. They alone had the legal power of making decisions and compelling compliance with their wills. Unity in any realistic sense was thus to be achieved only through the deliberations of an Assembly in which representatives of the national states would meet periodically, "to ensure cooperation in the fields of politics, economics, culture and of defence". The administrative donkey-work could be left to what de Gaulle described contemptuously as "certains organismes plus ou moins extra- ou supra-nationaux".[35]

What de Gaulle was describing appeared to be in essence the structure of a confederation. It therefore corresponded to the only form of international organization which the United Kingdom had apparently been willing to endorse. The task of the British Government thus seemed enormously simplified. Gaullist Europe could not be a federal Europe. There thus seemed no great difficulty in the way of the United Kingdom's retaining close relations with countries outside the Common Market. The major problem would therefore be merely the one of explaining to some of those other countries why it was necessary that their economic interests should be at least temporarily jeopardized in the interests of restoring the basis of British pretensions to a world power role. There was also the presentational difficulty of explaining why a policy which had been repudiated inflexibly since 1948 had now become both desirable and necessary.

This problem could not be dismissed simply by taking the attitude that those Commonwealth Governments which had formerly manifested any interest in European affairs had tended to support British entry into Community Europe. Two things were different. These earlier views had been expressed with reference to British entry into limited Communities, which could hardly be expected to have any significant material affect upon other Commonwealth countries; and they had been made at a time of far greater British authority and material predominance within Europe. Support which might have been expressed for British entry into the Coal and Steel Community in 1950, the Defence Community in 1951–54, or even the Economic Community in 1956 could not be predicated in the case of the Economic and the other Communities in 1960.

The British Government took preliminary soundings of Commonwealth views at the first meeting of the Commonwealth Economic Consultative Committee in Accra, 20–21 September 1960. It was noted that the British delegation was led by the officials of the Foreign Office and their Minister, Edward Heath, with Maudling and the Board of Trade taking a secondary role. Heath assured the Commonwealth Ministers that there were still no negotiations actually in train to bring the EEC and the EFTA closer together, and that the Commonwealth would not be confronted with any prior British decision. The response was hardly encouraging. Objections were perhaps expressed most memorably by the New Zealand Finance Minister, Arnold Nordmeyer, a politician of informed intelligence, commanding presence and impressively loud voice, who said, briefly, that New Zealand was clearly opposed to any move towards closer integration between the two trading blocs, as it had suffered from the effects of the EFTA already, and would necessarily suffer still more from any closer association with the EEC. Maudling tried to reassure the other Ministers that the United Kingdom would keep them closely informed of any negotiations, or any move towards negotiations, aimed at harmonizing economic interests in Europe. He said that the United Kingdom wanted to be associated with the EEC, and it was important that it should be, but he personally did not believe that association should be purchased at any price.

The question of price was of course the one exercising the minds of all present. Heath and Maudling nonetheless secured the agreement of the Commonwealth Ministers to a communiqué stating that the Committee recognized the need for political and economic unity in Europe, that the United Kingdom would be prepared to examine and discuss proposals for a satisfactory solution, and that it was accepted that in any negotiations the essential interests of Commonwealth countries should be safe-guarded, and full account taken of the continuing importance of Commonwealth trade. This impression of general agreement lasted about twenty-four hours. It was abruptly broken by the Canadian Minister of Trade, Donald M. Fleming, who announced at a press conference that Canada had given full value for any advantages it enjoyed in United Kingdom markets, and that it would be necessary for the Canadian Government to re-examine the terms of access of British goods to the Canadian market if there were to be any tampering with Canadian preferential rights. Fleming admitted that any approach to Europe was a matter for decision by the United Kingdom Government, but insisted that it should be taken with the full knowledge of the views of the other Commonwealth Governments. He was supported, though far more mildly, by the Rhodesian Trade Minister, who said that the EEC had already raised concern in the Federation with regard to trade in tobacco.

It was perhaps surprising that Canada and Rhodesia in parti-cular should have felt it necessary to express their misgivings in this way. Canadian trade with the United Kingdom had increased by about 16 per cent in the past two years, and Rhodesian by about 20 per cent. However, the Conservative Government of John G. Diefenbaker was experiencing intense domestic difficul-ties, with its huge majority in disarray, its policies degenerating into mere responses to the probings of the Liberal Opposition, and its efforts to restore momentum to the Canadian economy unsuccessful throughout 1960.

The response from the Commonwealth had scarcely been encouraging. However, Heath's primary concern was to prepare British and European opinion for the impending shift in the policy of his Government. Five days later, he told the Council of Europe that the existence of two trade blocs carried the danger of creating a serious division of the Continent. He then praised the creators of the EEC for having taken care to cement their welcome concord by economic means. The British also wanted to play their part in developing the unity of Europe. The Commonwealth and domestic agriculture were two factors which made it impossible for the British Government to sign the Treaty of Rome unconditionally as it stood. These difficulties were nonetheless not insuperable.

This in itself was enormously further than any British Minister had been prepared to go since the end of the war. But Heath now developed his argument still further. A fortnight later he told the Conservative Party Conference at Scarborough that:

> If we are a part of a vigorously expanding and united Western Europe, our power to help that Commonwealth politically, economically and militarily can be maintained. If we are outside, however, there is a risk that our economic position, relatively, and perhaps absolutely, will decline; our power to help the Commonwealth would then decrease.[36]

He added that if the United Kingdom were closely associated with the Common Market it might find a way to reduce the harmful effects of the protection accorded by the EEC to its associated overseas territories.

The posture of the British Government had thus changed totally. It had formerly been argued that one of the reasons why membership of the EEC was impossible for the United Kingdom was that it would be injurious to the Commonwealth. Heath was now claiming that membership of the EEC might well be necessary if the United Kingdom were to be able to continue to assist the Commonwealth. It was certainly arguable that the economic welfare of the United Kingdom might indeed be enhanced by entry to the EEC. However, it could certainly not be assumed that this enhanced economic capacity might be used effectively to the advantage of the Commonwealth. What was virtually certain was that Commonwealth countries would suffer some loss of access to the British market which would necessarily occasion short term injury. Even this could be advantageous to at least some of them in the long run, if it impelled them to rationalize their patterns of production. But the advantages could only be problematical. The injuries were assured. How great they would be would depend primarily upon the capacity of the United Kingdom to compel the EEC to adjust their own policies to take account of the interests of Commonwealth countries. And it could only be said that the probability of the United Kingdom's being able to do this was distinctly slighter than it would have been in 1950 or 1955. In the year of the Schuman Plan, the United Kingdom boasted a Gross National Product equal to about 48 per cent that of the Western European Six. In 1955 it was 41 per cent. In 1960 it was down to 39.5 per cent. Figures of world trade showed a similar decline in British economic power relative to the Six. In 1950 the United Kingdom had accounted for 11.7 per cent of world trade, in 1955 for 11.2 per cent and in 1960 for 8.5. In the same years, the Six accounted for 17.6 per cent, 22 per cent and 22.6 per cent. It was also evident that the United Kingdom was becoming increasingly dependent upon trade with the Six and less so upon trade with the Commonwealth. In 1950 44.7 per cent of British trade had been transacted with the Commonwealth, and 12 per cent with the Six; in 1955 46.7 per cent and 12.6 per cent respectively; and in 1960 34.2 per cent and 18.3 per cent.

These figures could of course provide a basis for quite contradictory arguments. It could be said on the one hand that the United Kingdom positively required to expand its access to a market whose importance was increasing so evidently. As against this, it could also be maintained that the fact that British trade with the Six had indeed been increasing so markedly showed that the tariff barriers of the Treaty of Rome did not impose any serious obstacle to commerce. It was in short not unambiguously clear either that the British would be able to join the EEC in such a way as to ensure that the Commonwealth would benefit ultimately from the move, or that their economic interests required them to. The interest of recovering their own status as a world power might indeed require them to, but this was not an argument which seemed immediately compelling to the Commonwealth.

It certainly did not seem so to the Canadians. The oldest, the longest independent and the richest of the Dominions had consistently found itself at odds with the United Kingdom throughout the postwar period. The Government of John G. Diefenbaker now seemed to be actively discouraging the United Kingdom from following the kind of course which the Governments of Louis St. Laurent and Lester Pearson had encouraged it to adopt. On the other hand, the Canadian Liberals had not been in the position of really expecting to have to pay some economic price for the merging of the United Kingdom with Continental Europe. The Conservatives did, and the prospect was peculiarly unwelcome. As British spokesmen began to refer repeatedly to the conditions which would be required before the British Government could accede to the Treaty of Rome, Diefenbaker insisted upon the necessity for prior consultation with the rest of the Commonwealth before the United Kingdom took any such move. He stressed particularly that such consultation should not be limited to separate meetings between interested Commonwealth countries. The fullest consideration should also be given to "collective Ministerial discussion and, if necessary, to a meeting of the Prime Ministers."[37]

Following further exchanges with the British Government, it was agreed that Duncan Sandys, the Secretary of State for the Commonwealth and the Colonies, should visit Ottawa in July, to acquaint the Canadians personally with the present policy of the British Government. However, the Canadians were at pains to point out that this was precisely not the kind of Commonwealth consultation that they considered appropriate. Diefenbaker said that he had made it clear to the British that he would not regard talks with Sandys as constituting the basis for any binding decision, or even any understanding of the attitude of Canada in the matter. He felt that the vastly complex issues concerned should be discussed by representatives of all Commonwealth Governments meeting together.[38] Fleming expanded this view, claiming that full consultations at the ministerial level were required now. The value of the Sandys visit would depend on the extent to which the British were able to provide specific information in advance. If Fleming was referring here to the circumstances under which the United Kingdom would consider entering the EEC, and the effect such entry could have on Commonwealth countries, it was of course going to be singularly difficult for the British to have anything like reliable information in advance. Fleming then repeated the principles he had expressed at the press conference in September, asserting that the keynote of the Commonwealth trading system consisted in free access to the United Kingdom market for agricultural products, industrial raw materials and most manufactured goods; that the Canadian Government sought to maintain the most favourable terms of access to the markets of both the United Kingdom and Europe; and that it would pursue whatever policies were necessary to achieve this end.[39]

The Canadians were not alone in expressing their misgivings

about the proposed change in British policy. In New Zealand, the Governor-General's Speech from the Throne referred to the deep concern of the New Zealand Government over the implications of current proposals for the association of the United Kingdom with the EEC, and confirmed that assurances had been received in London that prior consultations would be held with New Zealand and other Commonwealth countries before any definitive decision were made.[40] In Salisbury, Sir Roy Welensky, the Federal Prime Minister, spoke of the way in which recent developments had reduced the Commonwealth tie to "an almost slender thread", and considered that it might well be that the entry of the United Kingdom into the EEC could do irreparable damage to the whole Commonwealth structure. He insisted however that he could not believe that this was really envisaged.[41] His Minister of Economic Affairs, J.M. Caldicott, also stated that the Federal Government was seeking safeguards involving assurance of the continued political and economic well-being of the Federation, and of the Commonwealth as a whole, with a strong United Kingdom at its centre. It was particularly important that not only should the present market for Rhodesian exports be preserved, but that opportunities no less favourable than those existing at present should be afforded for the expansion and further diversification of Rhodesian exports.[42] These views were elaborated more precisely by President Nkrumah of Ghana, who first referred to the EEC as "an arrangement that used the unification of Western Europe as a cloak for perpetuating colonial privileges within Africa"; then stated:

> I am of the firm belief that the senior member of the Common-wealth should not join the EEC unless she succeeds, first, in eliminating from the present arrangements all those features which involve discriminatory trading relations between the European members and their colonies or ex-colonies; secondly, unless she can give assurances that her own treatment of her colonies and ex-colonies will be no less favourable than those which exist at present; and third, unless she can ensure that whatever financial assistance is offered by the European Powers to the newly emergent States of Africa is given unconditionally.[43]

Nkrumah ended by saying that if the United Kingdom were to join the EEC under conditions which prejudiced the position of Ghana as a member of the sterling area, Ghana would have to leave the area to safeguard its own trading position. He added that he would be sorry to see the United Kingdom become a member of the EEC in any event, because of the disruptive effects this would have upon the Commonwealth, which was an important force for good in the world.

It was not often that voices in Salisbury were likely to be found in accord with those in Accra. This unison was the more significant for the British Government in that the Rhodesians and Ghanaians seemed to be combining with the Canadians and New Zealanders in imposing terms on British entry which would in all probability prove unattainable. It was hardly possible that the Europeans would place so high a value on British entry that they would be prepared to rewrite their own agricultural policies, admit exceptions to the common external tariff, redirect their foreign aid and investment programmes in the interests of the Commonwealth and in general expose themselves to incalculable dislocation. British entry was virtually certain to involve repercussions for the Commonwealth. And some of the more important of those repercussions were manifesting themselves already. Not even over Suez had the United Kingdom been unable to enlist a single Commonwealth voice in support of British policy. Commonwealth disunity had never been manifested so extensively as it was now. And this in itself could only weaken the bargaining position of the United Kingdom when it came to approach Europe. It was not only that the Commonwealth Governments were making demands which could not provide a basis for negotiation because no European government would treat them as such. The extent to which these demands manifested the division and in some degree the irresponsibility of Commonwealth attitudes tended to suggest that the United Kingdom might indeed have no alternative but to seek access to Europe on any terms the Europeans proposed, if it were to discover a satisfactory power basis for itself. The Commonwealth had never looked less like providing such a basis than in the second half of 1961.

Sandys's tour of Commonwealth countries thus took place under singularly unpromising auspices. He flew first to New Zealand, the country traditionally most prone to follow the lead of the United Kingdom in international affairs, but also the country most likely to be directly and seriously affected by the circumstances of British entry to the EEC. Discussions were indeed not happy. They could scarcely have been otherwise in any case, but mutual disillusionment was certainly intensified by the distinctly unconciliatory manner adopted by the British Minister in circumstances in which conciliation would have seemed appropriate. For the first time in history, a representative of the British Government was booed by onlookers at Wellington airport as he walked to the aircraft waiting to take him to Canberra. Sandys had nonetheless achieved some measure of formal success in his mission. The final communiqué issued by the New Zealand Government welcomed his assurance that the British Government would not feel able to enter the EEC unless special arrangements were made to cover vital New Zealand interests. For their part, the New Zealanders agreed that they would understand if the United Kingdom decided to open negotiations with the EEC after consulting the Commonwealth.

New Zealand had certain grounds for hoping that it might be regarded by the Six as deserving special consideration because of the extreme degree of its dependence upon the British market. Australia could expect no such concession. There was hence even less basis for cordial discussions in Canberra than there had been in Wellington. Indeed, the day before Sandys left New Zealand, Trade Minister McEwen said that it was "unthinkable for Australians to contemplate that foreigners should obtain a preferred position in the United Kingdom market, or that by any contrivance foreigners should receive higher prices for the same commodities as the Commonwealth countries sell to Britain".[44] Discussions with Sandys proved to be both inconclusive and violently acrimonious. An essentially unsatisfactory communiqué reported merely that the Australian Government did not feel entitled to object, simply because the decision to open negotiations with the EEC was necessarily one for the British Government to make itself.

At this point, the New Zealand Government took pains to express reservations which had not been spelled out in the communiqué issued after Sandys's departure. Prime Minister Holyoake told the House of Representatives that he had fully expressed his "fears, doubts and reservations" to Prime Minister Macmillan. The New Zealand Government would have to reserve its position and insist upon its rights of duty-free and unrestricted entry to the United Kingdom market for its main exports, until acceptable alternatives were found. He referred to Macmillan's argument that the United Kingdom and Europe would both be stronger if the United Kingdom were inside the EEC, but insisted that this objective would not be satisfactory if it meant the sacrifice of the New Zealand economy. Holyoake went on to say that he had been assured that the New Zealand Government would be consulted before and during any negotiations; that the British would seek in any negotiations that took place to protect the vital interests of New Zealand; that they would not feel able to join the EEC until these arrangements were secured; and that the result of any negotiations would be fully discussed with New Zealand before the British took any final decision. He added that he knew from experience that when the British gave an undertaking, that undertaking would be honoured. Opposition leader Walter Nash agreed that the decision was one for the British Government to make, and that on the evidence the British ought to stay with the Commonwealth and let the EEC go, if New Zealand exports could not enter the British market.[45]

The most that could be said of Sandys's mission so far was that it had not been a total failure. The Australians had declined to support, but at least had not specifically opposed, British entry. The New Zealanders had accepted British entry, on condition that it did themselves no harm. It was left to the Canadians specifically to reject British arguments in the most discouraging terms available to them. The communiqué issued at the close of the talks in Ottawa stated bluntly that:

> The Canadian Ministers indicated that their Government's assessment of the situation was different from that put forward by Mr. Sandys. They expressed the grave concern of the Canadian Government about the implications of possible negotiations between Britain and the EEC, and about the political and economic effects which British membership in the EEC would have on Canada and the Commonwealth as a whole.[46]

On 3 August 1961 the House of Commons debated a Government motion to make formal application for membership of the Common Market under the terms of Article 237 of the Treaty of Rome. The case for entry was defended primarily as a means of conferring benefits upon the Commonwealth. After claiming that the rightful place for the United Kingdom was in the vanguard of a movement towards the greater unity of the free world, Prime

Minister Macmillan said that he had asked himself the question: "How can we best serve the Commonwealth? ... Britain in isolation would be of little value to our Commonwealth partners, and I think that the Commonwealth understands it." However, it could only be felt that it was unfortunate that the United Kingdom had not discovered its rightful place eleven or at least six years earlier, and that the New Zealand and Canadian Governments at least did not appear to understand the force of this argument. Opposition leader Gaitskell then moved a comprehensive amendment to the effect that the United Kingdom should enter the EEC only if the House of Commons approved, if the conditions were generally acceptable to a Commonwealth Prime Ministers' Conference, and if they were in accord with the pledges and obligations of the United Kingdom to the rest of EFTA. Harold Wilson, formerly President of the Board of Trade under Attlee, also raised the possibility of Australian and Canadian wheat and Australian meat being replaced by supplies from the Continent, and warned that "we are not entitled to sell our friends and kinsmen down the river for a problematical and marginal advantage in selling washing machines in Dusseldorf". The advantages might indeed be marginal, but Wilson of course could not have known that six years later he would himself be making the decision in favour of Dusseldorf. Sandys, who knew better than anybody how far his views were likely to be shared in Commonwealth capitals, argued in return that through the United Kingdom the Commonwealth and Europe would be brought closer together, and that this was to the advantage of both.[47] The Labour amendment was duly voted down by 318 votes to 209, and the Conservative motion carried by 313 votes to 5. The House of Commons had ruled that Britain should no longer be an island. Probably no more truly remarkable decision had been made in British history. The problem was how to carry it into effect.

And the Commonwealth was certainly still refusing support. Government after government expressed doubts as to whether British entry was worth purchasing at the price expected, or indeed at any price at all. In the Lok Sabha, Indian Finance Minister Morarji Desai regretted the loss of preferences, and particularly the danger that reverse preferences might be applied against Indian exports to the United Kingdom. However, he considered that his Government was prepared to acquiesce, provided suitable transitional arrangements were made. These would include a general lowering of the EEC tariff on imports from India, and the abolition of quantitative restrictions. In Australia, Prime Minister Menzies attacked the British decision on more comprehensive grounds, in perhaps the most rewarding speech of his life. He began by affirming that he was certain that the decision of the United Kingdom had been arrived at in the light of that country's "immense experience and ripe judgement". It was not for Australia therefore to substitute some opinion of its own. He nonetheless proceeded to do so. He discussed first Sandys's contention that competition with Continental countries in a market of 250 million would lead to greater efficiency in the United Kingdom economy. Menzies referred to the fact that Commonwealth countries still took nearly three times as great a volume of British exports as the EEC, and argued that the Commonwealth market would therefore have to grow if the overall strength of the United Kingdom were to increase. This might of course be considered to be a different argument from the one Sandys had been making, and of dubious validity in any case. It therefore weakened Menzies' further assertion that the Common-wealth market could not grow if British membership of the EEC were to inflict serious damage on the export earnings of Common-wealth countries. However, he was unquestionably being pertinent when he said that the danger did not come only from the tariff policies of the present EEC countries. Difficulties for Australia and New Zealand would be increased still further if other EFTA countries were to follow the example of the United Kingdom. Preferences enjoyed in the British market by Australian and New Zealand dairy producers might be reversed against them in favour of Denmark. However, he considered that the United Kingdom would not accede unconditionally to the Treaty of Rome because this would mean the end of the preferential system, which would be seriously damaging to Australia and disastrous to New Zealand, and also might mean the end of the preferential tariffs on British goods in the Australian customs schedule.

Menzies was perhaps on stronger grounds in dealing with the more intangible consequences of British entry. He conceded that the prospects of world peace might grow brighter if true European unity could be brought about. However, he asserted that Australia as a senior Commonwealth country felt bound to say that it did not think that the Commonwealth would be thereby strengthened as a political organism. The United Kingdom as the centre of the Commonwealth had formerly spoken for itself at Commonwealth conferences. It could no longer do so if it were a member of the New Europe. Nor could the growing interest and involvement of the United Kingdom in Europe leave untouched the present British interest in and around Asia and Africa. He concluded by saying that in the long run "the stern facts of contemporary history might require some abatement of the special Commonwealth relationship in favour of a powerful European community ... [but] ... it would be a mistake to pretend that there was no change when in fact there had been a great one".[48]

This might well have seemed the truest word that had yet been spoken on the issue. There was simply no doubt that the Commonwealth relationship was going to be changed massively by British entry to the EEC. It might be that the existing relationship had become too tenuous or unsatisfactory to be worth preserving. The British Government had fairly obviously decided that it had. But it was surprising that Commonwealth Governments themselves might be reluctant to admit this, particularly if the British decision were going to reduce their assurance of British markets, investment and protection. The element of sacrifice would not be confined to short term economic effects. And it was also possible that the British decision might have been simply mistaken. What was valid in the circumstances of 1950 or 1955 was not necessarily valid in 1961.

What was still lacking was a voice, experienced, involved and responsible, to assess objectively the rationality of the British position. In 1940 Ottawa had claimed to speak for the North American continent. In the 1950's it had certainly seemed at times to speak for the Commonwealth. In this new and extraordinary crisis it could not even speak for itself. Lester Pearson pondered in silence leaving his deputy, Paul Martin, to ask whether the Government of John G. Diefenbaker, with what he called its policy of "reluctant acquiescence", had made a full appreciation of the implications of the British move for the United Kingdom, for Europe and for Canada.

It might be doubted whether the Canadian Conservative Government was any better placed in 1961 than it had been in 1960 to make a full appreciation of anything except the election returns. But certainly "passive acquiescence" was not a suitable description of the position adopted by its representatives at a meeting of Commonwealth Finance Ministers in Accra, 12–14 September 1961. Fleming attended, accompanied by Trade Minister Hees. Unexpectedly, the Canadians found themselves required to take the lead in discussions, due partly to the fact that New Zealand was represented by a Minister who not only differed from Arnold Nordmeyer in all significant respects, but was also generally too indisposed to attend meetings. These indeed sometimes resembled pitched battles. After two days, the Commonwealth Ministers returned a communiqué which resoundingly proclaimed their total lack of confidence in the arguments of the British Government. They all "expressed grave apprehension and concern regarding the possible results of the initiative taken by the United Kingdom". They all

> reaffirmed the value and importance they attach to traditional Commonwealth trading arrangements under which most food-stuffs, raw materials and manufactures enter the United Kingdom free of charge from Commonwealth suppliers ... Many questioned whether the United Kingdom, with its other international and domestic obligations, could possible secure in the proposed negotia-tions an agreement which would protect Commonwealth interests adequately and effectively ... [such a] realignment could under-mine traditional multilateral trading arrangements to which all Commonwealth countries had given their support.[49]

They also considered that British membership of the EEC would fundamentally alter the relationship between the United Kingdom and Commonwealth countries. Indeed, they considered that this relationship could be so imperilled as to weaken the cohesion of the Commonwealth as a whole, and thus reduce its effectiveness as a world instrument for understanding, prosperity and peace.

All this might have been true. On the other hand, it was equally true that the Commonwealth had not recently given convincing proof of its utility as a world instrument for such pur-poses; that the divisions manifested within it by any significant crisis since 1945 raised doubts as to whether it could really be regarded as an instrument for anything likely to be affected by British entry; and that some of the governments most enthusiasti-cally expressing their belief in the Commonwealth relationship now were among those whose actions and words in the past had helped to render that relationship as insubstantial as it had become.

It was also at least incongruous that the Accra communiqué should bear so evidently the imprint of a country whose leaders had formerly been conspicuous for their measured support of British involvement in Europe.

So at least it was regarded in Ottawa. Hees and Fleming at first vigorously defended the "ginger" role they had played at Accra. The Trade Minister claimed that out of total Canadian sales to the United Kingdom in 1960 of $Can.915 million, $Can.691 million would be seriously affected by British entry; $Can.584 million would be faced with higher tariffs; and $Can.553 million would be faced not only with a loss of preference, but in most cases with reverse preferences. In some instances, the loss of preference itself would be sufficient to eliminate the Canadian product concerned from the British market. Hees considered that the communiqué adopted unanimously at Accra had accurately expressed the grave concern felt by members of the Commonwealth at the probable fate of their trading relations with the United Kingdom. However, he denied that he had at any time said anything that could be construed as an ultimatum to the United Kingdom to choose between the EEC and the Commonwealth. Hees was then taken to task by the Liberal member for Laurier, Quebec, Lionel Chevrier. He said that Canadians had been shocked to hear Hees and Fleming lecturing the British about British problems, and in effect telling them that they could no longer stay in the Commonwealth unless they did what the Canadian Government told them to. He said that it was clear that the Canadian representatives had taken the lead in "ganging-up in a negative and obstructive fashion against the British".[50]

It was something unusual for Ontario Conservatives to be criticized by a Quebecois Liberal for having been insufficiently courteous to the United Kingdom. Fleming certainly seemed to find it so. The mutual admiration society atmosphere of Ottawa was shattered by a furious speech from the Finance Minister. Fleming began by asserting that he had never before come across so much inaccuracy and misunderstanding in regard to any conference. He said that it was a blatant lie that Canada had taken an "anti-British line at Accra". The Conservative Party had traditionally stood for closer relations with the United Kingdom and the rest of the Commonwealth, and if the time ever came that Canadian Ministers took an anti-British line he would not be a

Canadian Minister. He nonetheless considered the issue to be one of great concern to Commonwealth countries. In the first place, there would be a changed political relationship involving the United Kingdom if that country were to accede to the EEC under the Treaty of Rome. All countries at the Conference had expressed the view that British leadership was essential to the Commonwealth. He then claimed that his critics appeared to be overlooking the importance of trade. The potentialities of trade within the Commonwealth had not yet been fully developed. All countries in the Commonwealth had affirmed their belief in the value of the preferential system at Montreal in 1958. This remained the policy of the Canadian Government, even though no well-informed person believed it possible for the British to negotiate terms with the EEC which would preserve the preferred position of Canadian foodstuffs in the British market, let alone Canadian manufactures.

Chevrier held his ground, as was indeed not very difficult under the circumstances. The position of the Conservative Government appeared to be that the United Kingdom should not enter the EEC under any conceivable circumstances. But Chevrier considered that the position of the Conservative Government was simply wrong. Drawing on the past speeches of Mackenzie King, Louis St. Laurent and Lester Pearson, in which Canadian leaders had been prepared to accept the admittedly then remote possibility of material loss to Canada in the interests of Western union, Chevrier argued that the Government should be trying to extend European achievements to the Atlantic Community. An Atlantic Economic Community would indeed strengthen the political cohesion of the Atlantic Alliance. This was the authentic voice of postwar Canadian diplomacy. But Hees argued in return that Canadian industry could not be developed if it were exposed to competition with the Europeans under conditions of free trade, as Chevrier had envisaged. He concluded that this meant that the Liberal Opposition were willing to see important Commonwealth preferences diminished, even if it made a great deal of difference to the production, livelihood and standard of living of Canadian producers.

But all the debate and depression in Commonwealth capitals was only prelude. It was indeed prelude to a drama that had no final act. The whole presumption of British hopes and Common-

140

wealth fears alike was that the United Kingdom did indeed have
a choice between the Commonwealth and Europe. On 8 November
Edward Heath flew to Brussels to begin negotiations on British
entry to the EEC. Their outcome was to suggest that the choice
in fact might no longer exist.

NOTES

1. These countries, which subsequently formed the European Free Trade
Association, became known as the "Seven" (United Kingdom, Sweden,
Norway, Switzerland, Denmark, Austria and Portugal) in contrast to the
EEC "Six" (France, Germany, Italy, Belgium, the Netherlands, and
Luxembourg). The "Six" soon became effectively "Seven" too, when
Lichtenstein became a member. However, it has normally seemed more
convenient not to count Lichtenstein.
2. U.K., House of Commons, *Debates,* Vol. DXCIX, cols. 1368-82.
3. *Times* (London), 16 March 1959.
4. *Observer,* 13 July 1959.
5. *Times,* 22 July 1959.
6. Australia, House of Representatives, *Debates,* 25 August 1959.
7. Canada, Department of External Affairs, *Statements and Speeches,* 17
October 1959.
8. *Ibid.,* 27 October 1959.
9. Australia, H. of R., *Debates,* 10 November 1959.
10. *Ibid.*
11. *Times,* 13 November 1959.
12. *Financial Times,* 26 November 1959.
13. WEU, Assembly, *Proceedings*, 30 November 1959.
14. *Yearbook of International Trade Statistics,* 1960.
15. I.M.F., *International Financial Statistics,* 1960.
16. *New York Times,* 11 December 1959.
17. *Ibid.,* 12 December 1959.
18. *L'Année Politique,* 1959, p. 572.
19. Canada, House of Commons, *Debates,* 18 January 1960.
20. *Ibid.*
21. Council of Europe, Consultative Assembly, *Reports,* 21 January 1960.
22. EEC Commission, *Press Release,* 29 February 1960.
23. *Financial Times,* 17 February 1960.
24. *Ibid.,* 14 March 1960.
25. *Corriere della Sera,* 2 April 1960.
26. U.K., H. of C., *Debates,* Vol. DCXXI, cols. 1671-72.
27. Australia, H. of R., *Debates,* 27 April 1960.
28. *Times,* 11 May 1960.
29. Australia, H. of R., *Debates,* 11 May 1960.
30. Canada, H. of C., *Debates,* 16 May 1960.
31. *Times,* 6 July 1960.
32. U.K., H. of C., *Debates,* Vol. DCXXVII, cols. 1094-101.
33. *Ibid.,* col. 1214.
34. *Le Monde* (Paris), 6 September 1960.
35. *Ibid.*
36. *Times,* 11 October 1960.
37. Canada, H. of C., *Debates,* 9 June 1961.

141

38. *Ibid.*
39. *Ibid.,* 13 June 1961.
40. N.Z., House of Representatives, *Debates,* 21 June 1961.
41. Federation of Rhodesia and Nyasaland, Federal Assembly, *Debates,* 26 June 1961.
42. *Ibid.*
43. Ghana, National Assembly, *Debates,* 4 July 1961.
44. *Age* (Melbourne), 22 February 1961.
45. N.Z., H. of R., *Debates,* 12 July 1961.
46. Canada, Department of External Affairs, *External Affairs,* 1961, p. 278.
47. U.K., H. of C., *Debates,* Vol. DCXLV, col. 1775.
48. Australia, H. of R., *Debates,* 16 August 1961.
49. *Times,* 15 September 1961.
50. Canada, H. of C., *Debates,* 29 June 1961.

6. The Europe of Realities

The negotiations began unluckily, under the shadow of the greatest economic threat that most of the Commonwealth countries had ever faced. In January 1962 the Council of Ministers of the EEC agreed on the principles of a Common Agricultural Policy (CAP), to be introduced throughout the Community in 1970. Copies of the draft policy were made available to the Governments of Australia and New Zealand. They were studied in Canberra and Wellington with considerable bewilderment and mounting concern. The first was due to the vexing obscurity of most of the text, resulting partly from the sheer unfamiliarity of the literally-translated French expressions of the original, and partly from the practical difficulty of envisaging how some of the extraordinary techniques envisaged by the EEC officials were actually supposed to be applied. But the main features of the policy were disturbingly clear. Very briefly, its operation was based on the relationship of three artificially determined prices, as applied to grain; and on a combination of minimum import prices and import levies, as applied to pigmeat, eggs and poultry. In the case of grain, the most significant trading item, arbitrary target prices would be established by the EEC Commission, representing the "ideal" market price within the Common Market. "Intervention" prices would then be fixed, representing the price level at which local marketing organizations would begin to buy up supplies so as to keep the actual market price as close as possible to the target price. "Threshold" or minimum import prices would be based on the target price applying in the area of greatest deficiency, less the cost of transport from the point of entry. Exports from outside the EEC would also be subject to a variable import levy, representing the difference btween the lowest import price at the port of entry, and the threshold price in the importing EEC country. The levies would be used ultimately to finance the application of the CAP itself.[1]

The most significant characteristic of the CAP was that it mobilized every conceivable technique of import limitation, short of exchange control, to protect the standard of living of European farmers from the consequences of external competition. It thus repudiated totally the principles of free competition and the open market. What it involved was indeed the sacrifice of almost any economic principles in the interests of European political exigencies. Farmers had votes. The governments of the Six were accordingly going to safeguard the interests of their farmers. And they could certainly afford to do so.

This obviously left almost no possible grounds for negotiation between the EEC and outside producers. But the governments of primary producing countries outside Europe could hardly accept this position without making some attempt to get it modified. Trading, financial, statistical and diplomatic officials in the public services of Canada, Australia and New Zealand sought throughout 1962 to find some common ground for negotiation with governments pledged to buy from outside producers what their own farmers were literally incapable of producing. Economists and mathematicians in the Commonwealth tried to find abstract answers to questions such as whether the target price should be as close to the threshold price as possible, so as to allow the greatest opportunity for imports, or as high above it as possible, so as to allow the greatest possible price; or whether they should quote as low as possible, so as to undercut other outside suppliers, or as high as possible, so as to avoid the application of the import levy. But calculations of this kind were substantially irrelevant in any event. There was no means by which the Europeans could be compelled to accept the suggestions of Commonwealth governments, and it could be taken for granted that they would apply whatever technique afforded the most effective means of protecting their own producers. They were nonetheless not allowed to ignore the Commonwealth case. And for the first time this case was presented on the basis of principles deliberately chosen because of their attractiveness to the Europeans themselves.

It might have been expected that such an approach would most typically have been made by the Canadians. But the Diefenbaker Government had abandoned any hope of a direct Commonwealth approach to the EEC. Domestic problems were too pressing; Canada was itself, as Fleming pointed out, exactly the kind of surplus producing country that the Europeans would least want to be associated with; and prospects of relief were allowed to rest on the possibility that the United States might use its huge bargaining strength to exact concessions from the EEC, which would then have to be granted to all other members of the GATT, under the terms of that Agreement. This virtual confession of impotence did not of course enhance the status of the Conservative Government. Feelings accordingly continued to run high on Parliament Hill. Lester Pearson castigated Fleming for his "childish hectoring and lecturing of the British". Fleming responded by describing the speeches of the Nobel Prize winner as a "tissue of distortions, errors, half-truths and selected anti-Canadian quotations".[2]

The initiative was left to the Australians. In March and April 1962 Trade Minister McEwen and the Permanent Head of the Department of Trade, Dr. J.C. Westerman, visited first Washington, then Brussels. In the latter capital, Westerman presented a profoundly serious attempt to reconcile the basic EEC principles of price stability and financial security for European producers with the demands of traditional suppliers to the EEC for continued access to the Common Market. In essence, Westerman approached the French as fellow surplus producers. His address remained the only meaningful response from outside Europe to the colossal schemes for world commodity trade floated by the French Minister of Finance, Baumgartner, and the Minister of Agriculture, Edgar Pisani. The basic principles of the Pisani-Baumgartner solution were that it was immoral to restrict agricultural production in the industrial countries when food shortages were endemic in the under-developed parts of the world; that it was completely in accordance with the logic of agricultural trade to fix world prices artificially, since all countries protected their agricultural industries in one way or another; and that the appropriate level for a world price would be slightly above the price already being received by French producers. The Westerman approach substantially respected these principles as a serious basis for discussion. However, the Australians were unable to gain any corresponding recognition by the Europeans of their own principle that there should be firm and effective safeguards for the trade of existing suppliers, until these world commodity agreements were operative.

Failure was virtually inevitable, given the basic reality that the producers of the temperate zones of the Commonwealth were precisely the people whom the French were most determined to admit to their own markets only as suppliers of emergency relief. Back in Canberra, McEwen began to see dangers everywhere. The United States had admitted that Australia was a worthwhile friend, but had also maintained that Commonwealth preferences were wrong in principle and ought not to be perpetuated. President de Gaulle had assured him of the high value he placed on the Commonwealth as a political unit and the high regard in which he held Australia, but had insisted that Australian interests would be adequately covered by the eventual introduction of world commodity agreements. McEwen stated that in any case the French obviously hoped to gain the greatest share of the United Kingdom market for their own agricultural exports. This meant that the United Kingdom would not be able to operate as a trading area separate from the rest of the EEC, which Australian goods could continue to enter on terms different from those available to exports from the EEC. McEwen's solution was that Australia should be granted permission to sell to the enlarged EEC on the terms obtaining for its exports in the British market at present, but in quantity no greater than was then being sold in the British market. This quota should have adequate provision for growth, and there should be no limit placed on whatever additional quantity Australia could sell by meeting the EEC tariff.

It was hardly probable that this suggestion would be accepted. It was nonetheless rather more responsible than the kind of statement being made in some other Commonwealth capitals. In Wellington, for example, Prime Minister Holyoake insisted that great harm would be done if New Zealand were to stir the British people to action against their Government's planned entry to the EEC. This drew the comment from Dr. Finlay, the President of the New Zealand Labour Party, that Holyoake was demonstrating "irresolute timidity" rather than "blessed meekness".[3] But even Harold Macmillan chose to describe the position of his Government in language that seemed strangely unsuitable to the occasion. On 2 May he told an audience of Canadian Ministers and officials in Ottawa that "every time we have tried to escape from the grasp of Europe, we have been drawn back". This certainly appeared to the Canadians as sounding more like a cry for help than a description of a daring change in British policy. As one of them said later, "it sounded as if he was saying goodbye to us forever".[4]

Commonwealth hopes were hardly raised by the news that on 11 May the British negotiators in Brussels had tabled a proposal under which Commonwealth exports of manufactured products to the United Kingdom would be exposed gradually to the impact of the full Common External Tariff of the EEC. It recommended that 30 per cent of the tariff should be applied in 1965, a further 30 per cent two years later, and the full tariff in 1970. Canada, the Commonwealth country most seriously affected, took the realistic line that the Commonwealth might well suffer worse terms if it tried to hold out for better. Some price would have to be paid. The Europeans could hardly be expected to make exceptions for manufactured goods, whatever they might be induced to do for agriculture. However, the Australian and New Zealand Governments seemed to take the contrary position, feeling that even the most unavoidable concessions on commodities in which they had little or no interest should be opposed, for fear that they might serve as precedents for restricting trade in areas in which they were interested. On 16 May Menzies invited Opposition leaders to join him in a visit to the United Kingdom in July. He left for London himself on 18 May, accompanied by John Marshall, the New Zealand Deputy Prime Minister and Minister of Trade.

On 30 May the British and EEC negotiators agreed on the application of the three stage tariff, or *"décalage"*, against imports of manufactured goods from the Commonwealth. A French representative said that this showed how easy things were once the British accepted the principles of the Treaty of Rome. However, the following day Menzies and Marshall issued a joint statement in London asserting that the outcome of the decision on industrial trade represented a disturbing development, as it fell far short of providing adequate safeguards for Commonwealth trade, and must not under any circumstances be taken as a pattern for the type of settlement to be reached on goods of greater concern to the Commonwealth.[5] On the same day, McEwen in Canberra, after assuring the United States of unqualified Australian support in matters of foreign policy, told the Americans to "just keep out of our hair" on the question of Commonwealth preferences.[6]

It was not surprising that signs of irritation were beginning to manifest themselves. Attitudes all round had scarcely been conducive to mutual trust. The British had certainly been less than frank, the Commonwealth Governments in general less than reasonable, the Americans less than helpful, and the Europeans less than sympathetic. Something of all this showed in a generally unrewarding debate in the British House of Commons in June 1962. Heath began by reiterating that the British Government would not enter into agreements with the EEC until after full consultation with Commonwealth countries. He insisted however that British membership of the EEC could be made compatible with both Commonwealth ties and the American connection, that the United Kingdom would be a more valuable partner for both if it did not remain outside the mainstream of European development, and that only a prosperous United Kingdom could provide an expanding market or adequate investment for the Commonwealth. He then said that the Europeans found it difficult to see why the United Kingdom should ask for specific arrangements about unforeseeable events in the future, since it would be possible to adapt to problems as they arose. In support of this view, he alluded to the compromise already reached on aluminium, zinc, woodpulp and newsprint. However, this in fact represented a compromise only in the sense that the British request for nil tariffs had not been rejected out of hand, but was still being considered.

The Leader of the Opposition, Gaitskell, made the appropriate points in reply, stressing that Menzies and Marshall at least were obviously anything but satisfied about the one concrete achievement of the negotiations to date, namely, the *décalage* on Commonwealth manufactures; and that if the Government really thought that it was necessary to expose British industry to the stimulus of freer competition, all they had to do was to negotiate tariff concessions on a multilateral basis in GATT. They did not have to go into the Common Market to do that. Gaitskell summed up:

> To go in on good terms would be the best solution ... Not to go in would be a pity, but not a catastrophe. To go in on bad terms which would really mean the end of the Commonwealth would be a step which, I think, we would regret all our lives and for which history would not forgive us.[7]

On the other hand, Liberal leader Grimond claimed that he did not despair of the United Kingdom's having some new relationship with the Commonwealth, and of its being able to provide the Commonwealth with more aid when once inside the EEC, than it would be able to do outside it. Sandys then began to explain away the commitments which the United Kingdom had undertaken to protect the economic interests of the Commonwealth. He said that the Government stood by its promise, unqualified and unaltered, not to join the EEC unless arrangements were made to safeguard the vital trading interests of the Commonwealth. Commonwealth producers had certainly taken it for granted that they would continue to have easy access to the United Kingdom market, even for commodities not covered by specific guarantees. But they had known that they could not count on free entry for unlimited quantities of all products for all time. The Government was trying to negotiate arrangements which would ensure Commonwealth producers comparable trading opportunities for an initial period. There would of course have to be some assurance of continuity after this period. But the Six were naturally reluctant to give precise guarantees of a kind which the United Kingdom itself had never been able to give.[8]

Nothing could of course have been less encouraging to the Commonwealth Governments than to hear the British explaining to them the superior reasonableness of the European position. Commonwealth officials also noticed the growing tendency of

British negotiators in Brussels to open discussions on the final position put to them by the Commonwealth. The fall-back line for the Commonwealth was invariably the front line for the British. This was indeed often merely a means of saving time, since the front line position nominated by the Commonwealth was customarily one which the Europeans would not have considered taking seriously. There was certainly no doubt that whatever the outcome of the negotiations, the element of mutual trust and regard in the Commonwealth relationship was being sorely diminished.

This was even the case in New Zealand, traditionally the most trusting of the British dominions. Prime Minister Holyoake pleaded that the whole economy of New Zealand had been geared and developed to meet the needs of the British market over the past hundred years. It was fair to argue that the United Kingdom must come to terms with the EEC, but not under conditions which would undermine New Zealand's vital economic interests. Finance Minister Lake also stressed the unacceptability of a situation in which the world's leading low-cost producer of butter, cheese, lamb and beef should be required to function as a producer of surpluses for disposal, because of its being excluded from its traditional market in the interests of less efficient producers.[9] At the same time, it had to be admitted that New Zealand's case had many unsatisfactory aspects. In the simplest terms, the New Zealanders had had a particularly good run for their money. They were also among the most protectionist peoples in the world in the field of industrial trade, despite their devotion to the principles of free trade in areas where they were competitive. Their claim to special consideration essentially rested on their failure to develop markets elsewhere to reduce significantly their dependence upon the United Kingdom.

There was nonetheless considerable reason to expect that the EEC would be prepared at least to mitigate the effect upon New Zealand of circumstances for which the New Zealanders themselves were at least only partly responsible. Optimism and philanthropy seemed to be in style in Brussels. EEC officials confidently drafted proposals to rationalize agricultural trade throughout the world. The British began to identify themselves with this moderately promising trend, employing terms like the "Seven Governments" and the "Enlarged Community", when referring to the Six and themselves. In July the "Seven" Governments announced that it was intended to take, "in the context of the Enlarged Community", an early initiative to secure long term agreements on a broad international basis for major agricultural products. The Six themselves were ready to conclude limited agreements of this nature with interested countries if world-wide agreements were found not to be practicable. However, these wider agreements would have to take into account the interests of other traditional suppliers to Europe outside the Commonwealth, such as the United States and Argentina. While the Commonwealth was digesting this prospect, Lord Home, now British Foreign Secretary, explained to the House of Lords that there was nothing in the Treaty of Rome which could effect the position of the Crown or the sovereignty of Parliament, except in the fields specifically defined in the Treaty. This interpretation contrasted interestingly with the insistence of Home's predecessors that the enabling treaties of the European Communities contained federalist implications which made them intrinsically unacceptable to the British Government. It would undoubtedly have saved much trouble if Home could have explained this mistake to previous British Governments between 1950 and 1955. The only real objection now made to this changed view was by Lord Attlee, who protested that the EEC represented a step backwards from the idea of world government to that of "the old one of Europe apart from the rest of the world, and a Europe which did not contain the best elements of democracy".[10]

This did not exactly assist the British Government in its present position. Neither did a sudden outbreak of dissension in the Australian Parliament. During the last week of July, the Australian Minister for Air, L.H.E. Bury, suggested that the economic consequences to Australia might be overcome without significant dislocation, despite the "severe emotional shock to the older generation".[11] These remarks certainly conflicted with those of McEwen, as well as being scarcely complimentary to Menzies. McEwen promptly accused Bury of undercutting Australia's negotiating position, although it was by now difficult to see that Australia had one at all. Menzies then requested Bury's resignation, insisting on the need for Cabinet solidarity in the context of the Brussels negotiations. Both he and McEwen then reaffirmed their previous positions. Menzies went on to argue that the economic processes of the Common Market would lead to pressure for an organic political structure in Western Europe, and this would mean that the United Kingdom, if it were a member, would then not be sovereign to the same degree as other Commonwealth countries. The Commonwealth would then have ceased to be an association of sovereign and self-governing states, for the ironic reason that the United Kingdom itself would have ceased to be in this category. McEwen reminded his audience that the present prospect after nine months of negotiations was that the enlarged Community was going to state that its policy would be to offer reasonable opportunities in its markets for imports of temperate foodstuffs from outside. In the meantime Australia faced the complete loss of all special conditions it had negotiated and paid for in the British market.

At the Prime Ministers' Conference in September the issue again was argued in terms of intangible benefits against tangible losses. Macmillan told an unresponsive audience that a new opportunity had opened up "for Britain to contribute to the ... progress of all peoples and all continents, and an opportunity to play her part in bringing nearer a world order towards which mankind must move or perish".[12] Diefenbaker replied that there was no real assurance that Commonwealth interests at least would not be damaged in the long run, referred to the obvious changes in British thinking since the Maudling speeches of 1959 and 1960, and suggested that the United Kingdom could surely continue to make its voice heard in the world, whether it was in Europe or out of it. Menzies asked if Australia was expected to give a blank cheque, and demanded that the Six should have to spell out what their "reasonable price policies" were really going to involve. Holyoake reserved New Zealand's position on the economic side. India feared for the consequences for under-developed countries, and also doubted if the Commonwealth could survive unless radical changes were made in the present proposals. The Jamaican Prime Minister compared the Treaty of Rome with a surgeon's knife thrust into the body of the Commonwealth, cutting one member off from the rest. Nkrumah simply denounced the Common Market as an imperialist device for exploiting the less developed countries of Africa. Support came only from Ceylon and Malaya, which did not expect the bulk of their trade to be affected; from Trinidad and Rhodesia, which proposed to associate

themselves with the EEC anyway; and Cyprus, whose two
mother-countries, Greece and Turkey, had been applying for
associate membership with the Common Market for the past three
years.

Coincidentally, this nadir of Commonwealth solidarity was
followed shortly by a situation which seemed at first to offer a
quite remarkable opportunity to reaffirm that solidarity. On 20
October, heavy fighting began in Ladakh between Chinese forces
and advance units of the Indian army, in an extraordinarily
ill-defined area claimed by both Governments. On 22 October a
state of national emergency was declared in India. On the same
day, Duncan Sandys announced that the British Government
profoundly deplored the Chinese attack, and arrangements were
made for the supply of military equipment from the United
Kingdom to India. The first airlifts of British automatic weapons
began to arrive only a week later. Australia followed the British
example. Menzies conveyed a message of sympathy and support
to Nehru on 26 October, and negotiations for the supply of military
equipment and other aid by Australia began immediately. Substantial assistance was offered on 28 October by the Canadians,
who had been preoccupied until then by the exigencies of the
Cuban missile crisis. Rhodesia followed with an offer of copper at
special rates of interest, and New Zealand with an offer of blankets
and butterfat. Good wishes came from Cyprus, Nigeria, Uganda,
Sierra Leone, the West Indies and Malaya. This was an impressive
display of unity. But it was questionable whether it was more
impressive than the departures from unity occasioned by those
Commonwealth countries which declined to align themselves
with India. Ghana clashed directly with the United Kingdom over
the issue of supplying India with arms; Ceylon condemned India
for acting "contrary to the principles of non-alignment"; and
Pakistan actually assisted China, by persuading Turkey to withdraw
offers of assistance to India. Greater unanimity was certainly
shown by the Associated Overseas Territories of the EEC, which
fell into line solidly with their European partners in condemning
the Chinese.[13]

The Commonwealth had not satisfactorily answered one of
its most serious challenges. And now Sir Roy Welensky offered
the view that the real danger to the Commonwealth did not lie
in British membership of the EEC, but in the immaturity and
lack of restraint of Commonwealth countries themselves.

Meanwhile, negotiations on British entry had reached dead-lock. This was not primarily due to the Commonwealth issue. Gaitskell indeed argued that the Government did not seem perturbed by the fact that the negotiations on Commonwealth access to the enlarged Community had achieved virtually none of their stated goals. Heath had asked for associate status for all less developed territories of the Commonwealth, but this had been turned down; he had asked for the United Kingdom to be allowed to continue to give duty-free access to the products of particular Commonwealth territories, but this was not available; he had asked for zero tariffs on aluminium, wood pulp, copper, lead and zinc, but all he had got was a duty-free quota for the second.[14] All these efforts undoubtedly testified to the endeavours of the British to safeguard Commonwealth interests. What was still lacking was any evidence that their failure to secure safeguards was going to deter them from entering. The present stalemate had occurred for quite different reasons. The Europeans had insisted that the British should terminate their system of deficiency payments to primary producers by 31 December 1967, and adopt the CAP instead. This would have involved British acceptance of the European system of consumer subsidies. Heath refused to agree to this. However, the French insisted that the only matter they were prepared to discuss was the procedure by which the British accommodated their existing system to the CAP. They were not prepared to discuss the possibility that the British should retain their own system.

This did not seem at first to indicate any estrangement between the United Kingdom and France. Both countries had indeed a common interest in their dissatisfaction with the policies of the United States. French susceptibilities had been affronted by the failure of President Kennedy to consult his NATO allies over the Cuban missile crisis. The British were similarly concerned by the decision of the Americans in November to abandon Skybolt, the air-to-ground missile to be used by the British V-bomber force. Anglo-French co-operation seemed to be symbolized by the agreement between the two Governments on 29 November to share production costs in building a new supersonic aircraft, hopefully named Concorde. Further American actions seemed positively to encourage this development. On 6 December Dean Acheson delivered a speech at West Point which might have been composed with the express purpose of driving the United

Kingdom into a European alignment. Dismissing British policy over the past seventeen years, he said:

> Britain has lost an empire and has not yet found a role. The attempt to play a separate power role ... based on a special relationship with the United States, a role based on being the head of Commonwealth which has no political structure, or unity or strength ... this role is about to be played out.[15]

This would obviously leave the British with no real power basis except in their relationship with Europe. This in turn would certainly require their forming the closest possible accord with France. British dependence on Europe could thus seem to favour the independent ambitions of General de Gaulle. But the fact was that the British never conceived their relationship with Europe as being exclusive. It was always intended to assist in some measure the development of relations with the United States and even the Commonwealth. A Britain which persisted in regarding Europe as of secondary importance to the world outside was of no use to General de Gaulle.

This fundamental divergence between British and French attitudes towards the American connection was abruptly and brutally demonstrated. On 9 December 1962 Dean Rusk, Kennedy's Secretary of State, assured the Europeans that the United States would not oppose the formation of a multilateral European nuclear force without American participation, even though such a duplication of weapons systems seemed wasteful and irrational. It was suggested that the European force might be based upon the American Polaris missile, mounted in submarines. The Europeans would thus be able to deploy a medium-range nuclear capacity, while the Americans would retain control over strategic long-range weapons. Rusk also indicated that the fate of the Skybolt missile would be discussed by Macmillan and Kennedy, when they met at Nassau later that month. The question was apparently not mentioned when Macmillan spoke with de Gaulle on 15 December. De Gaulle obviously chose to regard it as a purely Anglo-American problem, which he was presumably only too happy to observe. This first exchange between the British and American leaders seemed as unpromising as de Gaulle could have hoped. The Americans made clear their intention to abandon Skybolt. Macmillan then demanded that they provide the United Kingdom with some alternative delivery system for its nuclear weapons. They agreed on 19 December to consider the Polaris missile in the context of a multilateral NATO force. The participants would be the United States, the United Kingdom and France. The Americans would provide the missiles and the British and French the warheads. As the French were not present, it was left to the British and American leaders to draft the terms of their agreement. The conditions agreed upon certainly seemed to preserve the notion of British military independence. Paragraph 8 provided that the British nuclear forces would be used "for the purpose of international defence of the Western alliance in all circumstances", but allowed for independent use "where Her Majesty's Government may decide that supreme national interests are at stake". It was implied at first that the Americans regarded Paragraph 8 as being more binding that this proviso suggested, and that in any case the guidance systems of the Polaris rockets were so complex that they could be delivered only with American scientific co-operation. However, Kennedy himself said that Paragraph 8 recognized the fact that the United Kingdom "might be conscious that there may be a moment when it is isolated and when its national interests are involved";[16] and British military authorities professed themselves satisfied as to the reality of their independent control over the weapons.

There thus seemed little in the Nassau Agreement that need be basically objectionable to a country which intended to remain associated with the United States. But this of course was precisely what the French did not intend to do. Gaullism had always stood for French independence. It also stood for French predominance within Western Europe. Hence de Gaulle could neither enter into a binding military relationship with the United States himself, nor permit French predominance to be challenged on the Continent by a nation which had entered into such a relationship. This consideration would presumably have entailed British exclusion in any event. Nassau merely provided the excuse.

As always, de Gaulle moved according to a timetable which regarded no interests save his own. On 19 December it had become obvious that the British would not co-operate with France in the development of an independent nuclear deterrent. On 20 December France and Germany agreed to co-operate more closely in the nuclear field, thus in effect substituting German nuclear resources for British. More needed to be done yet. De Gaulle maintained for three more weeks the pretence that the Nassau Agreement was a purely Anglo-American affair, which did not call for French comment. As he said on 3 January 1963, France, unlike Britain, had undertaken the nuclear enterprise by its own means, and intended to pursue it by its own means. He became more explicit after Chancellor Adenauer had confirmed that he would be coming to Paris in person to assure the closer relationship of France and Germany. At a press conference on 14 January de Gaulle said directly that "France could not subscribe" to the Nassau Agreement. He then went on to claim that the United Kingdom was substantially different from the original Common Market Six in being "insular ... maritime ... linked through her exchanges, her markets, her supply lines to the most diverse and often the most distant countries". Nonetheless, he admitted that it was possible that "one day England might be able to transform herself sufficiently to become part of the European Community, without restrictions, without reserve, and in preference to anything else, and in that event ... France would raise no obstacle". However, it was "possible, too, that England might not yet be so disposed".[17]

It was remarkable that the leader of the Gaullists should be so prepared to condemn the British in 1963 for being in a similar position in relation to the world outside to that which his fuglemen had claimed for France in 1954. It was even more remarkable that the most determined enemy of the Community idea should accuse the British of having "earlier refused to participate in the communities which we (!) were building, and finally ... having put pressure on the Six to prevent a real beginning being made in the application of the Common Market".[18] An even more extraordinary version of the facts was given, however, by Harold Macmillan, when he asserted that the "movement for European unity was founded ... by the greatest English patriot of his or any other time, Sir Winston Churchill ... (and) was supported in Britain by leading Labour figures like Mr. Ernest Bevin."[19] But at least it was quite clear what had happened. The British had reaped the full harvest of their policy of disinvolvement in the 1950's. By refusing repeated offers to lead Western Europe, they had made it possible for the Gaullists to do so. By declining to enter Europe when they could have, they had made it possible for the Gaullists to exclude them. In the 1950's the British might well have been able to enter Europe without paying any significant price for admission. They were now in effect debarred from entry, no matter what price they might have been prepared to pay.

There were of course a number of extenuating points to be made. The first was that nobody could really have been sure in the early and middle 1950's that de Gaulle would eventually return to power in France. On the other hand, there was also no doubt that Maudling's conduct of the Free Trade Area talks had done not a little to create the conditions in France necessary for de Gaulle's return, and to ensure that he would have a ready fund of resentment towards the United Kingdom to work on. Nor was it certain that in pursuing this policy of grandeur in Europe de Gaulle was necessarily adopting the course of action most appropriate to French capacities. The rewards of great power status in contemporary international politics seem to be almost wholly psychological. The price it exacts is material and colossal. France's capacity to pay such a price for its satisfactions was called violently in question in the weeks of almost total national collapse in May and June 1968. But those weeks of protest culminated in the return to power, by the greatest popular vote in the history of Republican France, of the man against the consequences of whose policies the protests had been made. Finally, one must admit the correctness of Gaitskell's analysis. It was not a catastrophe for the British to have failed to get into the Common Market in 1963. There were still options open.

But there was no question that the United Kingdom had been made to suffer a savage humiliation. The French technique was the same in 1963 as it had been in 1959. Just like Jacques Soustelle before, the new Minister of Information Peyrefitte claimed that France was merely recognizing the fact that there was no way in which the negotiations with the British could be resumed fruitfully. There was "nothing dramatic" in all this.[20] There was also nothing true. The negotiations were not terminated because nobody thought that they could succeed. They were terminated because almost everybody thought that they would. And even the agricultural issue on which the talks had temporarily foundered had been allowed to reach this point primarily through French intransigence. France had deliberately worked to prevent its great rival from challenging or displacing French ambitions to world power status. That was the meaning of the Europe of Realities.

NOTES

1. See H.G. Gelber, *Australia, Britain and the EEC, 1961-1963* (Melbourne: Oxford University Press, 1966), esp. chaps. v – vii.
2. Canada, House of Commons, *Debates,* 24 January 1962.
3. *Times* (London), 7 May 1962.
4. *Ibid.,* 2 May 1962.
5. *Ibid.,* 31 May 1962.
6. *Age* (Melbourne), 1 June 1962.
7. U.K., House of Commons, *Debates,* Vol. DCLXI, col. 528.
8. *Ibid.* col. 699.
9. N.Z., House of Representatives, *Debates,* 26 June 1962.
10. U.K., House of Lords, *Debates,* Vol. CCXLIII, col. 431.
11. *Age,* 26 July 1962.
12. *Times,* 11 September 1962.
13. G. St. J. Barclay, "The Commonwealth Does Not Answer", *World Review,* IV, No. 2 (July 1965), 3-9.
14. U.K., H. of C., *Debates,* Vol. DCLXVI, cols. 1007-1008.
15. *Times,* 7 December 1962.
16. *Ibid.,* 24 December 1962.
17. *Le Monde* (Paris), 15 January 1963.
18. *Ibid.*
19. *Times,* 21 January 1963.
20. *Le Monde,* 25 January 1963.

7. Down the River to Dusseldorf

Blood dries quickly, as General de Gaulle assures us. The most remarkable thing about the British check at Brussels was how little discernible effect it had upon British relations with the Continent. United Kingdom trade with the EEC and the EFTA remained virtually constant as proportions of total British trade throughout 1963, while trade with the rest of the Commonwealth fell to about 30 per cent of the total. This decline reflected as much as anything the intensified efforts of Commonwealth countries to develop new markets to reduce their dependence upon the United Kingdom, in case the British were to try again. Otherwise, the EEC issue ceased to engage the attention of Commonwealth Governments. Only in Canada was there a general expression of an urgent need to strengthen the Commonwealth association after the extraordinary buffeting it had been exposed to over the past year. Diefenbaker again called for full and informal discussions among Commonwealth countries. Parliament Hill also witnessed the only display throughout the Commonwealth of the leaders of politically significant parties stating their regret at the exclusion of the United Kingdom from the EEC. Lester Pearson, R.N. Thompson, Leader of the Social Credit Party, and T.C. Douglas, Leader of the New Democratic Party, all professed their sympathy for the British bid and their disappointment at its failure.[1]

But it was not only Commonwealth ties which now had to be restored. While a Royal Tour of Australia and New Zealand was arranged as a demonstration of Commonwealth solidarity, Heath called a ministerial meeting of the EFTA in February. He reaffirmed there his intention of "working together to promote the creation of a large unified European market which would be outward-looking towards the rest of the world".[2] However, he considered that the present task of the Seven was to pursue the dismantling of trade barriers between themselves. This had immediate repercussions for New Zealand. In May the British Government suspended the 15s. per hundredweight tariff on imports of butter from non-Commonwealth countries. This would clearly benefit Denmark, New Zealand's most important non-Commonwealth competitor. The Australians and New Zealanders were then assured by the British that consultations would be held every year regarding the amount of butter to be allowed into the British market. The existing quotas would not be removed unless the circumstances which had led to their imposition changed.

They changed within five weeks. On 14 June the Irish Republic was authorized to supply a further 5,000 tons of butter to the British market, in addition to its existing quota. Less than a month later, Australia was given a similar dispensation to supply a further 10,000 tons. After another five weeks, the British invited exports from all sources of a further 12,080 tons of butter. New Zealand was allotted 2,000 tons of this. But the New Zealanders felt that the policy of inviting extra supplies destroyed the whole logic of applying quotas in the first place. Holyoake warned that "a clear difference of opinion" existed between the New Zealand and British Governments over the issue. However, the New Zealanders were in no position to protest too strongly, as their rights in the British market were due to terminate anyway in 1967. Whether the British made another bid for entry or not, the days of New Zealand's profitable dependence upon the United Kingdom market were obviously numbered.

And it undoubtedly seemed as if the British would be encouraged to make another bid. Chancellor Adenauer said that he had been astonished when the Brussels negotiations had broken down. He had no idea that "such a row" would develop from the Nassau Agreement. Nine days later, the Ministers of the EEC countries agreed that meetings of the Council of Ministers of the WEU should be held every three months and that an exchange of views on the European economic situation should always appear on the agenda, so as to keep open the possibility of the British joining the EEC. However, all Commonwealth representatives except the Canadian at the Parliamentary Conference held in Kuala Lumpur on 4 November 1963 expressed satisfaction that the talks had broken down. The British delegation said that the breakdown had been due to the determination of the British Government not to sacrifice the interests of the Commonwealth. In the same vein, Labour leader Harold Wilson asked if the Prime Minister would now give a pledge that no Government of which he was the head would go into the EEC on terms that meant a substantial reduction of Commonwealth imports. However, Butler insisted that the question of British membership was not an issue at the present time.[3]

This was clearly true, in the sense that there seemed little that the British Government itself could do to alter the situation created by de Gaulle in January 1963. It would also have been most unwise to have risked another setback, which could only have been even more humiliating and disrupting than the first. It therefore behooved the British to develop as much as possible the utility of the Commonwealth option, itself in need of some repair. The new Conservative Prime Minister, Sir Alec Douglas-Home, referred to the Commonwealth as the best guarantee against the horizontal development of the world into the northern rich and the southern poor, which he said would be "the worst horror the world had ever seen". Harold Wilson repeated that the Labour Party at least was not prepared to sacrifice Commonwealth interests to get into the EEC. He also condemned the failure of the Government to call a meeting of Commonwealth Prime Ministers since September 1962, the session which, according to Wilson, had almost broken up the entire Commonwealth relationship.[4]

A conference was indeed called on 16 July 1964. It ranged

widely, including consideration of a proposal for collaboration on programmes of economic development in individual Commonwealth countries. However, its main concern was again with the endless problems presented by the newly independent Commonwealth countries in Africa and their relations with the United Kingdom and with one another. European matters were tactfully left alone.

But de Gaulle would not leave the British and Americans alone. Barely a week after the Commonwealth Conference had closed, de Gaulle chose to launch a comprehensive attack on the logic of Anglo-American policies. He admitted that it was necessary for France to maintain an alliance with the United States as long as the Soviet threat lasted. But "the reasons which made that alliance one of subordination for Europe are daily receding. Europe must take her share of responsibility. Moreover, everything indicates that this development would conform to the interests of the United States ..." On the other hand, it was the British who were failing to conform to American interests, since they had declined to take their share of responsibility as an independent partner of the United States. "Great Britain had shown ... that her defence force ... could not be European for want of being independent of the United States." In conclusion, de Gaulle ridiculed critics who had spoken of the *force de frappe* as France's "baby bomb", pointing out that in six years France would possess a nuclear capacity equivalent to the "instantanous power of more than 2,000 Hiroshima bombs".[5]

It was undoubtedly ironic that the French should now be explaining to the British and Americans their failure to appreciate the best interests of the Atlantic system, just as the British had done to the French and Americans back in the days of the Schuman Plan and the European Army. There was certainly no likelihood that de Gaulle would be listened to much more respectfully than Bevin or Churchill. British spokesmen now rigorously denied any intention to involve themselves in European affairs for the present. The election manifestoes of both major British parties stressed the importance of the Commonwealth relationship. The Conservatives affirmed that:

> Entry into the EEC is not open to us in existing circumstances, and no question of fresh negotiations can arise at present. We shall work with our EFTA partners, through the Council of Europe

and through the Western European Union, for the closest possible relationship with the Six consistent with our Commonwealth ties ... [6]

The Labour spokesmen were more specific in their declaration of intention:

> Though we shall seek to achieve closer links with our European neighbours, the Labour Party is convinced that the first responsibility of a British Government is still to the Commonwealth ... Under the Tories the Commonwealth share of our trade has been allowed to fall from 44 per cent to 30 per cent ... Worse still, the Commonwealth itself came near to disintegration at the time of the Common Market negotiations ... We shall: Promote more effective and frequent consultations between Commonwealth leaders ... make a new drive for exports through a Commonwealth Export Council; Build a firmer base for expanding trade by entering into long-term contracts ... ensure that development and capital investment programmes are geared to Commonwealth needs ... [7]

The new British Labour Government certainly attempted to safeguard Commonwealth interests in applying a 15 per cent import surcharge on 26 October, to assist British balance of payments difficulties. Foodstuffs, tobacco and specified basic raw materials were exempted from the surcharge. This meant that commodities affected amounted to only 13 per cent of imports from the Commonwealth, compared with 57 per cent of those from the EEC, and 36 per cent from the EFTA. The Six responded philosophically, possibly not displeased to see this new evidence of British trading weakness. The reaction of the United Kingdom's EFTA partners was quite different. The Secretary-General of the Association said that the British action was illegal and in contravention of the Stockholm Agreement; the Danes described it as anachronistic and incompatible with the building of the EFTA; the Swiss asked if international agreements could be held to have any value when they were so flagrantly violated; the Norwegians said that it was not fair play; the Swedes considered that it was a serious matter if large countries were no longer to respect international treaties; the Finns professed themselves shaken; and the Portuguese said that it was hitting below the belt. This was only the beginning. On 4 November the Council of Europe formally regretted that the British had taken action which could not fail to have serious repercussions on international trade, without having had prior consultations with other trading countries, and called for new economic policy consultations to be held within the EEC. In an unusual display of voting behaviour, twenty members supported the resolution, while eighty abstained. The Austrian and Swiss Ministers of Trade and the Norwegian Foreign Minister then denounced the British measures again as contravening the obligations of the EFTA, and the Irish Taoiseach condemned them as a violation of the 1938 Anglo-Irish Trade Agreement, "which could force us to adopt protective measures".

The British Government could hardly please everybody. This unfortunate wrangle was merely another demonstration of the fact that the Commonwealth connection could prove distressingly hard to reconcile under existing circumstances with obligations to a European organization. It also tended to confirm the widely held suspicion that the EFTA was not an organization that was likely to strengthen the position of the United Kingdom. It was nonetheless perhaps unfortunate that Prime Minister Wilson should have chosen this time to say at the annual Lord Mayor's Banquet that the friends of Britain were waiting for another "clear British initiative". Nor was it at all clear from his speech what form this initiative was likely to take. He certainly rejected explicitly the idea of a separate European deterrent, warning in the words of John Foster Dulles that this might require the Americans to make a further "serious reappraisal of their attitude to Europe". He then sounded the note for a new upward movement in the British economy, and delivered the warning that:

> ... we have already taken urgent measures. We shall not hesitate to take any further steps that at any time are or become necessary. If anyone, at home or abroad, doubts the firmness of that resolve, and acts upon their doubts, let them be prepared to pay the price for their lack of faith in Britain.[8]

It was equally hard to guess from this what Wilson was going to do, what the doubters might be tempted to do, and what price they were going to have to pay if they did it. But there was no doubt that the events of the next eighteen months were sadly to cause many to falter in their faith in Britain. British claims to world regard since 1945 had rested upon economic preponderance in Europe, upon the Commonwealth connection, upon the moral prestige of victorious resistance to Hitler, upon the legacy of diplomatic and technical expertise, and upon the American relationship. By the end of 1966 the first had been decisively lost; the second had deteriorated to an extent that the most pessimistic observer could hardly have forecast; the third was in any event a wasting asset; the fourth was certainly being called in question; and even the American relationship appeared to be in a somewhat unfruitful stage.

The first setback to the prestige of the Commonwealth occurred in peculiarly unfortunate circumstances. A meeting of Commonwealth Prime Ministers from 10 to 17 July 1965 considered that the Commonwealth should approach the Government of North Vietnam in an attempt to initiate negotiations to bring the war in the South to an end. It was hoped that the wide membership of the Commonwealth might enable it to appeal to Hanoi as a form of honest broker, embracing as it did ex-colonial as well as colonialist peoples, neutrals as well as NATO and SEATO allies. It was certainly a logical role for the Commonwealth to play. It was also a role which one might most sincerely wish had succeeded. Wilson sent the Parliamentary Secretary of the Ministry of Pensions, Harold Davies, to Hanoi, to try to persuade Ho Chi Minh that the Commonwealth Peace Mission was actually genuine. Davies was not even accorded the courtesy of being allowed to speak to Ministers in Hanoi. He returned to London without having obtained an undertaking that the mission would be received.

This regrettable failure was followed a month later by another setback to Commonwealth policy. The British defence of Malaysia during the confrontation with Indonesia had been reassuringly successful. Its achievement was distinctly clouded however by the disruption of Malaysia itself, with the expulsion of predominantly Chinese Singapore by the politically influential Malays. Another experiment of the Colonial Office had failed to fulfil expectations. But far worse was to come. Nothing could be so obviously incompatible with the Commonwealth idea as the spectacle of two of its members fighting each other. This occurred through September between India and Pakistan. What was almost as damaging to Commonwealth prestige was the apparent belief among Commonwealth Governments that they could not themselves effectively intervene to halt the fighting. A cease-fire was ultimately achieved by the Soviet Union, following one of the rare displays of unanimity by the United Nations Security Council.

Prospects for the Commonwealth could hardly have worsened, but they certainly did not improve. On Armistice Day 1965 the regime of Ian Smith in Rhodesia made a unilateral declaration of independence from the authority of the British Government. Wilson denounced this as illegal, and ordered the application of sanctions against the Rhodesian rebels. A ban was imposed on exports of tobacco and sugar from Rhodesia to the United Kingdom. But this was far from sufficient for other Commonwealth Governments. Nkrumah told a press conference that it "was dangerous for the African states to wait any longer for the United Kingdom to do its duty".[9] They should rather take the initiative in their own defence. The Federal Prime Minister of Nigeria, Sir Abubakar Tafawa Balewa, insisted that the Rhodesians were committing an act of rebellion, and that there was no more effective remedy for rebellion than to crush it by force. President Kaunda of Zambia was too close to the site of the trouble to be quite as confident about this solution. He accordingly denounced Rhodesian African nationalists in his own country as "stupid idiots", while at the same time damning Ian Smith as "a rebel and a traitor".[10] He also demanded that British forces should be sent to defend the Zambian border. Wilson did send troops, though with the proviso that they should be used for defensive purposes only. He himself expressly ruled out the use of force against Rhodesia. Sanctions were however extended to apply to oil exports to Rhodesia. Even this was not sufficient for all the Commonwealth. Between 15 and 18 December nine African countries severed diplomatic relations with the United Kingdom. They included two members of the Commonwealth, Tanzania and Ghana. It was noteworthy that the Queen's message to the Commonwealth on Christmas Day 1965 merely expressed the hope that the next twelve months might be happier for the association than the last had been. It was not much to ask.

The Commonwealth had obviously not enhanced the political status of the United Kingdom since January 1963. Nor did it seem to have done much to improve its economic circumstances. During 1966 the material position of the United Kingdom deteriorated to its lowest level in modern history, relative to that of Continental Europe. Germany had already overtaken the British Gross National Product in 1959. But Germany had a rather larger population.

France achieved the same feat with a smaller population in 1966. Over the previous five years, France had indeed sustained a rate of economic growth of about 7.1 per cent, compared with 6.8 per cent for Germany, and 5.3 per cent for the United Kingdom. It was just enough to encourage the hope that France might once again become the strongest economic power in Western Europe. Meanwhile French material power and technological skill seemed symbolized by the launching of the A-1 satellite from Hammagaria in the Algerian Sahara on 26 November 1965, propelled by a French Diamante rocket. France had become the world's third space power, at however great a remove it might still be from the other two.

In these circumstances, it was understandable that British leaders should again look to the Common Market as a means of revitalizing their country's economy, and of providing it again with a rewardingly influential role in world affairs. They obviously faced great difficulties. In the first place, it would be particularly imprudent for a country in the inauspicious position of the United Kingdom to risk another rebuff. At the same time, it would also be essential to convince the Europeans that the objections presented to British entry in January 1963 no longer applied. This again needed to be done in a manner which did not suggest that the United Kingdom had no other options open to it. Wilson discussed the issue in general terms with de Gaulle on 3 April 1966. De Gaulle merely remarked that the successful conclusion of the tariff negotiation then in train in the GATT would make relations between the EEC and EFTA more fruitful. Now speaking from the Opposition benches, Sir Alec Douglas-Home promptly recalled the advantages that would accrue to the United Kingdom from being inside the EEC. However, Wilson briskly dismissed the suggestion by saying that the difference between the two parties was that the Conservatives were prepared to sacrifice Commonwealth interests to get into the EEC, while the Labourites were not.[11]

This of course had been said before. But events since 1963 had not exactly tended to augment the importance of Commonwealth interests for the United Kingdom. There was by now a very real case for believing that the embarrassments which the association involved for the United Kingdom might well outweigh its value. January and February 1966 continued the pattern of tension and distress. The Federal Prime Minister of Nigeria called a meeting of Commonwealth leaders in Lagos for 11–12 January 1966, to discuss the Rhodesian crisis. Differences appeared early. The Australian Prime Minister declined to attend, on the grounds, coincidentally held also by de Gaulle, that the Rhodesian question was one for the United Kingdom alone. The rulers of Ghana and Tanzania also refused to attend, since they had already broken off diplomatic relations with the United Kingdom. The Ministers present welcomed the assurance of the British Prime Minister that the illegal Smith regime might be brought to an end in a matter of weeks rather than months. But in fact it was not rebel Rhodesia that was in danger of dissolution. It was Nigeria itself, the country whose creation as an independent state had been regarded as the greatest achievement of British policy in Africa. The Federal Prime Minister was assassinated four days after the close of the conference he had summoned. A military junta entered office in Nigeria, amid the mounting prospect of massacre and civil war. The next African regime to fall was that of the most outspoken enemy of white Rhodesia. Nkrumah was deposed from rule in Ghana in his absence, by yet another military coup. Ian Smith could be grateful for his enemies.

It was thus not surprising that the Commonwealth received only passing mention in the manifestoes of the Labour and Conservative Parties, released before the general election of March 1966. What was noteworthy was their change in attitude towards entry to the EEC. The Conservatives promised to enter "at the first favourable opportunity". Labour would do the same, "provided essential British and Commonwealth interests are safeguarded". But a new tirade delivered by Wilson in Bristol on 18 March seemed to suggest that the safeguards that he would insist upon represented a positive hardening of British attitudes since the stalemate in Brussels three and a half years before. The basic differences between British agricultural policy and the CAP were apparently still irreconcilable. Further, the British people must continue to be "free to go on buying food and raw materials as we have for 100 years in the cheapest markets — in Canada, Australia, New Zealand and other Commonwealth countries — and not have their trade wrecked by the levies the Tories are so keen to impose".[12]

A Prime Minister's pre-election speeches should perhaps not

be taken too seriously. On the other hand, Wilson could hardly complain if people were still prepared to believe that he might mean what he said. It was indeed becoming very hard to know where the British Government stood upon almost any issue. In June, for example, the Chancellor of the Duchy of Lancaster, George Thompson, told the Council of Ministers of the WEU that "the political will to join the EEC exists in Britain today".[13] He also suggested that the problems of the neutral or under-developed countries associated with the United Kingdom in EFTA or the Commonwealth were less formidable now than they had been in 1962. French Foreign Secretary Jean de Broglie accordingly called on the British to make "concrete and precise proposals on conditions for entry". He added that France was not "doctrinally opposed" to British membership of the EEC. However, numerous difficulties remained and could not be resolved rapidly. France would therefore maintain a policy of "benevolent waiting".[14]

It waited for four months. Then on 10 November 1966 Wilson took up the French challenge. He told the House of Commons that the Government had been conducting a searching review of the whole problem of Britain's relations with the EEC. Every aspect of the Treaty of Rome and all the implications and con-sequences which might be expected to flow from British accession "had been examined in depth". The Government had now decided that a high-level approach should be made to see whether conditions existed for fruitful negotiations, and the basis on which such negotiations could take place. He said that it was vital to main-tain the closest relations with the other EFTA countries. He had accordingly invited heads of government of the rest of the Seven to London. It was intended afterwards to enter into discussions with the heads of government of the EEC countries. The Common-wealth Governments had already been informed, and the British Government would maintain the closest consultation with them throughout. The Government was entering the discussions with the determination to enter the EEC if, as was hoped, essential British and Commonwealth interests could be safeguarded.

Heath, Leader of the Conservative Opposition, assured Wilson that his party would support the Government in any genuine bid to enter the EEC. And there was no doubt that Wilson was genuine. For the first time a British Prime Minister deliberately sought to meet the Europeans on their own ground. He began at the top. In a speech at the Guildhall on 14 November Wilson actually proposed the creation of a new European Community. This was to be a "technological community to pool within Europe the enormous technological inventiveness of Britain and other countries ... in this field of technological cooperation on one has more to contribute than Britain ..."[15] This was notably deft. But rather the contrary impression was created by a speech by Foreign Secretary George Brown in the House of Commons, delivered only two days later. Brown asserted that the question was not "whether Britain should join Europe, but whether it could effectively be a leader of a unified Continent"; that "perhaps more than anything Britain would bring world standing and her position as head of the Commonwealth"; and that the Government was "resolutely opposed to any change in Britain's relationship with the United States ... particularly in defence, and any abandonment of the role Britain played in the outside world".[16] This was certainly true enough. However, it was precisely on considerations such as these that de Gaulle had based his decision to exclude the United Kingdom in 1963. It was at least unusual tactics to suggest that the position of the United Kingdom had not meanwhile changed. Douglas-Home accordingly warned that the enterprise could very well fail before it had begun unless there were some change in the Government's approach.

There was nothing wrong with Wilson's tactics, at least. By the end of the year he had gained the support of the EFTA countries for the British move as "an important step along the road to determining the prospects for a solution to the question of European economic integration..."[17] It was admittedly ominous that de Gaulle should have made no mention of the issue of British entry in a New Year's Day address to the diplomatic corps in Paris. But Wilson proceeded with his individual approach. He and Brown left London for Rome with the assurance that: "This is no empty probe. We mean business." His words were taken in Italy to mean that this time no external commitment would be allowed to impede British entry. This may well have been taking too much for granted. But there was no doubt about the personal success of the British leaders. Wilson and Brown were greeted by cheering crowds in the streets of Rome. Premier

Aldo Moro assured Wilson that he too meant business. British and Europeans must together "seek in our old Continent a new concept of European integration".[18] In a subsequent speech on 16 January 1967 Moro repeated the view, so familiar in the 1950's, that Western Europe would remain unbalanced until the United Kingdom became a part of it.

Wilson claimed in the House of Commons that the Italian talks had been a useful start to the round of conferences. They had undoubtedly been an encouraging beginning. But they had also been predictable. Traditional Italian friendship for Britain was reinforced in this case by a desire to have some counterweight within the EEC against the predominance of Germany or France. But Italy was not going to determine by itself whether or not Britain would actually be able to enter. The position of France remained the vital one, although this might conceivably be influenced by the other members of the EEC, if they were sufficiently strong in their support of British entry. Wilson had already made a tactical gesture to France by agreeing on 15 January to co-operate with them in producing a swing-wing aircraft for service in both the Royal Air Force and the Armée de l'Air. He also tried to allay fears that the United Kingdom might work to destroy the effective unity of the EEC when once inside it, telling the House of Commons that the British Government would "cooperate to the full on anything that can be done to achieve agreement on political unity if we enter the Common Market". He sounded this note again in an address to the Council of Europe on 23 January, when he said that:

> Over the next year, the next ten years, the next twenty years, the unity of Europe is going to be forged, and geography, history, interest and sentiment alike demand that we play our part in forging it — and working it.[19]

Now he approached de Gaulle. He began by claiming that Europe could not be great unless France and the United Kingdom were partners in it. Then he developed two new themes. The first was that the overseas associations of the United Kingdom could in fact lead Europe to a wider and deeper unity, as well as assisting Europe to play a greater role in world affairs. The Commonwealth and the special relationship with the United States were thus positive supports to Gaullist ambitions. Wilson's second argument was that Britain and France had really no diplomatic differences on important issues. For example, they both sought above all else a reduction of tension with Russia. They could thus well work together. Finally, he applauded the achievements of de Gaulle's pragmatism in Europe, and assured the French President that as far as the Common Market was concerned, the British were pragmatists too.

All this might have seemed conducive to restoring Anglo-French cordiality. But in fact this did not seem to have been the case. Wilson's diplomacy had apparently not been particularly successful with de Gaulle. Subsequent questioning in the House of Commons gradually revealed that nothing of any importance had actually been discussed in Paris. Only Brown had really established serious contact with the French, when he assured them that Britain no longer regarded the CAP as necessarily an impediment. Wilson tried to disguise his lack of success by claiming that: "We did not come to ask the French Government to answer yes or no, or to put any particular questions to it." But the whole objective of the mission had surely been to create in France a mood sympathetic to British entry, or at least to discover what the French mood was. It was thus virtually a confession of failure for Wilson to have to admit that he had not even discussed with the French the vital questions of the American alliance, defence, the independent deterrent or New Zealand.

There might have seemed little point in continuing approaches to the rest of the Six until these questions had been answered. Wilson may well have been hoping to mobilize support for British entry to force France's hand. But his next trip provided the most unexpected and serious disappointment of all. In Brussels Wilson received a welcome more appreciative and emotional even than the one he had enjoyed in Rome. Alone among the leaders of the Six, Belgian Prime Minister Paul van den Boeyants recalled the services and sacrifices which the British had made to defend the independence of his country in two world wars. In return, he pledged to make every effort to support British entry. As the Italians had done, he assured Wilson that he too meant business. He also agreed that the British now had the political will to join the EEC, and that when the political will was there all difficulties must be overcome. But Boeyants then recognized two serious difficulties which all the political will in the world might find it hard to overcome. These were the weakness of sterling as a reserve currency and the extraordinarily unsatisfactory performance of the British economy. Boeyants stressed that it was important that the United Kingdom should not enter the EEC in a condition which might require it to use escape clauses to evade its obligations under the Treaty of Rome. But this was very clearly exactly the position that the United Kingdom was in at the time. The value of external trade for both the United Kingdom and the EEC had risen by about 50 per cent in the past five years. But British reserves of foreign exchange had marginally fallen in that period. EEC reserves had risen by about 30 per cent. However, Wilson had clearly hoped that the British position would be improved if British producers could be exposed to European competition within the EEC. He was now in effect being told that he would have to restore British economic viability before the United Kingdom would be eligible for entry. This was equivalent to a bank manager's telling an applicant for an overdraft that he could have the money provided that he could show that he no longer needed it.

Some men would have given up at this stage. Wilson on the contrary announced on his return that: "We must keep up the urgency and momentum of this approach." If it were possible to open negotiations, then "clearly the earlier the better".[20] But this was only whistling past a graveyard. Yet another rebuff followed immediately, this time from Jean Rey, the Belgian expert on external affairs on the Commission of the EEC and soon to be its President. Rey had certainly hitherto seemed sympathetic to British entry. He now began by saying that there was now "no reason for the Six to have qualms regarding the entry of the United Kingdom".[21] He claimed that military and nuclear problems had practically disappeared; that there would be no greater difficulties over EFTA than before, and less over the Commonwealth; and that the United Kingdom had accepted the basic principles of the CAP, and so could be accorded a ceiling on levies, as had been done for Germany. But Rey then raised the problems of the structural weakness of the British economy and the role of sterling as a reserve currency. The United Kingdom could not be admitted to the EEC unless it could show its capacity to accept the responsibilities of belonging. It was unlikely to be able to do so while the present recession continued. Industrial production in the United Kingdom had remained for two and a half years at the level of the last quarter of 1964.

There was no doubt that this was Wilson's most obvious weakness. Macmillan had after all been able to offer the Europeans access to a booming British market, however unsoundly the boom might have been based. But even Macmillan had been unsuccessful. And there were other disadvantages as well. Personalities had changed. The new leaders of Germany were less inclined than Erhard had been to dismiss political considerations in the interests of securing new markets for German industry to conquer. Indeed, the last thing that Germany seemed to need in 1967 was wider access for its exports. What Germany needed was political support for its claims in Europe. The fact that this support was not likely to be forthcoming from the United Kingdom was indicated by a memorable indiscretion of Brown's. On the very eve of his departure with Wilson to Bonn, he managed to give the impression that the British Government recognized both the legitimacy of the German Democratic Republic, and the appropriateness of the Oder-Neisse line as the frontier between that state and Poland. It was unfortunate that the visit to Bonn should have followed closely upon the visit of Kosygin to the United Kingdom. Brown was doubtless still preoccupied with maintaining Anglo-Russian accord. Foreign Office officials tried to explain that their Minister had not been serious about East Germany, even though he might have been about the Oder-Neisse line. German diplomats noted that this was likely to be a difficult visit. It was certainly an unrewarding one. German leaders may well have been questioning the advantage of admitting the United Kingdom to a Community which they had hopes of being able to dominate eventually themselves. Chancellor Kiesinger was friendly, but non-committal. He said that his Government had been strengthened in its conviction that it should strive for the entry of the United Kingdom to the EEC. But there was no suggestion that Bonn would do anything to try to alter the position of Paris on this issue.

Meanwhile, opposition to the new British bid was beginning to appear in some unexpected quarters. In Wellington, Commonwealth Secretary Bowden said that it would be "a very long time" before the United Kingdom could join the EEC. This certainly contrasted with Wilson's personal insistence upon dynamism and urgency. More seriously, the President of the Board of Trade,

Douglas Jay, pointed out during Wilson's absence in Bonn that entry to the EEC might involve a rise of about 4 per cent in the British cost of living. Calculations of this kind tended to destroy the whole rationale of Wilson's bid to enter, since they suggested that the immediate dislocation involved in British entry might well wreck the nation's economy before it could gain the long-term benefits of freer competition. The British could now well be in the incongruous position that they could not afford to join the EEC when they needed to, just as in previous years they did not seem to need to join it when they could have afforded to. Perhaps still more significant was a sympathetic reminder that the options open to the United Kingdom might not yet be exhausted. On 21 February the *Times* published a letter signed by five American state Governors, ten U.S. Senators, five Chancellors of American universities, twenty-eight American university presidents and one acting president. It claimed that the "special relationship" between the two English speaking powers had produced "an enduring friendship, unique among sovereign states". It accordingly urged that the two Governments "should now begin to consider contingent means, including initiating beneficial trade and fiscal reforms, for saving and strengthening the historic relationship between our nations, whatever the outcome of the EEC negotiations".

This of course was the North Atlantic Union tirelessly raised for discussion by Pearson and Paul Martin, now Canadian Minister for External Affairs. Its logic had never been hard to appreciate. The British were obviously closer to the North Americans than to the Europeans in every sense save that of geography. Geography had been of little importance before the 1940's, and it might well have become so again. In the missile age, Washington might not be significantly further from danger than London. The real objection was of course that the United Kingdom might very well hope even now to dominate the EEC, but it could not possibly hope to dominate any union involving the United States. On the other hand, American control over the British economy was mushrooming anyway; British trade was increasing more rapidly with North America than with any other trading area; and subordination to the American economy did not necessarily mean subordination to Amerian policies, if the example of Canada was any criterion.

Wilson was still determined to admit neither alternatives nor opposition. He savagely rebuked Labour Party dissenters, reminding them that dogs were conventionally allowed one bite, but that they might not get their licences renewed if it seemed that they were continuing to bite because of evil temper. Jay pointed out the flaw in this analogy. As he said, it was the party that licensed the Prime Minister in Labour politics, rather than the other way about. Wilson then visited the Netherlands. He was there urged to "press hard for membership", but still had to report on his return that there were "three or four formidable problems remaining". A visit to Luxembourg on 8 March produced a wholly enthusiastic endorsement of British entry, as being beneficial in every way to the Community. But Luxembourg was not in a position to exercise a decisive influence within the EEC. In the House of Commons Wilson asserted that there would have to be a speedier conclusion to the negotiations this time. He claimed that "on the previous occasion the whole thing was treated rather as an operation in grocery and not ... high politics". But at least Heath had been able to bring negotiations to the brink of success. Wilson had not even been able to get them started so far. His chances of ever doing so seemed to be positively diminishing. At a meeting of the Anglo-German Society in Konigswinter on 12 March 1967 German parliamentarians argued that Germany's main priority had to be to get French support for a new policy in the East. This precluded any possibility of Germany's putting pressure on France in the meantime in support of British entry. Kiesinger himself made this clear in an interview with *Der Spiegel* on 20 March. He stressed the importance of retaining good relations between Germany and France, emphasizing that de Gaulle at least recognized the importance of achieving the reunification of Germany, which the Americans were not always prepared to admit. Germany might therefore support British entry to the EEC, but it could not and would not put any pressure on de Gaulle for this purpose; not that their putting pressure on de Gaulle was likely to be very effective.

The British had been encouraged by a German invitation to make their bid for entry in 1962. But failure to gain such an invitation was not enough to deter Wilson in 1967. No alternative to entry was admitted. On 15 March 1967 Paul Martin had spoken of the importance of developing "every reasonable link — political, economic, military, social and cultural" between North America, the United Kingdom and Western Europe, and had expressed Canadian disappointment at the failure of NATO to have provided the nucleus of a political community bridging the Atlantic.[22] But Wilson now specifically dismissed the idea of some kind of Atlantic Community, claiming, in the authentic language of General de Gaulle, that such an organization did not even exist, while the EEC was a reality. On 2 May the House of Commons was told that the Government had decided to make an application for membership of the EEC again, under the terms of Article 237 of the Treaty of Rome. Wilson listed what seemed to him to be the main difficulties. These were "the far-reaching changes in the structure of British agriculture" which would be required by accession to the CAP, the inequitable cost to the United Kingdom if the CAP were applied unconditionally to it, the special problems of New Zealand and the sugar-producing countries in the Commonwealth, capital movements, and the question of regional development within the United Kingdom itself. It was a formidable list. However, Wilson said that he believed that there was nothing in either the Treaty of Rome or the practical working of the Communities themselves which need make these problems insoluble. In any case, whatever the economic arrangements, the purpose of the British Government derived above all from their recognition that "Europe was now faced with the opportunity of a great move forward in political unity, and that Britain could, indeed must, play its full part in it". He argued again, as he had done with de Gaulle, that the overseas links of the United Kingdom could be positively beneficial to European aspirations, by ensuring that "Europe played in world affairs the part which the Europe of today was not at present playing".[23]

Commonwealth Governments had certainly had plenty of time in which to prepare their responses. The Canadian one had indeed been given already. Lester Pearson, now Prime Minister again, could speak with a singleness of resolve difficult under the circumstances of the Free Trade Area for St. Laurent, and quite impossible for Diefenbaker in the circumstances of the first British bid for entry. After a meeting in London of the Anglo-Canadian Committee he said simply that the Canadians "understand and appreciate Britain's desire to play its full part in Europe", pointing out that the "Commonwealth has not been regarded as an exclusive organisation".[24] The Australian response was also rapid. While the debate in the House of Commons was still in train, Prime Minister Holt expressed the hope in Canberra that the opportunity would be given for "meaningful consultations" between the United Kingdom and interested Commonwealth Governments. He noted that the British Government had repeatedly emphasized that British entry into the EEC would be subject to the provision of adequate safeguards to protect the essential interests of the Commonwealth. Wilson had referred specifically to the "special case" of New Zealand. Holt agreed that Australia too fully appreciated New Zealand's problems. But Australia had problems of its own, which tended not to be recognized to the same degree. "In recent years there appears to have developed, both in Britain and in Europe, a belief that there may be no great need to take special measures to protect Australia's export position because we have been diversifying our export trade ... "[25] McEwen developed this point in stronger terms. He said that he,

> like all other Australians, must wait with real anxiety to learn what arrangements the British Government believes it can achieve which would avoid seriously affecting the course of trade between Australia and Britain ... When previous negotiations between Britain and the EEC for British entry had broken down, only two proposals had been produced — a phasing out of preferences and international commodity arrangements covering the big bulk commodities.

He argued that no country was more obligated than the United Kingdom to press at once for the latter, since it was the British who intended to take a step which would disrupt the traditional pattern of bulk commodity trade.[26]

Such statements were probably required in the political climate of Canberra. It was difficult to believe that the British would be particularly influenced by them. There was no question that the British were in a substantially weaker bargaining position in 1967 than they had been five years earlier. It was therefore scarcely imaginable that they would obtain terms any more favourable than they had been able to secure then. In the discussion in the House of Commons the day after McEwen's speech, Wilson again referred only to the inequitable features of the CAP, and the need to seek safeguards for New Zealand and the sugar producers. He added that the Government sought no exemptions from the obligations falling upon every member of the EEC.

These could involve a rise of from $2\frac{1}{2}$ to $3\frac{1}{2}$ per cent in the cost of living in the United Kingdom. But in compensation British entry would "have a profound effect upon British industry by creating a new confidence, a new upsurge in investment, a new concentration on modernization, productivity and reduced costs. It would also impart to the Community a new dynamic. It would help to provide the basis for carrying the enormous research and development costs if European industry were to stay in the vanguard." Displaying a confidence he could hardly have felt, Wilson again slighted the previous attempts of the Conservatives, saying that it was not now a question of "Europe or bust" as the Continent might have believed five years before. "The Government was choosing the right, the best course for Britain and Europe." Heath again assured Wilson that the Conservative Opposition was also committed to a European policy. Duncan Sandys, forgetting his belittling of the ECSC in 1950, claimed to have been campaigning for the creation of a United Europe for over twenty years. The House endorsed the Government's motion to seek entry by 488 votes to 62, compared with a similar vote of 313 to 5 in 1961.

Wilson was at least spared the lingering torment of the Brussels negotiations. He was spared any negotiations at all. On the very day that the House of Commons voted on the British bid for entry, the President of the Commission of the EEC, Walter Hallstein, a long-standing proponent of British entry, announced that he would not be available as a candidate for the presidency of the unified Commission of the three Communities, scheduled to come into operation on 1 July 1967. The omen was distinctly unfavourable. Wilson nonetheless refused to appear perturbed. In a television debate the following day with the charming and eloquent Gaullist Servan-Schreiber, he determinedly took the offensive. Wilson claimed that the nuclear deterrent issue had changed since the time of the Nassau Agreement, since the Royal Air Force would be dependent upon Anglo-French aircraft in the 1970's. He also said that the United Kingdom was really more independent of United States predominance than Gaullist France was, since the British had refused to sell out their computer interests to the Americans. They were therefore in a position to help Europe to counter American domination. Two days later, the British application for entry under the terms of Article 237 was delivered to the Council of Ministers of the EEC. It consisted of one unqualified sentence. On 12 May, Wilson again struck fiercely at the opposition within his own Party. Seven British Cabinet Ministers were required to sack parliamentary under-secretaries who had disagreed with him on the EEC issue.

The ball was now squarely with the French. It did not stay there long. In his press conference of 16 May de Gaulle began by saying that: "The movement which seems at present to be leading Britain to link herself with Europe instead of keeping herself apart can only please France." He also promised that: "For our part there cannot be, nor moreover has there ever been, any question of a veto." But he then proceeded to deliver what on any basis was in effect a veto. He referred again as he had done in 1963 to the insular status and overseas commitments which had led the United Kingdom first to refuse to join the European Communities, and even to display a hostile attitude towards them as to "an economic and political threat". De Gaulle then affirmed that the United Kingdom was "declaring herself ready to subscribe to the Treaty of Rome, provided that she be granted exceptional and prolonged respites and that, in matters affecting her, essential changes are made in the Treaty's application". He argued that the United Kingdom could not submit to the provisions of the CAP because "her balance of payments will be overwhelmed by the levies and furthermore she will be obliged to raise the price of food to the level adopted by the Six, to raise the wages of her workers, and, thus, to sell her products at proportionately higher prices and with correspondingly greater difficulty". If on the other hand the United Kingdom were "to enter the Community without her being really subject to the agricultural system of the Six, then that system would collapse at a stroke, and this would upset completely the equilibrium of the Common Market and deprive France of one of the principal reasons that she can have to be a member of it ..." De Gaulle saw three alternatives:

> ... the creation of a sort of free trade area in Western Europe, while awaiting the Atlantic zone which would deprive our Continent of all real personality ...
> Or else, to set up between the Community on the one hand, and Britain and the various states of the free trade area on the other, a system of associations such as is provided for by the

Treaty of Rome and which could without upheaval facilitate and increase the economic relations of the parties.

Or else, finally, to wait before changing what exists, for a certain internal and external development, of which it seems Great Britain is beginning to show the signs, to come to a successful conclusion, that is, for this great people, so magnificently endowed with capacity and with courage to have accomplished itself the profound economic and political transformation desired so that its union with the Six continentals can be achieved ...

If one day Great Britain arrived at this point, how whole-heartedly would France welcome this historic conversation.[27]

There was obviously a great deal that this magnificently endowed but economically unpromising people would have to do to fit themselves for membership of the Europe of Realities. One prerequisite de Gaulle mentioned specifically was that they should become again "their own masters, notably in matters of defence". This seemed to imply that the British should hand their Polaris missiles back to the Americans and use Diamante rockets instead. They might also have to leave NATO. It certainly seemed that de Gaulle would not be satisfied with less, if indeed he would be satisfied with any British action. But Wilson continued to ignore negative indications from the Continent. At an industrialists' dinner on 18 May he told his audience that the United Kingdom must press on with the negotiations for entry.[28] George Brown acted the following day to make rapid negotiations more probable, by vetoing Bowden's proposal that a Minister of the Commonwealth Office should be made part of the British team in negotiations with the EEC.

Even before Brown's action, the New Zealanders began to register concern anew. Admittedly former Prime Minister Nash, now Sir Walter Nash, discovered reasons for comfort in British moves which had not been so obvious to other Commonwealth observers:

> Britain is going in with the Six on an undertaking that the trade of New Zealand and other Commonwealth countries including Australia is to be protected, and she is doing so not only to improve Britain's own standards, but also to enable her to exploit every possible and conceivable way in which she can help the countries of the Commonwealth where there are people dying because there is not enough food to eat.[29]

This was not the view of the New Zealand Government. Trade Minister Marshall warned members in the same debate that none

of the safeguards proposed during the previous Brussels negotiations would in fact have been any substitute for the continuity
of the present volume of New Zealand's trade with the United
Kingdom. He went on to argue that it was essential that any
arrangement made for New Zealand would have to be of a permanent nature. New Zealand had been part of the United Kingdom
market for over a hundred years.[30]

These seemingly impossible demands contrasted with the
objective stand sustained by the Canadians. This in turn admittedly
contrasted with the stand taken by that people five years before.
Donald Fleming had then adopted a view very different from that
of his successor Mitchell W. Sharp, who told a meeting of the
Canadian Manufacturers' Association in Toronto that:

> If Britain does join the Common Market, we stand to lose
> our preferred position in the United Kingdom market and, for
> many products, to face tariff preferences against our goods. But
> we do stand to gain from the greater economic strength of a Britain
> in Europe, and of a greater Europe.[31]

The New Zealanders were no more disposed in 1967 than
they had been in 1962 to admit the existence of any compensating
possibilities. The day after Sharp had spoken, Prime Minister
Holyoake moved in Wellington that:

> This House notes the application of the British Government
> for membership of the EEC ... reaffirms that it would be
> disastrous for the New Zealand economy if Britain entered the
> Common Market without adequate safeguards for New Zealand,
> and endorses the objectives of New Zealand in these negotiations
> as the continuity of the volume of our trade on a permanent and
> economic basis for our main exports, to an enlarged Community
> containing Britain.[32]

New Zealand negotiators had always been accustomed to begin
by asking for everything, in the hope that they might end by
getting something. But it seemed perhaps unduly hopeful to ask
in 1967 for conditions which they would clearly not have got in
1963. But there was no doubt that New Zealand's position of
dependence upon the British market had improved only marginally
in the meantime. In 1962/63 New Zealand had sent to the United
Kingdom 90.7 per cent of its exports of butter, 87.6 per cent of
its exports of cheese, and 88 per cent of its exports of mutton. In
the calendar year 1966 the respective figures were 85, 78 and 92

per cent. Overall dependence on the British market had fallen from 46 to 42 per cent. Overall Australian dependence had also fallen little in this period, from 19 to 17 per cent. But the Australians had managed to reduce substantially their dependence in the three vital commodities mentioned above. In 1962/63 the United Kingdom had taken 82 per cent of Australia's butter exports, 45 per cent of its cheese exports and 25 per cent of its mutton and lamb. In 1965/66 the respective figures were 80 per cent, 30 per cent and 11 per cent. It might indeed be true as Holyoake said that New Zealand was facing its most serious problem for many years, other than war. But it also seemed true that the problem was in large measure due to the failure of the New Zealanders to change the pattern of their external trade in a way which the Australians had not found it impossible to at least begin.

But the New Zealanders undoubtedly had the means of making it difficult for the British to disregard their pleas for consideration. The existing Trade Agreement between the United Kingdom and New Zealand did confirm the right of duty-free access to the British market for New Zealand meat and cheese, at least until 1972. New Zealand's position under the existing arrangement of butter quotas was similarly guaranteed. And there could be no doubt that New Zealand's problems would not be allowed to keep the United Kingdom out of an EEC anxious to welcome the British in. Several solutions had already been proposed in the context of the Brussels negotiations. These ranged from the official Commission proposal to establish New Zealand as a permanent producer of agricultural surpluses to feed the needy, to the unofficial suggestion of a French representative that the Six might agree to buy New Zealand's export production of butter at a determined price, and drop it in the North Sea. There was clearly general support in the Assembly of the WEU for Brown's argument that "New Zealand was a case of an altogether special kind".[33] But once again New Zealand interests seemed to be most effectively defended by the intransigence of General de Gaulle. There was not the faintest evidence to support the assertion of Maurice Edelman, in 1967 as in 1950 the most fickle of all protagonists of Western Union, that: "French resistance to British entry is crumbling. There is a movement in France in favour of British entry."[34] This assessment was followed almost immediately by a comment by Couve de Murville, that British membership would mean the transformation of the EEC into an Atlantic trading system, involving increased discrimination against the Latin Americans, among others.

It nonetheless seemed that British involvement in an Atlantic trading system could more sensibly be envisaged as an alternative to membership of the EEC, rather than as a consequence of it. Former Australian Prime Minister Menzies, now Sir Robert Menzies, was prepared to extend the Atlantic concept indefinitely. He said in Oxford that he was unable to grasp the logic of the change in the British attitude towards membership of the EEC, as the United Kingdom could have obtained good terms for the Commonwealth ten years previously if it had been prepared to enter then. It could of course have been said in reply that not a single Commonwealth Government had suggested that the British should enter the EEC in 1958 on this assumption. But Menzies then proposed as a present alternative a "closer association of the English-speaking peoples", embracing the United Kingdom, the United States, Australia, New Zealand, Canada and even South Africa, though not apparently Rhodesia. This possibility was again not even considered by the British leadership. The Minister in charge of the negotiations on entry, Lord Chalfont, insisted that no lack of response from Europe could make any difference to the British resolve. He told the Europeans at Strasbourg that he intended to go on

> sounding the British trumpet while there are still people who believe that Europe can be made without us ... The new Britain is still Great Britain, not Little England ... The only alternative to Europe is Europe ... We shall not take No for an answer. If we fail, if we are defeated, we shall go on ... What is at issue is nothing more or less than European independence.

American observers had just the same come to the conclusion that the British had already accepted that their efforts would be unsuccessful.[35] The Report of the European Commission itself explicitly rejected the basic logic of Wilson's approaches. It began promisingly by denying the basic French contention that British membership would "be of such a nature as to modify the fundamental objectives, the very character, and the methods of the European Communities..." It also recognized that the resources available for investment in technological research in the United Kingdom amounted to nearly two-thirds of those in the EEC.

But the Commission went on damagingly to argue that British entry "by itself would in no way solve the technological gap". Much of British research would merely duplicate European programmes. And it was also the fact that the British frequently engaged in "expensive and unproductive undertakings . . ." Their own domestic programmes were "inadequate either through lack of coordination or a real spirit of innovation".

There was probably only one thing the British Government could still do to try to make its determination yet clearer. This was to repudiate explicitly its particular connections with countries outside Europe. Chalfont did this on 10 and 11 October. He first of all asserted that henceforth the United Kingdom would have only a European relationship with the United States. The "special relationship" no longer was relevant. Neither apparently was the Commonwealth connection. Chalfont then said that the United Kingdom would merely "try to negotiate for a period of transition to enable the Commonwealth countries to have the opportunity to adapt themselves to the new circumstances".[36] There was no longer any talk of safeguards or permanent guarantees. But even this was ineffective. In the first place, one does not necessarily recommend oneself to a new group of prospective partners by affirming one's unqualified readiness to abandon the old; in the second place, the very existence of these overseas links had been used by Wilson as one of his strongest arguments in favour of British membership; and lastly of course, no one could believe that the British intended seriously to discard their special ties with the United States, or even with at least certain Commonwealth countries. On 24 October Couve de Murville again pronounced unmoved the final veto. France briefly reminded the other EEC countries that the United Kingdom would have to achieve equilibrium in its balance of payments position and abandon the reserve role of sterling before negotiations could even begin. This setback apparently provoked Chalfont to the kind of retort previously associated with Eccles and Maudling. Accounts of what he actually said varied from one reporter to the next. But it was generally agreed that he had referred to the possibility that the British might reconsider the position of the Army of the Rhine and their status in West Berlin. The national secretary of the Gaullists in France serenely described the incident as a venture in "vulgar and inferior blackmail". Chalfont's offer to resign was refused by Wilson, who assured the House of Commons that the Government would pursue an "unequivocal European policy based on Britain's adherence to the Community". Brown similarly stated that the British commitment to Europe was total, and that their "major field of operations must be in and through Europe".

But it takes two to participate. In these circumstances, it took seven. The British certainly took their most drastic and promising step yet to restore their external financial position, by devaluing the pound in November 1967. But this was welcomed by yet another crushing press conference held by de Gaulle. The President told his audience that they were watching "the fifth act of a play during which England has taken up very different and apparently inconsistent attitudes towards the Common Market". According to de Gaulle, the sequence of the acts was "refusal to participate ... deep-seated hostility ... negotiations aimed at bending the Community to England's conditions ... disinterest in the Common Market ... [and] This time Britain has made its application and has embarked upon all imaginable promises and pressures to get it accepted." But the application could not be accepted yet. As de Gaulle listed comprehensively:

> The Common Market is incompatible with the economy, as it is, of England. The chronic deficit of the British economy's balance of payments demonstrates its permanent disequilibrium ... The Common Market is also incompatible with the way the British get their food ... The Common Market is also incompatible with the restrictions imposed by Britain on the outward movement of capital which, by contrast, circulates freely among the Six ... [But] France is certainly quite prepared, in order to make things easy for England, to enter into any arrangements which, under the name of association or any other name, would favour, as of now, commercial exchanges between the Continentals and the British, the Scandinavians and the Irish ... [37]

This was second class membership, such as had been negotiated with Greece and Turkey. It might well have been enough, if the British had been concerned only with commercial interests. But it would not give them a role in Europe. It was indeed expressly proposed to prevent their having one. Once again a British bid to establish a power base in Europe seemed unquestionably to have failed. The most appropriate course remaining might have been to look for one elsewhere. Douglas Jay, delivering his first speech in the House on this issue, bowdlerized the memorable appeal of Oliver Cromwell, to make an obviously pertinent comment:

> To those who still refuse summarily to consider any solution other than conventional and full membership of the EEC, I would say: "For heaven's sake, conceive of the possibility that you may be mistaken."[38]

But perhaps the final word should be given to Lester Pearson. Speaking at the Mansion House luncheon in London on 27 November 1967 he stressed again the importance of preserving and developing the concept of the Atlantic system, rebuking at the same time British designs of entering Europe at the price of severing Atlantic ties, and French designs of keeping the British out as a means of keeping them severed:

> The idea of a strong and united Europe is surely a wise one, but only if it can be worked out without isolation from North America. That is why, as I see it, Britain should be a central and integral part of the new Europe, politically and economically. I see this as something which need not weaken ties across the Atlantic or with the rest of the Commonwealth. I see it rather as something which would help prevent Europe from becoming an isolated third force. If you like, I see Britain in the role of link between Europe and America ... Maybe we can give you some advice on how to perform that role![39]

He had been giving British Governments that kind of advice for the past twenty years.

NOTES

1. Canada, House of Commons, *Debates,* 29 January 1963.
2. *Times* (London), 19 February 1963.
3. U.K., House of Commons, *Debates,* Vol. DCLXXXVIII, col. 799.
4. *Ibid.,* col. 1356.
5. *Le Monde* (Paris), 29 July 1964.
6. *Times,* 16 September 1964.
7. *Ibid.*
8. *Ibid.,* 10 November 1964.
9. *Ibid.,* 20 November 1965.
10. *Ibid.,* 15 November 1965.
11. U.K., H. of C., *Debates,* Vol. DCCXXVII, cols. 552 and 1865.
12. *Times,* 19 March 1966.
13. *Ibid.,* 14 June 1966.

14. *Ibid.,* 28 June 1966.
15. *Ibid.,* 6 December 1966.
16. U.K., H. of C., *Debates,* Vol. DCCXXXVI, cols. 446-55.
17. *Times,* 6 December 1966.
18. *Ibid.,* 17 January 1967.
19. *Ibid.,* 24 January 1967.
20. *Ibid.,* 3 February 1967.
21. *Ibid.,* 4 February 1967.
22. Canada, Department of External Affairs, *Statements and Speeches,* 15 March 1967.
23. U.K., H. of C., *Debates,* Vol. DCCXLVI, cols. 310-14.
24. Canada, D. of E.A., *S. and S.,* 21 April 1967.
25. Australia, House of Representatives, *Debates,* 4 May 1967.
26. *Ibid.,* 7 May 1967.
27. *Le Monde,* 17 May 1967.
28. *Times,* 19 May 1967.
29. N.Z., House of Representatives, *Debates,* 18 May 1967.
30. *Ibid.*
31. Canada, D. of E.A., *S. and S.,* 29 May 1967.
32. N.Z., H. of R., *Debates,* 31 May 1967.
33. *Times,* 5 July 1967.
34. *Ibid.,* 12 July 1967.
35. *U.S. News and World Report,* 18 September 1967, p. 105.
36. *Times,* 12 October 1967.
37. *Le Monde,* 28 November 1967.
38. U.K., H. of C., *Debates,* Vol. DCCLIII, col. 386.
39. Canada, D. of E.A., *S. and S.,* 28 November 1967.

Postscript

The cataclysmic events of the first half of 1968 did not seem to bring the British Government any closer to finding a solution to the basic problem of choosing a new destiny for the United Kingdom. Drastic attempts were certainly made to restore British economic viability. These took the form of a rigorous cutback in January 1968 of British military capacity to support a world power role. All British forces in the Persian Gulf and the Far East, excluding Hong Kong, were to be withdrawn by the end of 1971; an order for fifty United States F-111 aircraft to give the RAF continuing strategic capability was cancelled; and it was decided that the carrier force of the Royal Navy should be phased out of operations. This indeed left British military capacity restricted to a European sphere. Couve de Murville noted approvingly what *Le Monde* described as a general and precipitate retreat.[1] He observed that the British financial cuts seemed to mean "a change in the emphasis given to Europe, by comparison with the rest of the world". But he also indicated that there was still no prospect of a change in French policy towards British entry to the Common Market.[2]

Nor was there any sign of a British change. Sir Frank Roberts, the British Ambassador to Bonn, specifically rejected on the same day the suggestions of de Gaulle that the British Government might be contented with some commercial arrangement which did not involve political participation. Roberts dismissed any notion of "association, pseudo-membership, some loosely-defined economic relationship or even customs union, (because) these would have no political content ... would do nothing to advance the closer political relationship which nearly all Europeans wanted".[3] But the Germans were still interested in increasing their access to the British market, whether this led to closer political relations in the future or not. German Foreign Minister Willy Brandt proposed directly to George Brown some kind of Free Trade Area relationship between the United Kingdom and the EEC. He also revived Profumo's old idea that the United Kingdom should be brought into Euratom before the three Communities were fused. But Brown could not accept even old British ideas as an alternative to the new British idea of total commitment. The EEC Council of Ministers nonetheless began seriously to discuss commercial relations between the United Kingdom and the Six, until de Gaulle intervened on 7 March 1968, demanding that all discussions of political, technological or free trade association should be postponed indefinitely.

The General could still give orders to Europe. But for an incredible few weeks in May and June 1968 it looked as if he would be unable to give orders to France itself any longer. Student protests against fantastically outmoded educational facilities and techniques set flame to general dissatisfaction with soaring prices, inadequate housing and what seemed to be the other domestic consequences of the policy of grandeur. The troubles began most appropriately while de Gaulle was absent on a policy-making visit to the Rumanians. For about three weeks, it seemed as if France, with its economy paralysed and half its labour force on strike against Gaullist leadership had finally eliminated itself from the great power race. Wilson tactfully refused to comment on the French strikes, and insisted that there was no question of ganging up on France. The British Government was prepared to deal with the Six as a whole. It would not take sides.[4]

It was perhaps fortunate that Wilson was so forbearing. Historical experience had shown France to be the most resilient and unpredictable of nations. And it had certainly never been safe to assume that a majority of the French electorate had rejected either de Gaulle or the policy of grandeur, however displeased they might be with some of its apparent side-effects. In any event, the nation which had appeared to be in almost total revolt against its regime swept that regime back into power with the greatest margin of electoral support accorded any French party since 1789. Europe and the world outside were confronted again in July 1968 with the implacable faces of de Gaulle, de Murville and Michel Debré, overwhelmingly if perhaps only conditionally back in power.

And real power was still in their hands. The French economy had indeed suffered a setback almost without parallel in the post-war world. French financial reserves were drawn on by at least a quarter of their strength to save the franc from a devaluation even more humiliating that that administered to the pound sterling. But there were few stronger economies and only two larger reserves in the world. In the past four years, French industrial production had climbed by 15 per cent, compared with 12 per cent for Germany and a little over 4 per cent for the United Kingdom. French reserves of foreign exchange approached the size of Germany's and were nearly three times the size of the United Kingdom's. The Republic born of the Resistance had developed into a country that was still one of the most formidable powers on earth. It was certainly not likely to be prepared to abandon its predominant role in the EEC. The new British Foreign Secretary, Michael Stewart, again pleaded his country's case for entry after the French elections. He received the usual reply. Nothing had changed. Nothing was likely to change until an alternative appeared in France to Gaullism or the present Gaullist leadership. And on the face of it, no group of men had ever been more unchallengeably established in power in the Republic.

By mid-1968 as by the end of 1967, it seemed evident that nothing that the United Kingdom could do itself could effect a change in the attitude of France. It therefore seemed more evident still that it was urgently necessary for the British to re-think their position. Persistence in a hopeless cause is not merely wasteful and degrading. Its greatest danger is that it tends to blind the unsuccessful striver to the possible existence of other more promising courses of action. In a letter to the *Daily Telegraph*,[5] Stanley Henig, a Labour Member of Parliament, argued that unwillingness to choose between Europe and the North Atlantic was depriving the British of their ability to play a meaningful role in either area. It was perhaps even more serious than that. The great error of British foreign policy before 1961 has been a failure to realize in time that Europe could offer a meaningful basis for a role in world affairs. It would be unfortunate indeed if their policy after 1961 were to be invalidated by the opposite error of not realizing in time that that offer was no longer open.

But the North Atlantic role did not seem to be open either. American thinkers and publicists were vocal enough in their support for a new pattern to the old "special relationship". Their political leaders were not. And perhaps the last thing that could reasonably be expected from the success of the Republican candidate, Mr. Richard Nixon, in the Presidential elections was that the United States was about to embark on a new departure in international organization. Nor did the Wilson Government evidence the faintest sign of having changed their minds. Britain's commitment was still to Europe.

This amounted to saying that its commitment was to waiting for something to happen. Powerless to create events, the British could only attend on them. And in May 1969 their patience received some kind of reward. In a gesture which reflected either seriously impaired judgment or simple weariness of office, Charles de Gaulle staked his tenure of power on the willingness of the French people to vote "Oui" again in yet another referendum of unclear relevance and enormous obscurity. The issues involved were set out in fourteen pages barely comprehensible to trained constitutional lawyers. The French people may well have decided that one of the main reasons for having politicians at all was so as not to have to read such documents. This strangely insignificant episode brought an end to the most rationally-directed regime in French history. It did not of course bring an end to Gaullism.

The old implacable Gaullist front was admittedly broken. The Great Implacable himself was gone. Couve de Murville also conveniently retired into aristocratic private life. And Michel

Debré was moved on to the honorific station of Minister of State and the portfolio peculiarly congenial to his temperament, of Minister of Defence. The new face presented by France to the world after Georges Pompidou's succession to the Presidency was flexible, pragmatic, conciliatory, and extraordinarily good-looking. It was simply that of dissident Gaullism. President Pompidou himself had been dismissed from the Premiership by de Gaulle after he had effectively brought the May 1968 Revolution to an end with the most impressive display of physical endurance and negotiating skill in modern times. Premier Jacques Chaban-Delmas had run against de Gaulle's own candidate for the presidency of the Assemblée Nationale in 1959, and had never been trusted by de Gaulle thereafter. Foreign Minister Maurice Schumann had been out of politics for the past five years, after disagreeing with de Gaulle over the issue of European integration. And the new Minister of Justice, René Pleven, bore perhaps the most highly honoured name in the whole history of the Fourth Republic, and certainly the one most consistently identified with everything antipathetic to Gaullism. The new Gaullist cabinet consisted to a very great degree of men who had been unable to get on with de Gaulle.

Changes could thus be expected. And the first allusions of the new French leaders to the question of British entry to the EEC might certainly have seemed encouraging. They insisted that there was no doctrinaire opposition on the part of France. But so had de Gaulle. The question had always been one of the price to be exacted from the British as a price of French endorsement. And there was no reason to suspect that Pompidou would set that price at a level any less prohibitive than it had been before. As the *Guardian* pointed out gloomily:

> Pompidou has said that Britain's entry should be reconsidered, but he has not said that France will agree to the changes . . . which would make Britain's entry possible . . . France is doing extremely well out of the common agricultural policy as it stands. M. Pompidou knows that Britain cannot join unless the policy is changed to France's disadvantage. Unless M. Pompidou changes it . . . nothing else he says about Britain's entry into Europe can matter much.[6]

And Pompidou was really hardly in a position to change it. Only one thing could save the Gaullist regime and French grandeur.

That was an early and unambiguous recovery in France's external trade position. The magnificently resilient French economy was again outmatching the German in its rate of expansion. But France's reserves of foreign exchange had fallen by about 45 per cent over the past twelve months, and were still falling marginally as Pompidou took office. There was no likelihood of his taking any steps in the foreseeable future that might have the slightest adverse effect on France's terms of trade.

This meant above all no change in the common agricultural policy. But the new Gaullist line was to avoid any appearance of intransigence. At his first press conference President Pompidou explained:

> First of all, the Community exists. It is made up of Six. I will even say that if it happened it was not entirely, at the start, thanks to Britain. *N'est-ce pas?* We feel, I feel, that the first thing to do is to pursue the construction of this Community . . . despite several recent disappointments we have no objection in principle to the possible membership of Britain or of any other country in the Community. But we think it is right, first of all, that the Six agree among themselves on the conditions of that membership and the consequences it could have on the future and the very nature of the Community . . . I am sure that if the Six really want in good faith and in all freedom of mind to view the problem squarely, they will see that Britain's membership could not fail to be accompanied by the membership of a certain number of other countries, which raises first of all, at the outset, some difficult questions and brings about profound changes in the Community.
>
> We are not, I repeat, opposed to discussion. We are not opposed to study, but we do not want a negotiation to start without first knowing the difficulties which might arise, the perspectives which it might entail, and what might be the attitude common to the Six.

And all this might take a long time to work out. The new Gaullists were certainly firmly resolved that nothing should be rushed. Even gestures which appeared to imply a complete reversal of traditional Fifth Republic policy proved on examination to be simply techniques for delaying any real steps towards British entry. Thus at the meeting of EEC leaders in July new Foreign Minister Maurice Schumann was at pains to quote in English the phrase most memorably associated with Wilson's abortive démarche in 1967. "We mean business", he assured German Foreign Minister Willy Brandt. Schumann then proposed that the EEC heads of government meet in The Hague in October to debate the question of British membership. But what Schumann had really done was to torpedo an earlier proposal by Dutch Foreign Minister Luns that the British be invited immediately to participate in talks on their entry. There was no doubt that the Gaullists meant business. Their business was to preserve French predominance within the system of Continental Europe.

This could mean that a third British bid for entry might be talked to death or despair for years, until French economic expansion had left the United Kingdom hopelessly far behind. It could equally well mean a sudden decision by a failing France to bring the British in as a counterpoise to impending German domination. And it was of course always possible that the British might not be able to pay the price of entry, even if they were so invited; just as it was always possible that in such circumstances a French veto might be replaced by a German one. There thus seemed to be just about as many practical difficulties in the way of British entry as ever. The conditions of Franco-German rivalry made it unlikely that either would ever want the United Kingdom in, except to be used against the other; and the British would be unable to afford the cost of the agricultural levies, for at least as long as the French would be unable to afford to do without them. But one thing at least was certain. It was now less than ever a question of choice between the Commonwealth and Europe. The concepts which had seemed the wave of the future in the forties and fifties had lost all substance with the close of the sixties. Nationalism was coming back on all fronts. The Commonwealth was merging into a complex of business relationships and fading protocol. And the West Europeans were looking forward to a relationship of mutually beneficial collaboration which would resemble the traditional concept of the Concert of Europe, more closely than any federal dream of the Resistance. The age of internationalism was over. Federalism had missed the bus again. Thirty years after Attlee's prophecy that "Europe must federate or perish", the British could reflect that their entry to Community Europe, if it ever came about, would be uncomplicated by any fears for their own sovereignty in a European Federation, or for its effect upon the Commonwealth. No European government had the faintest intention of federating with anybody else, and nothing that the British could do in this regard would have any significant

196

effects upon economic or diplomatic alignments within the Commonwealth. History had provided its own answer to the question: *Commonwealth or Europe*?

NOTES

1. *Le Monde,* 17 January 1968.
2. *Times* (London), 19 January 1968.
3. *Ibid.,* 20 January 1968.
4. *Economist,* 1 June 1968, p. 12.
5. *Daily Telegraph* (London), 26 June 1968.
6. *Guardian,* 24 June 1969.

Conclusion

Obviously, no final verdict can yet be handed down on the conduct of British relations with Community Europe. This will be available, if ever, only when the British have either completed a successful bid to enter the EEC, or alternatively entered some other international association which precludes or renders irrelevant their acceptance of the Treaty of Rome. But some comments at least are possible on the events dealt with in this study.

The first obviously is that what has been at stake is the nature of the role available to the United Kingdom in world affairs since 1945. The most rewarding role was that of a Britain dominant in Western Europe, mediating between the Continent and the United States through its preferred position in the Atlantic system, and with its presence sustained in every part of the world through the Commonwealth relationship. But this depended upon three factors over which the British could exercise little direct control.

They were that no Western European power should present itself as a more influential rival to challenge British predominance; that the United States should continue to treat the United Kingdom as its most important and respected partner within the Atlantic system; and that the Commonwealth should preserve a credible appearance of unity and value. The first of these was the most serious. It was also the one where the British had the greatest likelihood of being able to take direct action to restore the situation in their favour.

There is no question that their efforts to do so suffered from both bad luck and bad judgment. The return of General de Gaulle to power undoubtedly falls in the first category. So on a charitable estimate might the failure of the British economy to match the performance of first the Germans, then the French. But the errors of judgment certainly make a long and melancholy catalogue. It was imprudent initially to give support to federal aspirations on the Continent, without some clear declaration of intention either to participate or not to participate in them. The statements of Churchill at Zurich in 1946 and Strasbourg in 1950 impress in particular as deliberate attempts to mislead or confuse European auditors, in a way which could only have unfortunate consequences later on. It would also certainly seem to have been a mistake not to have entered the ECSC, at a time when Western Europe still welcomed British leadership, if only as an insurance against more serious and exclusive organizations of this kind being developed in the future. It was of course pointed out that for the British to do this without being convinced of the virtues of the Community system would leave them open to charges of bad faith. But they were being accused of this anyway. And the policy adopted by the Conservatives, in or out of office, towards both the ECSC and European army could scarcely merit any other description. The EDC episode indeed did as much as anything could have done to re-open Western Europe as an arena for conflicting nationalisms. It therefore helped to leave the British face to face with their dedicated rival. It also tended to provoke such rivalry by making British power pretensions evident and British goodwill to the Continent suspect. But obviously British predominance in Europe was not lost by the defeat of the EDC. It was indeed temporarily enhanced. The Common Market and Euratom Six certainly counted despairingly upon British support, and for a time on

British participation. Undoubtedly, the Common Market presented an unusual difficulty. This was a phenomenon which unquestionably involved the relationship of the United Kingdom with the Commonwealth. The attempt to reconcile Common Market and Commonwealth in the Free Trade Area was probably the most thoroughly rational economic proposal of the century. But its handling left literally everything to be desired. A very little prior investigation could have revealed the impossibility of getting general support in the OEEC for the proposals as they were originally presented; a very little subsequent reflection would have shown the desirability of making quick and conciliatory modifications after opposition had become manifest; and the readiness of the British negotiators to observe and accelerate the isolation and ruin of the Fourth Republic was at best shortsighted.

EFTA may be described as a partial failure rather than as a mistake. Its economic aims were reasonable and substantially achieved. Its political aims depended on American support which was not forthcoming, which on past record was certainly unlikely to be granted, but which could not be dismissed as totally unattainable. Much the same may be said of the Brussels negotiations. They certainly had their unsatisfactory aspects, in that they seemed increasingly to involve the abandonment by the British of positions which they had repeatedly affirmed could never be given up. But the crushing of the British bid came from circumstances over which they had no control, unless they were frankly prepared to accept a role in relation to France considerably more subservient than that which they had with the United States.

Failure is of course scarcely more creditable than error. It is indeed probably worse. The most damaging thing that can be said of a government is that it failed to do what it clearly set out to accomplish. And the bid made in 1967–68 by Wilson to achieve what Health had not been able to secure seemed to combine both error and failure. It may well have been presumptuous for him to have made the attempt in the first place, when de Gaulle gave no indication of having altered his fundamental position; it could certainly only have served to discredit his own Government when he abandoned positions to which he had previously committed himself, and gave assurances which could simply not be taken seriously; and it would certainly have seemed fatally imprudent for him to have so emphatically denied the existence of any viable alternatives to a policy which he in fact proved, at least temporarily, incapable of bringing to fruition.

Governments have of course never been remarkable for admitting alternatives to whatever policy they have embarked upon at the time. However, the totality of Wilson's new-found commitment to Europe not only invited the Europeans to make no concessions on their part, but also tended to obscure the reality of the option still possibly available. It is easy to believe that the British economy could be rejuvenated only by being exposed to far freer competition with more efficient producers. It is also very likely that no British Government would be prepared to do this unilaterally, by simply reducing tariffs around the United Kingdom. Economic integration thus may continue to seem the most politically attractive course. But what also seems very probable is that the British would receive far more gentle treatment if they were to merge themselves with the United States and Canada, than they could hope to receive from Western Europe. Even the objection that the United Kingdom would then be totally absorbed into the North American system is perhaps less important today. In the first place, American investment and British military decline seem likely to produce this effect anyway. In the second, it seems that the British are unlikely to be admitted to Europe so long as there is any possibility of their effectively challenging either French or German predominance there. One could hardly assume that American predominance within a North Atlantic system would be any more inconsiderately exerted or inimical to British interests than the kind of control the British would be exposed to within the EEC. It would certainly be exercised with no more disregard to the interests of the Commonwealth, whatever form these might take in the seventies.

This of course has been the kind of proposal associated with the Canadians since 1947. Lester Pearson may have been premature in suggesting such a prospect for serious consideration in the 1940's and 1950's. But circumstances have very clearly altered enormously since then. And it can at least be said of the solutions propounded by the Canadian Liberals that they represented a genuine attempt to accommodate the interests of other peoples as well as of themselves. There is no doubt that it was in Canada's most direct interests to try to hold London, Washington and Paris together as closely as possible. But it was also of the greatest importance to the survival of the Atlantic system as a whole. And it was a task to which no other country brought anything like the same urgency and capacity. On repeated occasions, the Canadians gave the impression of being the only English-speaking people who really cared what the French thought.

Diefenbaker was certainly no less alert to French suscepti-bilities than Pearson or St. Laurent. But there is also no doubt that Diefenbaker's leadership robbed Canada of any chance it might have had of playing a meaningful role during the Brussels negotiations. Canada had been the only Commonwealth country to have exhibited any appreciation of the issues at stake in connec-tion with NATO, the ECSC or the European army. But Canada like the rest of the Commonwealth made no intervention during the Brussels negotiations inspired by anything more than a desire to retain and enhance every possible short-term economic advantage. The Canadians at least could claim to have had the realism to see earlier than the rest that their efforts were hopeless. But the efforts they did make combined with those of the other Commonwealth countries to frustrate the very purpose they were intended to achieve. If the British frequently abandoned positions at Brussels which they had undertaken to hold, Commonwealth Governments repeatedly demanded that they adopt positions which nobody could have regarded as tenable. The result was as damaging to both as could be. By the end of 1962 it looked as if the British were prepared to pay any price and the Common-wealth none.

But the Commonwealth connection did not keep the United Kingdom out of Europe in 1961-63. It certainly did not keep it out in 1967-68. The question, Commonwealth or Europe? has indeed always been somewhat irrelevant to the real situation. Up to 1961, the British claimed to be choosing the Commonwealth, when in fact they could in all likelihood have had both. After 1961, they very obviously chose Europe, but could not have it. Before 1958, no choice need have been necessary. After that year, no such choice seemed to exist. The basic weakness of postwar British policy has been its failure to recognize these essential facts in time and act accordingly. More than two decades after World War II, the United Kingdom is still seeking its appropriate role in the postwar world. The options are running out.

Select Bibliography

Australia, Department of External Affairs, *Current Notes on International Affairs.*
Australia, House of Representatives, *Debates.*
Canada, Department of External Affairs, *External Affairs.*
Canada, Department of External Affairs, *Statements and Speeches.*
Canada, House of Commons, *Debates.*
Council of Europe, Consultative Assembly, *Reports.*
France, Assemblée Nationale, *Débats.*
France, Conseil de la République, *Débats.*
France, Senat, *Débats.*
Journal of the Parliaments of the Commonwealth, 1946-67.
New Zealand, House of Representatives, *Debates.*
Rhodesia and Nyasaland, Federal Assembly, *Debates.*
Royal Institute of International Affairs, *Documents on International Affairs,* R.I.I.A., London.
United Kingdom, Conservative Party, *Reports of Annual Conferences.*

United Kingdom, Labour Party, *Reports of Annual Conferences.*
United Kingdom, House of Commons, *Debates.*
United Kingdom, House of Lords, *Debates.*
United Kingdom, Government White Papers, Cmd. 9525, Cmnd. 7970, Cmd. 641, Cmnd. 648, Cmd. 72.
United States, Congressional Record, *House.*
United States, Senate, Foreign Affairs Committee, *Hearings.*
United States, State Department, *Bulletin.*
Western European Union, Assembly, *Proceedings.*

STATISTICS

International Monetary Fund, *International Financial Statistics.*
United Nations, *Economic Developments in the OEEC.*
United Nations, *Economic Surveys of Europe.*
Yearbook of International Trade Statistics.

NEWSPAPERS AND PERIODICALS

Age (Melbourne).
L'Année Politique.
Combat.
Corriere della Sera.
Daily Herald (London).
Daily Telegraph (London).
Daily Worker (London).
Economist.
Le Figaro (Paris).
Financial Times.
L'Humanité.
Johannesburg Star.
Manchester Guardian.
Le Monde (Paris).
New Statesman and Nation.
New York Herald Tribune.
New York Times.
News Chronicle (London).
Observer.
Le Populaire.
Reynolds' News.
Scotsman (Edinburgh).
Times (London).
U.S. News and World Report.
Yorkshire Post.

ARTICLES

Barclay, G. St. J. "Background to EFTA", *Australian Journal of Politics and History,* XI, No. 2 (August 1965), 185–97.

————. "The Commonwealth Does Not Answer", *World Review,* IV, No. 2 (July 1965), 3–9.

Delzell, C. "The European Federalist Movement in Italy: First Phase 1918–47", *Journal of Modern History,* XXXII, No. 3 (September 1960), 241–50.

Gerbet, P. "La Genèse du Plan Schuman", *Revue Française de Science Politique,* VI, No. 3 (1956), 525–53.

Luthy, H. "When Zeus Took a Fancy to Europa", *Der Monat,* October 1960.

Mansergh, N. "Britain, the Commonwealth and Western Union", *International Affairs,* XXIV, No. 4 (October 1948), 491–504.

Reuter, P. "La Conception du Pouvoir Politique dans le Plan Schuman", *Revue Française du Science Politique,* Vol. 1 (1951).

Strange, Susan. "The Schuman Plan", *Yearbook of World Affairs.* London: Stevens, 1951, pp. 109–30.

Walton, C.C. "Background for the European Defense Community", *Political Science Quarterly,* LXVIII, No. 1 (1953), 42–69.

Vernon, R. "The Schuman Plan", *American Journal of International Law,* XLVII, No. 2 (April 1953), 183–202.

BOOKS

Bonnefous, M. *L'Idée Européene et sa Réalisation.* Paris: Editions de Grande Siècle, 1950.

Churchill, W. *Europe Unite.* London: Cassell, 1950.

Crawford, J.G. *Australian Trade Policy, 1942-1966.* Canberra: Australian National University Press, 1968.

Eden, A. *Memoirs.* London: Cassell, 1960.

Einaudi, M., Bye, M., and Rossi, E. *Nationalization in France and Italy.* New York: Cornell University Press, 1955.

Fitzsimons, M.A. *The Foreign Policy of the British Labour Government, 1945-51.* Notre Dame, Indiana: University of Notre Dame Press, 1953.

Gelber, H.G. *Australia, Britain and the EEC, 1961-1963.* Melbourne: Oxford University Press, 1966.

Greenwood, G., and Harper, N. (eds.). *Australia in World Affairs, 1961–1965.* Melbourne: Cheshire, 1968.

Grove Haines, C. (ed.). *European Integration.* New York: Johns Hopkins, 1957.

Harrod, R. *The Life of John Maynard Keynes.* London: Macmillan, 1951.

Heiser, H.-J. *British Policy with Regard to the Unification Efforts on the European Continent.* Leyden: Swythoff, 1959.

Lerner, D., and Aron, R. *France Defeats the EDC.* New York: Praeger, 1957.

Nutting, A. *Europe Will Not Wait.* London: Hollis and Carter, 1959.

Political and Economic Planning (PEP). *European Organizations.* London: Allen and Unwin, 1959.

Price, H.B. *The Marshall Plan and Its Meaning.* New York: Cornell
   University Press, 1955.
Robertson, A.H. *European Institutions.* London: Stevens, 1959.
Royal Institute of International Affairs. *Britain in Western Europe.*
   London, R.I.I.A., 1956.
United Kingdom Labour Party Executive. *European Unity.* London:
   1950.
Williams, F. *Ernest Bevin.* London: Hutchinson, 1952.
Zupnick, C. *Britain's Postwar Dollar Problem.* New York: Columbia
   University Press, 1957.

Index